D1536728

Wrong Diagnosis —
Wrong Treatment

The Plight of the Alcoholic
in America

by

Joseph D. Beasley, M.D.

Essential Medical Information Systems, Inc.

New York

Distributor:
Creative Infomatics, Inc.
1-800-225-0694

First Edition Published in the United States in October, 1987

ISBN: 0-917634-29-2

Printed in the United States of America
Library of Congress Catalog Card Number:
87-071211

Table of Contents

To all those who suffered needlessly from the disease of alcoholism—and those who still do.

ACKNOWLEDGMENTS

Roger Williams, who formulated the relation between nutrition and alcoholism.

Arthur Sackler, for his pioneering insights into alcoholism and psychiatric illness as biochemical and nutritional disorders.

Sir George MacDonald and Prof. A. W. Woodruff for enlarging my view of medicine and helping me take a more comprehensive, ecological path.

Dr. Grace Goldsmith, who taught me that without knowledge of nutrition and toxicology neither diagnosis nor therapy could be practiced well.

Linus Pauling, whose recognition that medicine must shift to the molecular basis has fundamental significance beyond the current controversies that swirl around him.

Drs. Benjamin and Douglas Stein, for their foresight and support of my work.

Leon Botstein and Dimitri Papadimitriou of the Bard Center for the Bard Fellowship and environment to study health policy issues.

Frank King and Loretta Shum, who helped me research and write this book, and Lorraine Miller, who typed and proofed the manuscript.

Barbara McGinley and the staff of Brunswick House.

Bill W. and Dr. Bob, whose inspired and brilliant understanding of the physiological aspects of alcoholism still lights the way for us today—body, mind and spirit.

Alcoholics Anonymous and the millions of members who helped bring the disease of alcoholism into the light of day.

Introduction

Some 11,000 alcoholics committed suicide in the past twelve months in the United States. At least double that number attempted suicide and failed.

Thousands upon thousands of alcoholics die each year in auto accidents, domestic squabbles and industrial accidents.

Untold thousands of alcoholics are incarcerated each year in prisons and mental institutions for alcohol-related behavior.

And no one can even estimate the enormous number of deaths each year which are attributable to gastrointestinal disorders, cardiovascular disorders, infectious disease and other *alcohol-induced* pathologies.

Alcoholism is *the* American health problem. All others pale before it.

Alcoholism yields the most gruesome harvest of individual and social dislocation—but it is virtually ignored by the medical profession, and when not ignored, *misdiagnosed*.

I am writing this book to save lives. I am writing this book to give physicians and lay persons the information they need to understand the disease and treat it correctly.

The book is built around four themes:

- I deal with the fatal error which has emerged in the American health care system pertaining to alcoholism.
- I take the reader on a demystifying tour of alcohol and alcoholism in time and space.
- I provide the first in-depth case history of a real alcoholic—covering all behavioral and physiological aspects of the disease.
- I provide a simple program which enables an individual or his loved ones to determine whether they have the disease of alcoholism; a strategy for the intervention necessary to get a patient into treatment; and the necessary treatment and continuing care program to achieve and maintain an alcohol and drug free state.

Throughout this book I have tried to present and compress an enormous amount of new information clearly and simply. This information is crucial to our understanding of the disease because it *substantially contradicts* most of the well-known theories pertaining to alcoholism.

I have not sought controversy in this book but since my views are now substantially at odds with the prevailing medical theory and practice—controversy cannot be avoided.

The point of the book is not to attack or to applaud—it is to diminish the gruesome harvest of alcoholism now.

Joseph D. Beasley, M.D.

Chapter 1

A Profession Blinded by Popular Myths

How does one judge the severity of a medical problem? Traditionally, there are three criteria.

First, how many fatalities are directly or indirectly attributable to the problem in a given year?

Second, how much of the health care dollar is spent dealing with the medical problem, directly or indirectly—hospital beds, fees, etc.?

And third, what are the costs to the society as a whole in lost man-hours of productivity, etc.?

There is now evidence that by these three criteria, alcoholism is the largest medical problem in the United States.

But that evidence is largely ignored by the medical profession for a variety of reasons—the most important one being that the American health care system has been unable to understand the disease called alcoholism. Their profound misunderstanding of the disorder perpetuates the "wrong diagnosis-wrong treatment" which characterizes the health care system's activities vis-à-vis alcoholism.

A recent editorial by one of the most esteemed physicians in America, Arthur M. Sackler, M.D. (writing in the *Medical Tribune*, October 24th, 1984) illustrates this point.

It is important to understand that Sackler's life and contributions have been characterized by a unique openness and commitment to medical research and clinical practice. When Sackler was given the facts he eventually disclaimed the words I will quote shortly. But, if one of the finest physicians in America was temporarily blinded by popular myths vis-à-vis alcoholism, the reader can intuit the scope of the problem in the profession.

In fact, recent surveys carried out in some of the most prestigious U.S. medical centers showed that more than 75% of the professional staff still considered alcoholism as a moral or psychiatric disorder.

Dr. Sackler wrote, after condemning the current and continuing reduction of health care services to the very young and the very old:

> "The other new option would be to make diseases, such as alcoholic cirrhosis of the liver, nonreimbursable by either Medicare or Medicaid, leaving the individual who chooses to abuse alcohol the responsibility of individual personal insurance to cover the cost of alcohol related disorders . . . The American people should not accept a constriction of health care services to children, a reduction of entitlements under Medicare and Medicaid or the placing into jeopardy of both the health of the elderly and our social security system by the contributory negligence of those who wittingly abuse alcohol or other toxic recreational substances."

Essentially, two very disturbing charges are made in this paragraph.

- First, that the alcoholic "wittingly . . . chooses to abuse alcohol."
- Second, that the costs of current alcoholic treatment programs are one of the main causes in the reduction of services to the young and the old.

The first charge is crucial because it illustrates how the medical profession has essentially abandoned the disease concept of alcoholism and returned to the long-repudiated model of alcoholism that existed from the first written records to the 1950s.

Margaret Bean, M.D. characterizes that view of alcoholism as the "moral" model and describes it succinctly:

> "The moral model assumes that alcoholism is a result of voluntarily chosen behavior (excessive drinking) which results from either immorality (not knowing or caring that one's

behavior is bad) or defective will power (knowing but not behaving well) because of poor self-discipline or impulse control." (Bean 1983:92)

This is a sophisticated description of the "moral" model. In more everyday terms it simply means that alcoholics are considered by people to be ethically inferior: the alcoholic drinks because he or she is bad.

There is a frightening trend towards a return to this 'moral' theory of alcoholism on the part of many clinicians, government and insurance administrators, labor and corporate officials—and such a return means an abandonment of the disease concept of alcoholism.

Why is this happening?

When the disease concept of alcoholism was finally accepted by the AMA in the 1960s, it was accepted as a behavioral disorder—what Bean calls the symptom model:

"The symptom model of alcoholism, while psychiatric in its language, is often a disguised variant of the moral model. At its best, it asserts that in alcoholism each drink taken is a behavioral outcome of inner psychic forces, some conscious and some out of the patient's awareness. It often ignores addiction and physiological factors in drinking. According to this model, behavior can be interpreted, for example, as resulting from unconscious suicidal impulses or primitive oral drives or poor impulses control, and can be resolved by psychotherapy." (Bean 1983:92)

The behavioral and psychiatric models of alcoholism are virtually identical—with the latter postulating that individuals drink to treat the symptoms of their mental illness.

We can all agree that the treatment of alcoholism over the past thirty years has been based on the behavioral/psychiatric model of the disease.

And we can all agree that this model has been found wanting as a means of diagnosis and treatment.

Over the last thirty years, hundreds of studies have been done on the effectiveness of alcoholism treatment. A review of this literature reveals rates of complete abstinence from alcohol ranging from 15% to 40%. (LeMere 1953; Brunn 1963; Emrick 1974; Alford 1980; Gordis et al.

1981; Pettinati et al. 1985). A 1975 review of 384 such studies found that alcoholics who received no treatment at all were just as likely to stop drinking as those who received psychologically oriented treatment! (Emrick 1975)

There have been studies which report higher abstinence rates (Welte et al. 1979; CATOR 1986), but these, like most studies, are limited by high "drop out" rates (34% and 47%, respectively). On the average, approximately 50% of alcoholic patients drop out of treatment within 3 months. (Baekeland & Lundwall 1975; Alford 1980; Gordis et al. 1981) One evaluation of a hospital based program found that 73% of patients who should have been under observation were lost by 12 months, with only 9% both under observation and totally abstinent! (Gordis et al. 1981) Can any treatment approach call itself truly effective if more than half the patients are lost before a year is out?

Yet this approach continues to dominate the field in the face of repeated failure and new information to the contrary—and this approach is the main reason why many important segments of the health care establishment are foolishly abandoning the disease concept of alcoholism.

Alcoholism *is* a disease but *not* a behavioral one.

In the last decade or so evidence has surfaced which reveals alcoholism as a multifactorial genetic/metabolic disorder more closely related to diabetes than to any behavioral disorder, or even, to use Vaillant's multifactorial analogy—"like coronary atherosclerosis." (1983: 15)

This evidence—twin and sibling studies, tolerance/addiction formation, nutritional links, etc.—is now so strong that "the theory that vulnerability to alcoholism is inherited . . . has generally been accepted by the scientific community." (Benowitz 1984)

But this new disease model has not been integrated into existing treatment programs.

That's why the treatment failure rate remains high. We are still wedded to alcoholism as a moral/behavioral disorder.

Instead of fighting for new programs based on the new evidence, the American health care establishment is going backwards . . . once again starting to talk about penalizing the alcoholic who chooses to drink. If alcoholics 'choose' to drink, then diabetics 'choose' not to metabolize glucose.

This backsliding on the part of regulators represents a loss of nerve by the 'powers that be' based on a long-standing prejudice toward, lack of information on and shortsightedness pertaining to the disease concept of alcoholism.

It's like the inventor who builds a new internal combustion engine, and the test-drivers keep trying to run it on chicken soup.

No matter how they vary the texture of the soup, the engine won't kick over. So, finally, those who underwrote him decide to cut off all funds on the grounds that the engine is flawed.

The tragedy is compounded by the fact that we are very close to success.

All the current scientific data indicates that by the next decade we will be able to:

1. identify susceptible individuals before they begin drinking

2. identify problem drinkers early in the disease, and

3. realize dramatic improvement in recovery rates for those in crisis (Clark 1976; Brennan 1975; Kahan 1975; Guenther 1983)

The Guenther study, for example, established the validity of a nutritional approach to the treatment of hospitalized alcoholics.

While the study results, for a variety of reasons, were not validated correctly, it is still, even with these important limitations, a landmark event.

Just by adding four variables to a classical alcohol treatment program—improved diet, nutritional supplements, nutrition education, adequate nutritional follow-up—Guenther achieved very promising results (Clayton Foundation Biochemical Institute, University of Texas).

At the end of six months, contact had been maintained with 89% of discharged patients. Of these, 37.8% of the control group had remained sober and 62.2% had resumed drinking, whereas 81.3% of the experimental group had remained sober and only 18.8% had resumed drinking, a statistically significant difference ($p \leq .001$). (Guenther 1983)

The experience of myself and my staff has confirmed the value of such an approach. A wide ranging treatment protocol, with a strong nutritional component, results in comfortable abstinence for more than

13

70% of our patients with very low attrition. We have observed this kind of success even in patients cross addicted with drugs (a condition we find in 40% of those we treat).

I and my staff have just completed a study at Brunswick House utilizing a strong nutritional component in a wide-ranging new treatment protocol and preliminary findings indicate that 73.3% of the 117 male and female alcoholics in the study were sober after a 12-month period.

And similarly promising results are being achieved with other interventions based on sophisticated diagnostic workups including detailed studies in allergy and immunology, endocrine system malfunctions, insulin-catecholamine relationships, malabsorption, nutritional individuality, and enkephalin/prostaglandin/serotonin metabolism.

The charge that alcoholism funding is responsible for runaway health costs is equally pernicious.

Why not blame cancer? Or the mentally retarded? Or schizophrenia? Or the coronary by-pass industry?

Why is alcoholism the culprit?

It has become the culprit because the medical establishment no longer believes that alcoholism is a disease—they have returned to the archaic belief that the alcoholic is somehow morally unfit and therefore drinks.

In fact, the reality of the situation calls for a diametrically opposite economic approach.

The "masked" disorders associated with alcoholism are so extensive that one of the few avenues available to cut medical costs significantly (particularly hospital costs) is by doubling or even tripling the funding for effective new treatment programs.

As Milam and Ketcham point out graphically (1983:83), the causes of death in a group of 1,823 male alcoholics were as follows:

Cardiovascular disease - 20%
Cirrhosis - 16%
Upper G.I. and Lung Cancer - 10%
Alcoholism - 9%
Suicide, Homicide, Accident, etc. - 33%
Pneumonia - 5%
Other medical causes - 7%

Thus, only 25% of the deaths are from traditional 'alcoholic' diseases—and, in my clinical experience, this figure is high, very high.

Vaillant of Harvard Medical School notes that "in the United States alcoholism is involved in a quarter of all admissions to general hospitals." (1983:1). This figure, I have found, is low.

But these figures serve to point out that the best way to cut hospital costs is to cut hospital use by what appears to be the *largest single category of general hospital users in the United States—unrecognized and untreated alcoholics.*

If one adds to alcoholism, drug abuse and addiction, plus the mental consequences of these two diseases, various estimates indicate 40% of the hospital usage in the United States.

I can cite any number of real-life horror stories in support of this economic argument, but one recent case sticks in my memory because it sums up the whole tragedy.

A 57 year old patient on medical disability payments was admitted to our clinic for alcoholism. Let's call him Larry.

Larry had been an alcoholic for 16 years but this was his first admission for alcoholism per se.

However, during that 16 year span, he's had 17 admissions to general hospitals for everything from aspirative pneumonia to G.I. bleeding and at least two admissions to psychiatric hospitals.

Since each admission cost an average of about $15,000, literally hundreds of thousands of dollars were paid out for hospital and other medical expenses for this one individual—yet at no time during those years was Larry ever treated for alcoholism or recognized as an alcoholic.

To compound this idiotic tragedy, when he finally sought treatment for alcoholism, the agency disallowed payments for treatment of the condition which had caused the disability in the first place.

The National Institute on Alcoholism & Alcohol Abuse conservatively estimates (1981) that there are 10 million known adults and 3 million teens who seriously abuse alcohol—and all authorities point out that drinking among the young is rising very fast.

There are millions of "Larrys" walking around right now and their numbers will only swell in the next decade if we don't proceed full-force in developing effective treatment programs for them based on the recognition that alcoholism is a genetic/metabolic disease.

To continue to base programs on the existing view of alcoholism as a behavioral/moral disorder will only perpetuate the gruesome harvest from year to year.

Chapter 2

Epidemiology of a Chronic Disease

We cannot understand the present view of alcoholism unless we follow the substance and its abuse far back into time and then bring it forward.

The mountain tribes of Uganda have for millennia brewed a powerful beer out of the whole banana. While all other food preparation tasks are performed by the women of these tribes, the preparation of this banana intoxicant is reserved for men who have exhibited unusual bravery or hunting skills.

Certain Eskimo groups net and ritually kill small seabirds during the short Arctic spring, then sew them up in the hollowed-out carcass of a harp seal and bury it in the ground for almost a year. The sole purpose of this enormously laborious process is to obtain an intoxicant mash.

Central American Indians use corn. South Sea Islanders ferment peppers. Nomadic tribes of central Africa prefer the palm.

In fact, it is one of the more amusing truisms of anthropology that virtually all cultures in time and place—whether hunter - gatherers or farmers; whether technologically advanced or primitive—share two universals: the development of a noodle and the discovery and use of the natural fermentation process.

It is this universality of ethyl alcohol as a powerful cultural artifact that makes the disease of alcoholism even more difficult to understand and treat. If our earliest written mention of beer is circa 5,000 B.C. on Babylonian clay tablets, and if the manufacture and distribution of this product was already controlled by priestesses, then the discovery of fermentation long antedated the discovery of writing and emerges somehow entwined with homo sapiens' most powerful impulses concerning his powers and destiny.

Hundreds of our traditions, particularly those which deal with death and life, with comradeship and celebration—from the birth of a child to a wake, from launching a ship to a marriage ceremony—have their roots entwined with ethyl alcohol.

Our language preserves hundreds of words and phrases associated with alcohol—the origins and meanings only dimly understood.

When, for example, a parent cautions a child to 'mind your P's and Q's'he doesn't realize this expression comes from the medieval English alehouse, with its pint and quart tankards and the barmaid noting the 'P's' and Q's' on a slate.

Antiquity's fascination with wine, beer and mead gradually shifted to their stronger cousins.

In the eighth century an Arabian scientist named Geber discovered the process of distillation. Five centuries later, a physician at the University of Montpellier in France rediscovered it and named his distilled product "aqua vitae"—the water of life.

Arnauld de Villeneuve claimed that here was the elixir of health that all men craved. He was believed.

In the centuries that followed, the newer and purer forms of ethyl alcohol—brandy, rum, gin and so forth—were used to treat everything from venereal disease to the pox.

So another layer was added to the tradition. Now Christian Europe used wine for its most sacred religious ritual, the mass; used ale for communal gatherings of all kinds; and used distilled 'spirits' for physical therapy. In addition, a vital new industry had been created which was linked to the State, the Church, the Nobility and even benefited the poor farmer.

But it was in the American colonies that ethyl alcohol was to find its most powerful role.

The English, French, Scotch, Irish, Scandinavians and Germans who settled the North American colonies represented a very diverse spectrum of political, social and religious opinions. But they all shared an affection for, and a belief in, the curative, social, ceremonial and other powers of alcohol.

More significantly, they knew the arts of brewing and distilling. The land in which they settled was filled with uncommon dangers: swift changes in seasons, hostile Indians, teeming wildlife, often treacherous terrain. In this new milieu—characterized by danger, freedom, and wide swings from bounty to scarcity—"spirits" (i.e. distilled to 90 proof) became one of the most common and powerful cultural factors in the emerging society.

In fact, early visitors to the colonies, in their extant writings, are always struck by the enormous consumption of spirits by the colonists. Some even elaborated far-fetched theories in an attempt to explain or excuse this very noticeable American alcohol phenomenon.

Dependence on alcohol became so omnipresent that on the northern, western and southern frontiers of the established colonies, spirits were often the most valued medium of exchange.

Note well; this was not merely a form of barter—whiskey was money. On the frontier, where currency was short, if you wished to purchase a cow you were often expected to pay the farmer in rum, brandy or hard cider (beer and wine were usually excluded from this role).

But alcohol was to play a far more important economic role in the development of the nation.

Brewing, distilling and importing alcohol developed into one of the largest, most complex and historically influential of the colonial industries, one which, for lack of a better term, was called simply the 'rum trade.'

Merchants in New England and the Middle Atlantic colonies, for example, purchased molasses from the West Indies. They distilled the molasses into rum. A large portion of the rum was then shipped to Africa and traded for slaves. The slaves were brought back to the West Indies where they were traded for molasses and the vicious circle started again.

This triangular exchange had far-reaching implications. The origin of the Republic as a future maritime power stems in good part from the ship-building efforts required to conduct that lucrative trade.

The West Indian merchants sold the slaves to the Southern Planters—building American agriculture and exacerbating the slavery conflict.

And the molasses tax, enacted by the Crown to combat American purchase of molasses from the French and the Spanish Indies, became one of the most inflammatory issues between the colonies and Mother England.

19

In addition, the growing taste for rum fueled tastes for other distilled spirits, particularly since these gave farmers a major new market for their wheat, barley, rye, corn and apples.

By 1830 the per-capita consumption of distilled spirits (90 proof/45% alcohol) had reached an astonishing five gallons for every man, woman, and child in the land. That is at least three times higher than consumption today. After 1830 there was a leveling off of demand in the face of increased taxes and a rising temperance movement.

Given the U.S. love affair with alcohol, it is not surprising that an American, Dr. Benjamin Rush, was one of the first to identify alcoholism as an illness. His influential treatise was published in 1784 but it was not until the 1950's that the AMA formally recognized alcoholism as a disease.

We now know even more clearly that the AMA's recognition was correct—alcoholism is a medical disease by any criterion of measurement or identification.

But it is also an unusual disorder epidemiologically in that it is rooted in age-old genetics yet triggered by the most contemporary of customs and pressures. Unmistakably, these customs and pressures, long woven into this society's social fabric, represent our social dynamics at a most basic level.

The British philosopher Gilbert Ryle used to tell an amusing story that everyone who wishes to understand alcoholism should keep in mind.

A visiting Asian diplomat with a minimal command of English expressed a desire to see Oxford University. Ryle was selected to squire the diplomat around. He showed him the labs, the classrooms, the libraries, the chapels, the playing fields, the students, the professors; even the janitorial staff.

At the end of an exhausting day, the diplomat thanked his guide (Ryle) profusely but said that what he really wanted to see was Oxford, not just a bunch of people and buildings, and maybe next time Ryle could show him the famous university.

The diplomat, of course, had made a simple conceptual mistake, perhaps because of his lack of fluency in English.

He didn't understand that the word Oxford is merely an umbrella term for all the people and buildings he was shown. He didn't understand that the whole, Oxford University, is simply and only the sum of its parts.

Anyone attempting to come to grips with the disease of alcoholism today is faced with the mirror image of that diplomat's problem; but unlike

Oxford University, alcoholism is made up of parts which are only visible sometimes or are scarcely discernible—or even totally submerged.

The word alcoholism seems to mean something, but what, in reality, does it refer to?

Let us look at some of the more visible parts—statistical, epidemiological and etiological—that make up this enormous national tragedy encompassing all age levels, classes and geographical areas.

From 10 to 15 million Americans are alcoholics, exhibiting classical symptom formation: increased tissue tolerance to alcohol; adaptive cell metabolism; appetite derangement and malnutrition; withdrawal symptoms and physical dependency; loss of control and other gross behavioral changes.

An additional 10 million can be considered on the cusp of alcoholism and that includes three million teenagers.

In a nation that is growing older statistically, the median age of the drinker is growing younger and younger.

More than 30% of all successful suicides in any given year are alcoholics. Sixty percent of suicide attempts are related to the disease of alcoholism.

More than 60% of county jail inmates in the United States are there for alcohol-related crimes—and the heavy role that alcohol plays in violent felonies has long been recognized.

Losses to U.S. industry from alcohol-related absenteeism, errors, accidents, reduced productivity, and so forth, are conservatively estimated at $45 billion a year. And, as we all know, more than half of the deaths reported in car accidents (approximately 500,000 in the past decade) are alcohol related.

No other present disease is so destructive of life, property and institutions on a daily basis. No other disease has shown itself so adaptable to changing social mores—witness the enormous growth in the number of persons who now combine a drug dependency (cocaine, heroin, amphetamines, tranquilizers, etc.) with alcohol dependency.

Most crucial of all, no other disease elicits so little medical help; the number of alcoholics who receive medical treatment for their condition from qualified physicians is minuscule, and that care is usually given only after the alcoholic has reached a life-threatening stage.

A complete epidemiological profile of alcoholism—one which conclusively establishes the disease's prevalence and its rates and patterns of occurrence—does not yet exist, for a variety of reasons.

First and foremost, the sources of our statistics are not standardized and are often unreliable; mainly clinic admissions, arrests for repeated drunkenness, deaths from alcohol poisoning, etc.—put together on a varying state-to-state basis.

Second, the symptom formation of alcoholism is imprecise and shifting—and besides, many symptoms are shared by drinkers who are not alcoholics.

We can, however, quantify to some extent, with a degree of confidence.

The average drinker in the United States today consumes approximately 12 liters of absolute alcohol per year.

Of that consuming population, some 10 million adults and 3 million youths are alcoholics or serious problem drinkers.

Out of this population there are about 250,000 alcohol-related deaths of all kinds annually—some 30,000 of which are from liver cirrhosis.

The mortality rate of the alcoholics will be twice that of the general population and is largely attributable, in addition to cirrhosis, to neoplasms of the upper digestive and respiratory tract, heart disease, alcohol poisoning, pneumonia, suicide, accidents, homicide.

About 80% of these individuals will develop the disease between the ages of 30 and 55. Given the prevalence of teenage drinking in the United States, this points to a long gestation for the disease.

Each alcoholic will consume an average of at least 150 ml of absolute alcohol per day. This figure has been laboriously obtained from the horse's mouth—from hospitalized alcoholics detailing their consumption after the disease took hold. There is good reason to believe that this figure is on the low side.

According to epidemiologists, the ratio of males to females in this alcoholic group will be six to one. Here, however, is another area where the recorded evidence is contradicted by medical experience. The real ratio is probably nowhere near that lopsided toward males.

Cultural and social factors tend to inflate the ratio, since alcoholic women are particularly loath to enter clinics for treatment, and their relatives or employers are quite reluctant to send them there.

Furthermore, the gains that women have achieved during the past decade toward economic, social and professional parity have dramatically increased alcohol acceptance and use among them, probably by roughly the same factor as smoking.

Even more disturbing, female alcoholics appear to show a much higher incidence of pathology than their male counterparts, mainly because they enter treatment at a later stage of their disease.

While the six-to-one statistic is obviously misleading, much of our dependable quantitative data works the other way—upsetting many long-held beliefs.

For example, there is the cliche that drunkenness leads to alcoholism. Yet Finland, a country where there is a tradition of sudden celebratory bouts of drunkenness, has a rather low rate of alcoholism.

Or take the popular belief that the more one drinks distilled spirits, rather than wine or beer, the more likely one is to become an alcoholic.

The United States, which holds the world's record for consumption of distilled spirits as a proportion (about 45%) of total alcoholic beverage consumption, trails Italy, Portugal and France in alcoholism rates—three countries in which distilled spirits were traditionally relatively ignored.

The highest rates of alcoholism occur in three job categories; the bar and restaurant business; stevedore and laboring trades; and musicians, authors and editors.

We also know that the white-collar occupations in sales and marketing are closing in fast. And we should keep in mind that alcoholism in black and Hispanic communities is seriously underreported. Certainly anyone who has lived in an inner city ghetto and observed the line-up of middle aged and older workers and unemployed in neighborhood bars for their morning ration of blackberry brandy or vodka and Coke is well aware of this gaping statistical lacuna.

As you can see, we know very little about the incidence of the disease.

But we are beginning to learn an enormous amount about the disease itself. In the past decade scientists, researchers and physicians have provided us with data that substantially contradicts established diagnosis and treatment.

To make all this new data comprehensible and relevant, in the following pages I am going to present an in-depth case history of an alcoholic and integrate these new findings in explaining his actions, his reactions, his psychology and physiology, his metabolism and genetics.

To put it bluntly—alcoholism is not what 'they' said it was. And it will never be dealt with successfully until physicians and administrators absorb and act upon this new information.

Before I proceed, however, I want to present the following facts, compiled in tabular form, which provide a unique overview of the alcohol problem in the United States today. The first section deals with the general problem as it impinges on the entire society. The next two sections deal with women and children and youth respectively. The tables were provided by the National Council on Alcoholism, Inc., a national nonprofit voluntary health organization founded in 1944 which has become the most important information, training and patient consultation resource on alcoholism in the U.S. through its network of 184 state and local affiliates.

A. Facts On Alcoholism and Alcohol-Related Problems

- Alcoholism is a chronic, progressive and potentially fatal disease characterized by tolerance and physical dependency or pathologic organ changes, or both. All are the direct or indirect consequences of the alcohol ingested. (National Institute on Alcohol Abuse and Alcoholism (NIAAA), *Fourth Special Report to the U.S. Congress on Alcohol and Health*, ed. John R. DeLuca, DHHS Pub. No. (ADM) 82-1080, 1981, p. 36)
- Alcoholism and alcohol abuse occur in every socioeconomic group, although the problems may manifest themselves differently across groups. (Congress of the United States, Office of Technology Assessment, Health Technology Case Study 22: *The Effectiveness and Costs of Alcoholism Treatment*, prepared by Leonard Saxe, Ph.D., et al., OTA-HCS-22, 1983, p. 3)
- Alcoholism is one of the most serious public health problems in the United States today. Among the 18.3 million adult "heavier drinkers" (those consuming more than 14 drinks per week) 12.1 million have one or more symptoms of alcoholism, an increase of 8.2 percent since 1980. (NIAAA, Department of Biometry and Epidemiology, 1985. *Working Paper: Projections of Alcohol Abusers, 1980, 1985, 1990,* prepared by John Noble, pp. 5 and 6.)
- Alcohol is the most widely used—and abused—drug in America. In 1981, the equivalent of 2.77 gallons of absolute alcohol was sold per person over age 14. This is about 591 12-ounce cans of beer, 115 fifths of table wine or 35 fifths of 80 proof whiskey, gin or vodka. A tenth of the drinking population consumes half the alcohol beverages sold. (NIAAA, *Fifth Special Report to the U.S. Congress on*

24

Alcohol and Health, from the Secretary of Health and Human Services, DHHS Publication No. (ADM) 84-1291, 1983, p. xiii)

- Alcohol abuse accounts for approximately 98,000 deaths annually. This includes cirrhosis and other medical consequences, alcohol-related motor vehicle accidents and alcohol-related homicides, suicides and non-motor vehicle accidents. (R.T. Ravenholt, M.D., *Addiction Mortality in the U.S.* National Institute on Drug Abuse (NIDA), March 1983)

- $116.7 billion was the economic cost to the nation resulting from alcohol abuse and alcoholism in 1983. The economic impact in 1980 (current dollars) was $89.5 billion. (Research Triangle Institute (RTI). *Economic Costs to Society of Alcohol and Drug Abuse and Mental Illness: 1980*, Herick J. Harwood et al., June 1984, pp. G-16 and 7)

- Alcoholism treatment reduces total health care costs. In a study of over 20 million claim records between 1980 and 1983, alcoholic families used health care services and incurred costs at twice the rate of similar families with no known alcoholic members. The average alcoholic's treatment cost was offset by reductions in other health care costs within 2 to 3 years following the start of treatment. (NIAAA, *Alcoholism Treatment Impact on Total Health Care Utilization and Costs,* U.S. Dept. of Health and Human Services, February 1985, pp. 1, 3)

- Alcohol is known to cause or contribute to other fatal illnesses, including cardiac myopathy, hypertensive diseases, pneumonia and several types of cancer. (Ravenholt, *Addiction Mortality,* NIDA, March 1983)

- One out of three American adults—56 million Americans—says that alcohol abuse has brought trouble to his or her family. This is about four times the number of families that say other drugs have troubled their homes. (P. Regans, ABC News/Washington Post Poll. Survey #0190, May 1985)

- Chronic brain injury caused by alcohol is second only to Alzheimer's disease as a known cause of mental deterioration in adults. Alcoholic mental deterioration is not progressive. If the patient stops drinking, the deterioration is arrested and substantial recovery can occur. (NIAAA, *Fifth Special Report*, p. xv)

- Children of alcoholics have a four times greater risk of developing alcoholism than children of nonalcoholics. There are 28.6 million children of alcoholics in the U.S. today, 6.6 million of whom are under the age of 18. (Children of Alcoholics Foundation, *Children of Alcoholics: A Review of the Literature,* 1985, Introduction and p. 2)

- Genetic influence is identifiable in at least 35 to 40 percent of alcoholics and alcohol abusers, and it affects both men and women. People with family histories involving parental alcohol abuse face increased risk. Futhermore, many types of alcohol abuse may exist, each with its own genetic predisposition interacting with a particular environment. (NIAAA, *Fifth Special Report,* p. 22)

- An estimated 3.3 million drinking teenagers aged 14 to 17 are showing signs that they may develop serious alcohol-related problems. (NIAAA, *Third Special Report to the U.S. Congress on Alcohol and Health,* 1978, p. 14)

- Recent surveys conducted in the United States indicate that the first drinking experience today usually occurs around age 12, in contrast to ages 13-14 in the 1940s and 1950s. It is no longer unusual for 10-12 year-olds to have serious alcohol abuse problems. (Nancy P. Gordon and Alfred McAlister, "Adolescent Drinking: Issues and Research" in *Promoting Adolescent Health* (New York, Academic Press, 1982), pp. 201, 203, 210. David W. Brooks and Judith S. Brooks, "Adolescent Alcohol Use," Editorial, *Alcohol and Alcoholism,* Vol. 20, No. 3 (Great Britain, 1985), p. 259)

- Since 1966, the number of high school students nationwide intoxicated at least once a month has more than doubled, from 10 percent to more than 20 percent. (Dorothy G. Singer, "Alcohol, Television and Teenagers," *Sex, Drugs, Rock 'N' Roll,* Yale University Family Television Research Consultation Center (New Haven 1985, pp. 668, 671)

- Most youth begin to drink in adolescence. A recent study on adolescent alcohol abuse relevant to prevention efforts found that alcohol is the most widely used drug by youth between the ages of 12 and 17. (NIAAA, *Fifth Special Report,* p. 125)

- About 30 percent of fourth grade respondents to a 1983 "Weekly Reader" poll reported peer pressure to drink beer, wine or liquor. (Weekly Reader Publications, *A Study of Children's Attitudes and Perceptions about Drugs and Alcohol,* conducted by the Weekly Reader, Xerox Education Publications, 1983, Table 2)

- Of 27,000 New York public school students, grades 7 through 12, 11 percent described themselves as being "hooked" on alcohol. (New

York State Division of Alcoholism and Alcohol Abuse, Drug and Alcohol Survey, 1983)

- By ninth grade, more than half (56 percent) of high school seniors responding to a 1982 national survey had tried alcohol. By their senior year, more than 9 out of 10 had done so. (NIAAA, *Fifth Special Report*, p. xiii)

- Fetal Alcohol Syndrome (FAS) is the third leading cause of birth defects with accompanying mental retardation and the only preventable one among the top three. The incidence of FAS is approximately 1 in 750 live births, or 4,800 babies per year in recent years. Thirty-six thousand newborns each year may be affected by a range of less severe alcohol-related fetal alcohol effects (FAE). (REI, *Economic Costs to Society*, p. B-3)

- Women frequently engage in the high risk practice of abusing other drugs in combination with alcohol. In a 1983 Alcoholics Anonymous Survey, 40 percent of female A.A. members reported addiction to another drug. The number increased to 64 percent for women 30 years and under. (General Service Office of Alcoholics Anonymous, Inc. Membership Survey, 1983)

- In 1984 there were 44,241 highway deaths, of which 23,500 (53 percent) were alcohol-related. (National Highway Traffic Safety Administration, *Alcohol in Fatally Injured Drivers*—1984, Washington, D.C.)

- About 65 out of every 100 persons in the U.S. will be in an alcohol-related crash in their lifetimes. (National Highway Traffic Safety Administration, U.S. Dept. of Transportation, *Drunk Driving Facts*, National Center for Statistics and Analysis, June 1984)

- Alcohol-related highway deaths are the number one killer of 15-24 year-olds. (*Health, United States*, 1980. National Center for Health Statistics, Public Health Service, U.S. DHHS Pub. No. (PHS) 81-1232, December 1980)

- Alcohol is a contributing factor in at least 15,000 fatal and six million nonfatal injuries in non-highway settings. (NIAAA, *Alcohol Health and Research World*, Summer 1985, Vol. 9, No. 4, p. 25)

- Between 400 and 800 boating fatalities annually involve alcohol. Alcohol is implicated in from 65 to 69 percent of all reported drownings. (NIAAA, *Alcohol Health and Research World*, Summer 1985, p. 28)

- Alcoholics are 10 times more likely to die from fires than non-alcoholics, 5 to 13 times more likely to die from falls and commit

suicide from 6 to 15 times more frequently than the general population. (NIAAA, *Fifth Special Report*, pp. xix and xx)
- Drinking is estimated to be involved in about 50 percent of spouse abuse cases and up to 38 percent of child abuse cases. (NIAAA, *Fifth Special Report*, p. xx)
- Fifty-four percent of jail inmates convicted of violent crimes were drinking before they committed the offense. Sixty-two percent of those convicted of assault had been drinking. Forty-nine percent of those convicted of murder or attempted murder had been drinking. (Bureau of Justice, Statistics Survey, 1983)
- Between 2 and 10 percent of people 65 and over experience some type of alcohol-related problem. Approximately 25 percent of the 65-plus population is on some form of medication. By most measures, older people consume more medication than any other group, putting them at high risk for drug and alcohol interaction. (NIAAA, *Alcohol Health and Research World*, Spring 1984, Vol. 8, No. 3, pp. 4 and 6)

B. Alcoholism and Alcohol-Related Problems Among Women

- Our society has traditionally had strong feelings regarding women and alcohol. Relatively little research into the specific aspects of women's drinking was performed prior to the 1970s, when a nationwide movement spearheaded by the National Council on Alcoholism and the National Institute on Alcohol Abuse and Alcoholism focused attention on the problem. Prior to the 1970s, nearly all the classical studies done on the physiology, biochemistry and metabolism of alcohol had been done on males. (S. Blume, M.D., "Psychiatric Problems of Alcoholic Women," *Alcoholism and Clinical Psychiatry,* 1982, p. 180)
- 60 percent of adult women 18 and over drink, while 40 percent are abstainers. 55 percent of adult women who drink do so moderately (defined as less than 60 drinks per month) while 5 percent are heavy drinkers (more than 60 drinks per month). (W.B. Clark, L. Midanik et al., *Alcohol Use and Alcohol Problems among U.S. Adults,* Results of the 1979 Survey, Working Draft, Social Research Group, School of Public Health, University of California at Berkeley, 1981)
- Women's drinking problems are often viewed as less serious than men's and their condition may be more frequently misdiagnosed.

Stigmatization and the unwillingness of many physicians, mental health professionals, police and the courts to label women as "alcoholic" are detrimental to early intervention and treatment. (L. Beckman and H. Amaro, "Patterns of Women's Use of Alcohol Treatment Agencies," S. Wilsnack and L. Beckman, Eds., *Alcohol Problems in Women, New York*: The Guilford Press, 1984, p. 342)

- Thirty percent of Alcoholics Anonymous membership is female. (General Services Branch of A.A., Inc. 1983 Membership Survey)
- Regular drinking is common among high school girls, and a sizable number engage in heavy drinking. In a 1983 survey, 31 percent of 12th grade girls had consumed at least five or more drinks at least once in the preceding two weeks. (K. Thompson and R. Wilsnack, "Drinking Problems Among Female Adolescents: Patterns and Influences," *Alcohol Problems in Women*, 1984, p. 39; Johnston et al., *Use of Licit and Illicit Drugs by American High School Students*, 1975-1984, University of Michigan, Institute for Social Research, 1985)
- Women frequently engage in the high-risk practice of abusing other drugs in combination with alcohol. In a 1983 Alcoholics Anonymous survey, 40 percent of female A.A. members reported addiction to another drug. The number increased to 64 percent for women 30 years and under. (General Service Branch of A.A., Inc., 1983 Membership Survey)
- Alcohol and drug dependent women report a high incidence of sexual abuse, including rape and incest. In one recent study up to 74 percent of alcohol and drug dependent women reported incidents of sexual abuse. (S. Wilsnack, "Drinking, Sexuality and Sexual Dysfunction in Women," *Alcohol Problems in Women*, 1984, p. 33)
- Among alcoholic women, the incidence of suicide attempts exceeds that of the female population as a whole and that of alcoholic men. (S. Hill, "Vulnerability to the Biomedical Consequences of Alcoholism and Alcohol-related Problems," *Alcohol Problems in Women*, 1984, p. 126)
- Women are more likely to develop liver disease with a lower level of alcohol consumption than men, and women have a higher risk of dying once the liver has been injured. (S. Hill, "Vulnerability to the Biomedical Consequences of Alcoholism and Alcohol-Related Problems," *Alcohol Problems in Women*, 1984, p. 126)

- Fetal Alcohol Syndrome (FAS) is the third leading cause of birth defects, with accompanying mental retardation, and the only preventable one among the top three. The incidence of FAS is approximately 1 in 750 live births or 4,800 babies per year in recent years. Thirty-six thousand newborns each year may be affected by a range of less severe alcohol-related fetal alcohol effects (FAE). (Research Triangle Institute, *Economic Costs to Society of Alcohol and Drug Abuse and Mental Illness*, 1980, p. B-3)
- Women continue to be under-represented in most alcoholism treatment programs. On a national level, they constitute less than 20 percent of all clients in alcohol treatment, although estimates indicate that women represent a much higher percentage of the total alcoholic population. (NIDA, CODAP: State Statistics, 1978, NIDA Statistical Series, Series E, No. 13, U.S. Government Printing Office, 1980; J.D. Homiller, "Alcoholism Among Women," *Chemical Dependencies: Behavioral and Biomedical*, 1980; M. Sandmaier, *The Invisible Alcoholics*, McGraw Hill, 1980)
- Most treatment programs do not provide child care or adequate alternatives for women entering treatment. Women may not seek to continue treatment because of the difficulty of finding acceptable child care arrangements. (L. Beckman and H. Amar, "Patterns of Women's Use of Alcohol Treatment Agencies," *Alcohol Problems in Women*, 1984, p. 329, p. 332)
- Most practitioners in the field believe that arrests for drinking and driving serve as a major opportunity for treatment intervention for the problem drinker, but female drinking drivers are far less likely than their male counterparts to be arrested. In a recent study, 7 percent of women classified as lighter drinkers and 45 percent of women as heavier drinkers reported driving while high or drunk during the preceding 12 months. (R. Ference, "Prevention of Alcohol Problems in Women," *Alcohol Problems in Women*, 1984, p. 418)
- Women are now heavily targeted for marketing of alcoholic beverages. According to *Impact,* a liquor industry newsletter, women will spend $30 billion on alcoholic beverages in 1994, compared with $20 billion in 1984. ("Betty Briefcase Buys More Bottles," *Advertising Age,* Thursday, September 12, 1985)
- Among blacks who drink, twice as many black women as black men report health problems due to drinking. (J. Leland, "Alcohol Use and Abuse in Ethnic Minority Women," *Alcohol Problems in Women*, 1984, p. 79)

- Native American women between the ages of 15-34 have rates of cirrhosis of the liver 36 times the white female rate. The corresponding black female rate is a little over 6 times the rate for white women. (J. Leland, "Alcohol Use and Abuse in Ethnic Minority Women," *Alcohol Problems in Women*, 1984, p. 126)
- Hispanic and black women report higher abstinence rates than white women. With acculturation, abstinence rates among Hispanic women significantly decrease. (R. Caetano, "Ethnicity and Drinking in Northern California: A Comparison Among Whites, Blacks and Hispanics," *Alcohol and Alcoholism*, 19: 31-44, 1984; A.M. Alcocer, "Alcohol Use and Abuse Among the Hispanic American Population," NIAAA, *Special Population Issues*, Alcohol and Health Monograph No. 4, DHHS Pub. No. (ADM) 82-1193, 1982, pp. 361-382)

C. Alcoholism and Other Alcohol-Related Problems Among Children and Youth

- Alcohol is America's No. 1 drug problem among youth. In 1985, an estimated 4.6 million adolescents aged 14 through 17 experienced negative consequences of alcohol use (e.g., arrest, involvement in an accident, impairment of health or job performance). (NIAAA, Projection of data in Alcohol and Health Monograph 1, *Alcohol Consumption and Related Problems* 1982, p. 85, updated with Bureau of the Census 1985 Population Projections)
- Alcohol is over twice as popular among college students as the next leading drug, marijuana, and over five times as popular as cocaine. Ninety-two percent of college students reported using alcohol in a twelve-month period compared to 42 percent who had used marijuana and 17 percent who had used cocaine. (Institute for Social Research, University of Michigan, Ann Arbor, MI., *Drug Use Among American High School Students and Other Young Adults.* 1985)
- Only 42 percent of fourth graders know that alcohol is a drug, compared to 81 percent who consider marijuana a drug; the percentage of students considering alcohol a drug drops with age to 28 percent in the upper grades. (Weekly Reader Publications. *A Study of Children's Attitudes and Perceptions About Drugs and Alcohol*, Middletown, CT, Apr. 25, 1983)
- The earlier in life a child starts using any dependence-producing drug, the more likely he or she is to experience dependence and

other health problems, and go on to other dependence-producing drugs. (Robert L. Dupont, "Substances Abuse," *Journal of the American Medical Association,* Vol. 254, #16, Oct. 25, 1985: p. 2336)

- Lower expectations for the future, alienation and boredom are associated with drinking among children in all socio-economic groups. (Nancy P. Gordon & Alfred McAlister: "Promoting Adolescent Health," *Adolescent Drinking: Issues and Research,* New York: Academic Press, 1982, p. 205)

- Approximately 10,000 young people aged 16-24 are killed each year in alcohol-related accidents of all kinds, including drownings, suicides, violent injuries, homicides and injuries from fire. (US DHHS, NIAAA Public Health Service, "Questions and Answers: Teenage Alcohol Use and Abuse," *Prevention Plus: Involving Schools, Parents and the Community in Alcohol and Drug Education,* Publication No. ADM/84-1256, Rockville, MD., 1983, p. xiii)

- Alcohol-related highway deaths are the number one killer of 15 to 24 year olds. (US DHHS National Center for Health Statistics, Public Health Service, *Health, United States, 1980,* Pub. No. (PHS) 81-1232, December 1980)

- It takes less alcohol to produce impairment in youth than in adults. Younger drivers in fatal crashes have lower average blood alcohol concentrations (BACs) than older drivers. Blood alcohol concentration is the amount by weight of alcohol in a volume of blood, and is typically expressed as percent weight by volume. A BAC of .05 percent is equal to 50 mg of alcohol per deciliter of blood (approx. 3.5 fluid oz.). ("Blood Alcohol Concentrations among Young Drivers, 1983," *Morbidity and Mortality Weekly Report* (MMWR) 33: 699-701, 1984)

- Drivers 16-24 years old represent 20 percent of licensed drivers and less than 20 percent of total miles driven, and yet account for 42 percent of all fatal alcohol-related crashes. (US DOT Fatal Accident Reporting System, 1982. DOT No. HS-806-566, 1984(h))

- Of 27,000 New York public school students, grades 7 through 12, 11 percent described themselves as being "hooked" on alcohol, with 13 percent admitting to attending classes while "high," "drunk" or "stoned" on alcohol. (New York State Division of Alcoholism and Alcohol Abuse, Drug and Alcohol Survey, 1983)

- Nearly 100,000 10 and 11 year olds reported getting drunk at least once a week in 1985. Over 185,000 sixth graders have used hard liquor by age 10. Alcohol use at least once a week by sixth graders more than doubled from 1983 to 1984. (Ronald Adams and Thomas Gleaton, Parents' Resource Institute for Drug Education, PRIDE—Drug Usage Prevalence Questionnaire, 1985)

- About one-third of fourth-graders (9 year olds) said children their age pressure others to drink beer, wine or liquor; the figure increased to nearly 80 percent by high school. (Weekly Reader Publications. *A Study of Children's Attitudes and Perceptions About Drugs and Alcohol*, Middletown, CT 1983)
- Alcoholics are more likely than non-alcoholics to have an alcoholic father, mother, sibling or distant relative. Almost one-third of any sample of alcoholics had a least one parent who was also alcoholic. (*Alcoholism: An Inherited Disease,* US DHHS. Pub. No. (ADM) 85-1426, 1985, p. 3)
- Children of alcoholics have a four times greater risk of developing alcoholism than children of non-alcoholics. There are 28. 6 million children of alcoholics in the U.S. today, 6.6 million of whom are under the age of 18. (Children of Alcoholics Foundation, *Children of Alcoholics: A Review of the Literature,* 1985, Introduction and p. 2)
- While no one is predestined to become an alcoholic, genetic factors may increase or decrease the level of vulnerability toward alcoholism. (Marc A. Schuckit, M.D., "Genetics and the Risk for Alcoholism," *Journal of the American Medical Association*, Vol. 254, No. 8, 1985, p. 2616)
- At present, first drinking usually occurs around age 12, in contrast to age 13-14 in the 1940s and 1950s. (Gordon and McAlister, *Adolescent Drinking: Issues and Research,* p. 204)
- Nearly a third of high school seniors have said that most or all of their friends get drunk at least once a week. (L.D. Johnston, P.M. O'Malley and J.G. Bachman, *Use of Licit and Illicit Drugs by America's High School Students, 1975-1984*, US DHHS Pub. No. (ADM) 85-L394, Washington, D.C., Supt. of Docs., US Govt. Print. Off., 1985)
- Up to half of heavier youthful drinkers also use marijuana at least once a week, and a third of the youth who use marijuana more than once a month also are classed as heavier drinkers. (Research Triangle Institute, *Economic Costs to Society of Alcohol and Drug Abuse and Mental Illness: 1980*, RTI/2734/00-DIFR, June, 1984, p. 114)

- Many surveys suggest that the best predictor of the drinking habits of adolescents is the attitude and behavior of their parents with regard to alcohol use. Adolescent heavy drinkers tend to come either from homes where one or both parents are heavy drinkers, or from homes where both are abstainers. (Gordon & McAlister, *Adolescent Drinking: Issues and Research,* p. 206)
- Annual surveys of 17,000 high school seniors aged 17 and 18 years old consistently show that 85 percent of the participants have had at least one drink in the preceding year and that more than 66 percent have consumed at least one drink in the preceding month. Forty percent of seniors have participated in the "party drinking syndrome," that is, consumed five or more drinks on one occasion, at least once in the preceding two weeks. Thirty percent did so on two or more occasions, and 10 percent did so three or more times in the designated two-week period. In response to a related question, only a third of the seniors thought there was great risk in this type of binge drinking. (Johnston, O'Malley and Bachman: *Drugs and American High School Students: 1975-1983*)
- A child will see alcohol consumed an average of 75,000 times on TV before he or she is of legal drinking age. (Dr. Thomas Radecki, Chairman of the National Coalition on Television Violence and Psychiatrist with the University of Illinois School of Medicine,1983)
- Adolescents and young adults more heavily exposed to alcohol ads on TV and in magazines are more likely to perceive drinking as attractive, acceptable and rewarding than are those who have been less exposed. The heavily exposed group in a recent study was more likely to engage in drinking liquor—31 percent vs 15 percent—than was the less exposed group. (C. Atkins and M. Block, *Content and Effects of Alcohol Advertising,* Bureau of Alcohol, Tobacco and Firearms, US Govt., Washington, D.C., Report of Michigan State University Study, 1981)
- Drinking differences between boys and girls are diminishing. The number of young female drinkers has been increasing more rapidly than the number of young male drinkers. Girls also tend now to experiment with a wider variety of substances. (Robert H. Coombs, David K. Wellisch and Fawzy I. Fawzy, UCLA School of Medicine, Los Angeles, CA. *Drinking Patterns and Problems Among Female Children and Adolescents: A Comparison of Alcohol Abuse,* II (3 & 4) pp. 315-348 (1985))

- It is estimated that increasing federal excise taxes on beer, the favorite alcohol beverage among youth, would reduce alcohol-related motor vehicle fatalities by 55 percent among 18 to 20 year old young men and by 45 percent among 18 to 20 year old young women. (Henry Saffer, Kean College of New Jersey and National Bureau of Economic Research, and Michael Grossman, City University of New York Graduate School and National Bureau of Economic Research, *Effects of Beer Prices and Legal Drinking Ages On Youth Motor Vehicle Fatalities*, November 1985)
- Alcoholism is a chronic, progressive and potentially fatal disease characterized by tolerance and physical dependency or pathologic organ changes, or both. All are the direct or indirect consequences of the alcohol ingested. (National Institute on Alcohol Abuse and Alcoholism (NIAAA), *Fourth Special Report to the U.S. Congress on Alcohol and Health*, ed. John R. DeLuca, DHHS Pub. No. (ADM) 82-1080, 1981, p. 36)
- Alcoholism is one of the most serious public health problems in the United States today. Among the 18.3 million adult "heavier drinkers" (those consuming more than 14 drinks per week) 12.1 million have one or more symptoms of alcoholism, an increase of 8.2 percent since 1980. (NIAAA, Department of Biometry and Epidemiology, Working Paper: Projections of Alcohol Abusers, 1980, 1985, 1990, prepared by John Noble, 1985, pp. 5 and 6)
- One out of three American adults—56 million Americans— says that alcohol abuse has brought trouble to their families. This is about four times the number of families that say that other drugs have troubled their homes. (P. Regans, ABC New/Washington Post Poll, Survey #0190, May 1985)

Chapter 3

Cooper Takes One Drink Too Many

Consider this scenario.

Cooper, Ross and Bernini are senior vice presidents at the Chicago headquarters of a nationwide and very aggressive retail chain.

Each one earns about $75,000-100,000 per year.

Each one is married and has from one to three children between the ages of 6 and 17.

Each one is a moderate drinker; two or three drinks during lunch; a drink before dinner; wine or beer with dinner; and possibly a drink at night.

Each one has been drinking since his late teens.

Each one is proud of the fact that he has not been drunk in over 20 years even though he will occasionally drink heavily at social events.

Each one is scornful of the person who cannot hold his booze.

Each one has experimented with marijuana for a brief period. Ross is the only one of the three who used cocaine—at parties. He enjoyed the sensation but considered it too expensive and impractical—unlike alcohol.

Each one recently passed a company-required physical examination. Each one is free of classifiable mental disorder. Each one has always been able to handle the stress accompanying his position.

In fact these three individuals—Cooper, Ross, and Bernini—are archetypal mainstream Americans in their hobbies, purchases, political beliefs, lifestyles and aspirations.

They are the American middle-class corporate version of Jefferson's 'yeomen'—updated into the late 20th century.

But suddenly, one of the three, Cooper, becomes an alcoholic.

Notice the term 'suddenly.' Isn't this a bizarre characterization? After all, he has been drinking for more than 20 years. He may live another 20 years as an alcoholic. How is the word 'suddenly' justified?

The addiction to alcohol, per se, appears to occur at a point in time, just as a mountain road somewhere passes its unmarked summit, beyond which the way will be persistently downwards.

In alcohol dependence there seems to be a threshold and a trigger. At point A in time, Cooper does not need a drink. At point B in time, once that addictive trigger has fired, Cooper must have a drink. And so starts his decline, which is sad, for no matter how long it takes he will destroy his career, his family and most assuredly, himself.

What triggered his alcoholism? What sent him over the threshold? Why not Bernini or Ross, who drank just as much as Cooper?

We don't know for sure. This is the central problem of alcoholism. This is the etiological puzzle.

We do have many theories and much hard evidence which has emerged from recent research attempting to explain the etiological puzzle; all of which will be presented to you in some depth in subsequent chapters.

For now, I would just like to identify the kinds of evidence we have.

There is solid hereditary evidence, for example. Adopted children with an alcoholic biological parent have four times the probability of developing alcoholism as adopted children whose biological parents are not alcoholic. Similarly, if one identical twin becomes an alcoholic, the other twin has a 50% chance of becoming an alcoholic, too. (Goodwin 1976:72, 80)

There are gene theories based on the association between color blindness, liver cirrhosis and alcoholism. (Hillman 1974)

There is an interesting theory which postulates a genetic defect in the adrenal-hypophyseal axis.

There are very suggestive metabolic/nutritional theories similar to the diabetic model of disordered carbohydrate metabolism.

And we know now that ethanol, through a series of biochemical transformations, alters brain concentrations of B-endorphin, enkephalin and other opiate peptides.

There are psychological theories which identify specific personality types prone to alcoholism.

And there are social theories based to a large extent on the heroin-addiction epidemics which periodically sweep large American cities.

The complexity of the disease called alcoholism is such that each of the above may contribute a portion of the truth.

Let's deal with that complexity in our $100,000 a year good family man Cooper who has suddenly become a morbidity statistic. Or, to put it another way, Cooper, after many years of 'free will' drinking no longer has any options vis-à-vis alcohol—now he must drink, steadily.

Let's explore what is going on in Cooper-metabolically; what distinguishes him now from his fellow vice presidents Bernini and Ross, in whom no alcoholism 'trigger' fired, even though they drank just like Cooper.

The human body can, on the average, eliminate only about one ounce of l00-proof whiskey per hour. (Milam & Ketcham 1983:19) The rest goes into the bloodstream and is diffused throughout the body's cells.

What remains in the bloodstream forms the blood alcohol level, defined as the percentage of alcohol to blood (a BAL of .10%—that is, one part alcohol to a thousand parts blood—is generally regarded as legal intoxication).

The simple molecular structure of alcohol enables it, once ingested and in the bloodstream, to pass through the cell membranes and infiltrate the liver, heart, pancreas, lungs, kidneys and other organs and tissues, including, most importantly, the brain—where the usually impregnable blood/brain barrier also fails to stop it.

Since alcohol and some of its metabolites are highly toxic substances and since its infiltration throughout the organism is swift and virtually total, how will Cooper survive and manage under almost constant intoxification?

Cooper, like other alcoholics, will survive quite well (even thrive) for a while by means of the organism's many adaptive mechanisms.

By developing a provisional tolerance, a sort of 'deranged' homeostasis in the midst of heavy drinking, Cooper's body and mind will strike a temporary but wide-ranging compromise with the systemic toxification.

But the price paid for this new homeostasis is addiction. To maintain the adaption, biochemically, Cooper must maintain the ethanol intake around which the alcoholic adaption is built. Whenever he doesn't, he will experience painful and in some instances life threatening withdrawal symptoms that will soon have him seeking metabolic relief: booze. This is what we mean when we say he has become an alcoholic: probably at risk all along (by genetic/enzymatic predisposition), he has succumbed to the metabolic disease.

Lieber, Noble and other distinguished researchers have begun to piece together the adaption puzzle in alcoholism. A great deal remains to be uncovered. In his path-breaking *Under The Influence: A Guide To The Myths & Realities of Alcoholism,* Milam has recently constructed a working model of the adaptive mechanisms involved. (Milam & Ketcham 1983:47) Three critical adaptions are changing Cooper's relationship to alcohol.

1. As an alcoholic, he is less able than his nonalcoholic colleagues to eliminate acetaldehyde—a toxic breakdown product of alcohol. The devastating effects of the acetaldehyde are buffered and masked, however, by the alcohol. So, unwittingly treating himself, Cooper drinks more and more. The liver adapts by gearing up a second alcohol processing system called the MEOS (microsomal ethanol oxidizing system), which of course yields additional acetaldehyde, to be buffered by still more alcohol.

2. The mitochondria, the cell's power units that release energy from absorbed food, become enlarged and misshapen in an attempt to burn the high caloric energy in alcohol. These distortions provide Cooper with energy even though he is eating less and less, but the end result is widespread cell injury and death.

3. The CNS cell membranes, which mediate the complex chemical and electrical processes necessary for nerve cell maintenance and transmission, are endangered by the massive alcohol consumption. They adapt by literally changing their structure and functioning, enabling them to handle the barrage of alcohol quite well—so well, in fact, that they begin to require it.

Cooper, in other words, has developed a remarkable, integrated, homeostatic infrastructure that enables him, indeed, requires him, to drink continuously.

His metabolic processes, formerly alcohol-sensitive, have now become tolerant of alcohol, so tolerant that they need alcohol. Cooper is, as we say, addicted.

It is the biochemical resolution of this seeming contradiction between hard-core addiction and easy tolerance that now enables Cooper to drink his associates under the table (where once he had no such ability) and often, astonishingly, improve his performance in sex, business, sports (while his nonalcoholic drinking colleagues are wiped out).

He has even developed a foolproof homeostatic feedback device— the BAL. Cooper's body 'knows' that the BAL must be kept high—at the fine line on which the adapted organs' tolerance/addiction balances. And this level is invariably higher than the BAL that would inebriate a nonalcoholic drinker.

It is, on the whole, an elegant, even imposing system. One major problem—time. Sooner or later the toxicity of alcohol will overwhelm all the adaptions that have coalesced in homeostasis and the whole system will come tumbling down.

Cooper is simply biding time. He is waiting for the poisoning or the life-wrecking behavioral changes or one of the secondary disorders which alcoholism and its adaptions pave the way to: diabetes, pneumonia, a heart attack, a car accident.

Perhaps the most difficult intellectual challenge facing the individual who attempts to deal with an alcoholic is to repudiate the time-worn view of alcoholism (passed down through the culture) that this disease is somehow 'metaphysical' . . . that it has something to do with will and character. Of course these qualities are important, but only before the 'trigger' fires.

One must understand that the alcoholic patient, no matter what he or she is being treated for, has developed an almost demonic homeostatic adjustment that is as powerful and automatic as the mechanism which regulates the body temperature through sweating and shivering.

Chapter 4

Fathers and Sons

Now that I have identified Cooper's biochemical adaptions we can pose once again the two questions which I asked previously, and phrase those questions more specifically.

- How can one use the word 'trigger' to explain such a systemic process?
- Why can't one be more specific in identifying why Cooper became an alcoholic and not Bernini or Ross, since all three were basically drinking men?

In answer to the first question . . .

I used the word 'trigger' not because there is a single organ or even process that 'fired'—there is no one thing that can be identified or placed under a microscope or removed surgically.

'Trigger' was simply a metaphor for that moment in time of the onset of the adaptions.

Let's follow the sequence again: A) Cooper 'fired' because of a metabolic response to ethanol toxicity; B) Cooper's particular response was adaption in the liver function, in the cells, in the CNS; C) The adaption(s) formed the tolerance/addiction homeostasis controlled by the BAL feedback.

In other words, 'trigger' is merely a code word for the coalesced, activated ensemble of adaptions.

In answer to the second question . . .

I briefly outlined, if you recall, several possible theories as to why Cooper and not Bernini or Ross became alcoholic. Each theory has its distinguished proponents.

My opinion, based on my clinical experience and reading of the relevant literature, is simply this: There is now overwhelming evidence that the genetic/hereditary factor is, like the Bishop of Rome, primus inter pares, first among equals.

This factor entails an inherited predisposition for metabolic dysfunction vis-à-vis ethanol . . . which of course can be influenced by many environmental factors.

The hereditary element has been amply documented in Goodwin's adoption studies and others in the United States, Denmark and elsewhere. Goodwin found that the children of alcoholics have a four times greater risk of becoming alcoholics than the children of nonalcoholics—despite having no exposure to an alcoholic parent after the first weeks of life. (This latter finding did great damage to the many etiological theories which included the concept of alcoholism as a learned behavior or a learning disorder.)

Various twin studies have been equally important in establishing the hereditary connection. As Vaillant notes in his acclaimed new work, *The Natural History of Alcoholism* (1983:65): "there have been four well-executed twin studies of alcoholism. In each study, identical twins exhibited much greater concordance for drinking behavior—and in some studies greater concordance for alcohol abuse—than did fraternal twins, who in theory shared the same family environment but not the same genes."

Vaillant also confirms Goodwin's importance in establishing the current scientific consensus on the primacy of hereditary factors (p. 64): "Goodwin (1976, 1979) has persuasively marshalled evidence that the observed increased rate of alcoholism in the descendants of alcoholics appears to correlate with alcohol abuse in heredity, not in the environment."

It is the specific genetic component of the hereditary predisposition which is still mysterious, although it appears that what is inherited is the inability to process alcohol so that toxic breakdown products of alcohol remain in the body and alter the brain concentration of opiate peptides.

Alcoholism, in fact, might be closely related to a host of enzymatic disorders, of which phenylketonuria is one of the more graphic examples.

The description of that disorder from Dorland's (1985) is quoted in part below:

> "phenylketonuria . . . an inborn error of metabolism attributable to a deficiency of or a defect in phenylalanine hydroxylase, the enzyme that catalyzes the conversion of phenylalanine to tyrosine. The lack permits the accumulation of phenylalanine and its metabolic products in the body fluids. It results in mental retardation . . . neurologic manifestations (including hyperkinesia, epilepsy, and microcephaly), light pigmentation, eczema, and a mousy odor, unless treated by administration of a diet low in phenylalanine. The disorder is transmitted as an autosomal recessive trait. Abbreviated PKU."

The paradigmatic similarities are intriguing—particularly when one keeps in mind how the alcoholic deals, metabolically, with the acetaldehyde problem.

So—why Cooper? Why not Bernini or Ross?

I must answer—genetics.

In fact, Cooper's father was a confirmed (nontreated) alcoholic who died at age 36 in an auto accident during a summer vacation with the family in Canada. Cooper's paternal grandmother was at least a heavy drinker (port), entered a state medical hospital at age 54 (diagnosis unknown), was released two years later and died at age (approx.) 61 possibly of pneumonia.

And now we are led to a third question: how important is etiologic identification in the successful management of the disorder?

Well, since in the real world an alcoholic may exist for anywhere between 5 and 20 years before he first enters a clinic or medical institution for alcoholism (of course the odds are good that he will be hospitalized or die before that from one of the many 'masked' disorders which alcoholism elicits)—the genetic/etiologic factor is important only prior to the trigger firing or after he enters a clinic for treatment.

To put it another way—his family should have known that Cooper was at severe risk during his years of nonalcoholic drinking; they should have understood that Cooper's heredity condemned him, genetically, to relative abstinence. But, in fact, their only response was, as we shall see later in more detail, bewilderment.

The physician who eventually treats Cooper first and foremost must dig into his family's history to locate any and all drinking and allied disorders—particularly those dealing with sugar and carbohydrate metabolism. If the physician doesn't do that, he's just 'whistling Dixie' because the genetic etiology of alcoholism has one very crucial diagnostic import: there is a radical difference between a heavy drinker and an alcoholic.

The former drinks for a host of reasons, but if not genetically predisposed will probably never become an alcoholic. He can and does drink for years and the telltale tolerance/addiction homeostasis is never activated. Moreover, this drinking will be cyclical.

The accomplished alcoholic is a different species altogether. He has been overwhelmed by his genetic blueprint. He can only drink more and more. Outside forces will now be important only in speeding up or slowing down the breakdown of his adaptions—his poisoning. Remember, it is not the appetite for alcohol which has been passed down to Cooper; it is the deranged metabolism in the face of the substance which assuages the appetite.

Chapter 5

A Deadly Trade Off: Nutrition for Energy

Now I want to discuss one of the most basic aspects of alcoholism—nutrition. Alcohol contributes only about 5% of the calories in the American diet. However, in the heavy drinker, alcohol supplies up to 50% of the total caloric intake—day in and day out (based on average national consumption figures). (Winick 1980:183)

Let me begin on a personal note.

I have treated thousands of alcoholics, both for alcoholism per se, and for ancillary disorders.

I have treated fat ones and skinny ones, tall ones and short ones—blacks and whites, sinners and saints, men and women, corporate presidents and day laborers, lunatics and wise men.

They all shared two fundamental things in common.

First, of course, was their addiction.

And second was the fact that they were all, in one way or another, malnourished.

Now, I am not using the term 'malnutrition' in the popular sense, but in the classical sense—that is (following *Dorland's*, 1981), as "any disorder of nutrition" that "may be due to unbalanced or insufficient diet or to defective assimilation or utilization of foods."

To be honest, for many years I ignored this fact.

I treated it as inevitable but unimportant—in the same way that a physician understands that hospitalized alcoholics, under the pressure of detoxification, will sooner or later manifest some behavioral peculiarity in the ward.

And in much the same way that practitioners of sports medicine deal with baseball teams. Players in certain positions will have minor chronic injuries that are considered irrelevant because they are always present. They are basically a function of the position that cannot be avoided. But the same injuries in players at other positions will be disabling.

For example, all major league catchers will have many bent and badly bruised fingers that a physician will ignore, except maybe to apply some spray, ointment or hot and cold packs to ease the discomfort. But such injuries when sustained by a pitcher or a shortstop will remove them from the competition until those injuries are treated extensively and healed.

So I ignored the bleeding gums, scaling skin, dry hair, mental derangement, vision impairment and the wide and often bewildering variety of malnourishment symptoms that alcoholics exhibit and, like other physicians, I just used thiamine or quick vitamin and nutrient fixes and then got onto the business at hand—detox.

Four factors made me change my mind.

First, there was the human factor. Like many other physicians who treat alcoholics, I was becoming increasingly depressed over my lack of success. I was experiencing the normal high failure rate, but that wasn't good enough for me, because it meant that out of every 10 alcoholics I treated, at least 7 would be hospitalized again for the disease or would be killed in a car accident or take his own life or be hospitalized for an allied disorder. I didn't really care that my failure rate was the national norm—I knew I was doing something wrong, seeing something blurry, missing something important.

Second, there was the diagnostic factor. New tests were becoming available (detailed analyses of carbohydrate metabolism, enzyme and vitamin metabolism tests, etc.) which showed that the gross malnourishment symptoms such as bleeding gums were only the tip of the iceberg.

Third was the research factor. New findings were firming up the genetic etiology of alcoholism. New metabolic findings were beginning to shed light on the many unexplained phenomena that had surfaced in my clinical practice—such as the statistical correlation between alcoholism and disturbances in the carbohydrate metabolism and the insulin-catecholamine relationships.

Fourth, and in many ways the most important, was the emergence of a new paradigm to explain the new empirical evidence.

- the paradigm of malnutrition was dramatically broadened by Professor Herman Baker of the New Jersey Medical School and others to encompass the entire human organism over time rather than merely deficiency disease. This broadening of the paradigm—panmalnutrition and subclinical—placed nutrition in a new perspective: as the systemic process which supports virtually all the body's homeostatic mechanisms . .
- the once revolutionary theory called "biological individuality" of Dr. Roger Williams was especially confirmed. This theory states that each individual has a unique, inherited pattern of susceptibilities and resistances . . . each individual deals with essential nutrients differently . . . each individual has different nutritional needs . . .
- the moral/behavioral model of alcoholism was found to be wanting—scientifically, diagnostically, therapeutically

All these factors contributed to my growing understanding that nutrition is one of the key, ignored factors in alcoholism, an awareness that is now being confirmed by research.

Enough of me, now let us deal with our alcoholic subject because we know a great deal about what is happening to Cooper, nutritionally.

Once the disease was triggered—once Cooper developed a new balance of tolerance/addiction which forced him to drink continuously, then the statistic we threw out before, off hand, becomes relevant and crucial. As long as Cooper stays in the world as an alcoholic, he will more or less consume 50% of his total calories in booze . . . And he will, indeed, become very much what he eats; a severe nutritional casualty.

First of all, Cooper will stop eating his normal food for very good biochemical reasons which will be explained shortly. As a good family man, and relatively affluent, his eating habits prior to addiction were: breakfast with wife and family, lunch with colleagues, dinner with family. This eating pattern goes by the wayside quickly. No alcoholic eats three meals a day of any kind. Alcoholics cannot. They have become metabolic cripples.

Not only does he stop eating as he has done before, but a fascinating dialectic emerges—a chain between his consumption of a bottle and half of vodka a day (with orange juice in the morning, straight and in martinis the rest of the day) . . . his inability to consume and/or utilize the nutrients required for the simple maintenance of health . . . and his desire for a host of 'antinutrients.'

There are in my opinion six major links in this chain—and probably at least four out of six of these links are verifiable in all alcoholics. These six links—energy, appetite, glucose, gut, metabolism, sugar—are patterns taking place within Cooper, large scale patterns which emerge from his addiction.

But before I describe those patterns, I must identify the very specific biochemical activities which underlie them and which have been identified by researchers.

Myron Winick, M.D. of Columbia University's College of Physicians and Surgeons has provided a remarkably cogent summary of important recent findings on specific ethanol toxicity vis-à-vis human nutrition (1980:184)

1. The major nutritional consequences of excess alcohol are due to its direct toxic effects, especially on the liver . . . fatty liver, hepatitis, cirrhosis—and the most serious complications, encephalopathy or ascites.

2. A second organ system on which ethanol exhibits direct toxicity is the gastrointestinal tract . . . Ethanol can affect gastric acid secretion and gastric emptying time and is a cause of acute gastritis.

3. It is directly injurious to the mucosa of the small intestine, and impaired absorption of fat, xylose, folate, thiamin and B 12 has been described.

4. All of these changes in the G.I. tract may lead to a malabsorption syndrome.

5. When ethanol is given as an isocaloric replacement for carbohydrate, protein breakdown is stimulated and urea content in urine increases.

6. Alcohol has been reported to alter amino acid metabolism in the liver.

7. Experimentally, a single large dose of alcohol may inhibit protein synthesis.

8. Lipid metabolism depends in part on liver function and may be abnormal in the alcoholic . . . Increased hepatic ketogenesis, decreased fatty acid oxidation and increased fatty acid synthesis may lead to an increase in triglycerides.

9. Chronic alcohol intake raises all the lipoprotein fractions in serum.

10. The consumption of alcohol may impair vitamin metabolism at many levels. Vitamin intake may be reduced as a result of poor diet or anorexia. Absorption may be impaired because of the effects on the gastrointestinal tract. Hepatic stores, particularly of folate, pyridoxine, B 12, and niacin may be depleted. In addition, the utilization of certain vitamins has been reported to be impaired. Particularly important in this respect are folate, thiamin, and pyridoxine. There is evidence that increased hydrolysis of pyridoxal phosphate takes place in the liver of alcoholics, resulting in deactivation of the vitamin.

These and other biochemical specificities coalesce into six major patterns of malnourishment operating in Cooper.
They are:

A. *Energy Link*. Although alcohol liberates 7.1 cal/g, it has virtually none of the essential nutrients such as vitamins, minerals or trace elements. So, our friend Cooper gets calories for energy on a temporary basis, but, by depriving himself of badly needed nutrients (either by not eating food which contains them because of Link B or not absorbing them because of Link D), precipitates both chronic and acute malnutrition.

51

B. *Appetitive Link*. Ethanol reduces the desire for food by acting on the appetite control center of the midbrain with the result that the alcoholic increasingly relies on alcohol for calories, with the attendant lack of essential nutrients.

C. *Glucose Link*. Almost uniquely, alcohol is like glucose in that it can pass the blood/brain barrier. Cooper's brain probably adapts metabolically to the ethanol as a fuel, and this concomitantly weakens his ability to burn glucose (this may account for the strong statistical correlation between alcoholism and hypoglycemia).

D. *Metabolic Link*. Simply, the toxicity of alcohol reduces Cooper's ability to digest, absorb, metabolize and store the limited amounts of nutritious food he does ingest.

E. *Gut Link*. The poor digestion of food and alcohol's continuous irritation of the colon and small intestine precipitate a form of chronic diarrhea in Cooper, entailing the wholesale loss of key nutrients and fluids and a disruption of the basic electrolyte balance of cells. More nutrients are lost through the 'leaky gut' syndrome, where partially digested matter seeps through the gut wall into the bloodstream and induces adverse food reactions and other sensitivities.

F. *Sugar Link*. As Cooper's life-style begins to deteriorate, he becomes desperate for more and more energy (it is a heroic and losing battle)—and thereby, while becoming more dependent on alcohol, he also becomes dependent on sugar, highly refined flour products, nicotine, and caffeine, using those substances, correctly called 'antinutrients', to sustain his level of energy and balance his glucose.

Patients with alcoholism trigger a series of addictive behaviors in their desperate attempt to balance their addictions. Alcohol, sugar, caffeine, refined carbohydrate, nicotine and increasingly drugs.

Many other researchers, physicians, and scientists have reached the same conclusions as myself, although the articulation of the links differ widely in their nomenclature.

Charles S. Lieber characterizes the alcohol-nutrition interactions thusly (1979:48):

- Primary Malnutrition (deficient intake)
  - 'empty' calories
  - economic factors
  - impaired appetite secondary to GI-liver disorders
- Secondary Malnutrition (deficient nutrient utilization)
  - ethanol-induced GI damage (maldigestion-malabsorption)
  - deficiency-induced intestinal dysfunction
  - energy wastage
  - decreased activation or increased inactivation of nutrients

It is obvious from this list that Cooper is gradually losing the capacity to extract the necessary nutrients from the environment—and the reasons are a poisoned metabolism which induces an equally poisonous set of eating behaviors.

Many physicians are fooled by alcoholics because their (the physicians') view of malnourishment is, like their view of alcoholism, very old-fashioned.

Most alcoholics are not quiescent skeletons. They are often robust and extremely active (often manic—depending on the phase they present) and therefore the diagnosis of acute malnutrition seems absurd to the physician who is confronted with a muscular 40-year-old male who plays squash twice a week and seems to show at the time none of the fatigue or gross symptoms that are normally associated with a nutrient cutoff. In fact, in the early stages of the disease, only rigorous testing will reveal the alcoholic's malnourishment.

It will be a long time, if ever, before Cooper looks like a concentration camp victim. But, in truth, he is literally starving himself to death (while poisoning himself) and masking it with an energy high/nutrient low lifestyle characterized by candy bars and black coffee with lots of sugar, and white bread smeared with cherry jam, and vodka—always vodka, night and day, more and more.

When I understood that simple fact, I finally understood that no treatment program for alcoholics would ever be successful unless a large component of that regimen is nutritionally based.

Before we leave this brief discussion of Cooper's nutritional problems while he is an at large alcoholic, I want to mention another, even more controversial area of nutrition—Roger William's etiology of alcoholism, his genotrophic theory.

Williams believes that alcoholism is a condition predisposed to by heredity and precipitated by nutritional factors—one of the most important being an impairment of the cells in the appetite-regulating mechanism in the hypothalamic region of the brain.

This thesis has been neither proved nor disproved—although Lieber and coworkers in 1975 showed in their baboon experiments that even a nutritionally adequate diet will not prevent the baboons from developing alcoholic fatty liver when their alcohol consumption approximates that of human alcoholics. (Lieber & DeCarli 1977)

But William's idea is an important one, conceptually, because it was the first theory that tried to situate the disease in a genetic/nutritional matrix, and more and more evidence is emerging that this may well be the case.

The therapeutic possibilities appear to be far reaching, as we have seen in Chapter 1.

One cannot leave any discussion of alcoholism and nutrition without dealing with the direct toxicity of alcohol on the gastrointestinal tract.

We have already seen that one of the major nutritional aspects of this toxicity is the inevitable malabsorption syndrome in alcoholics which in turn calls forth all kinds of deficiencies: the nutrients that the alcoholic does ingest simply cannot be dealt with by the body.

There are many other, often severe, GI consequences for the alcoholic.

Needless to say, the mild nausea which is a constant companion of the alcoholic is a function of that specific toxicity.

The most common serious GI symptom seen in alcoholics is bleeding.

Acute gastritis accounts for 25 percent of upper gastrointestinal bleeding in alcoholics as compared with 5 percent in nonalcoholic populations. The Mallory-Weiss syndrome, which refers to bleeding caused by lacerations of the stomach lining near its junction with the esophagus, is another common cause of bleeding in alcoholics. It accounts for 5 to 14 percent of gastrointestinal bleeding episodes in hospital populations of whom 60 to 80 percent reported heavy alcohol intake prior to the episode. Symptoms of retching and vomiting often precede the vomiting of blood, which suggests that the lacerations of the stomach lining may be caused by a sharp increase in intragastric pressure. (Mezey 1986:7)

Mark A. Korsten and Charles S. Lieber have provided one of the best surveys of research and clinical findings (1979).

Let me encapsulate partially their review:

- Esophagus
  - Increased risk of esophageal cancer in alcoholics has now clearly been related to alcohol per se, and to be independent of smoking habits.
  - Functional abnormalities of the esophagus have been described in the alcoholic . . . prominent changes included a decrease in frequency of primary peristaltic waves in the distal two-thirds of the esophagus as well as an increase in tertiary, nonpropulsive activity after swallowing.
- Stomach and Duodenum
  - Acute intragastric administration of ethanol results in the augmented secretion of hydrochloric acid.
  - Alcohol alters the permeability of the gastric mucosal 'barrier' and the subsequent ingress of hydrogen is potentially injurious.
  - The occurrence of gastritis after the acute administration of alcohol has been clinically well established.
- Biliary Tract
  - Acutely, ethanol decreases the volume of bile flow and the output and concentration of bile salts.
- Pancreas
  - Pancreatitis is one of the leading causes of morbidity and mortality in the alcoholic patient.
  - If it does not lead to early demise, chronic, incapacitating complications such as diabetes mellitus, pseudocysts and steatorrhea may ensue.
  - Ethanol stimulates the pancreas either indirectly by causing the secretion of gastric acid (and secondary release of secretin) or by the direct release of duodenal secretin.
  - Chronic intake of ethanol alters the exocrine response of the pancreas.
  - Abnormalities in pancreatic exocrine function are found in alcoholics even in the absence of clinical pancreatic disease.

- Small Bowel
  - The effects of alcoholism on small bowel function and morphology can be attributed to alcohol per se and concomitant nutrient deficiency, and both these factors may interact synergistically to impair the absorption of important foodstuff.
  - Hepatic and pancreatic injury may further accentuate defects in digestion and absorption and aggravate the tendency toward malnutrition in the alcoholic.

Chronic alcohol intake is particularly devastating to the mouth.

It increases the excretion of calcium phosphorus which leads to erosion of the tooth enamel.

The systemic malnutrition of the alcoholic affects the gums, making them more susceptible to infection, pyorrhea and loosening of the teeth in the sockets.

The pain from neglect of teeth and gum problems prompts the alcoholic to drink more and to search for additional narcotics.

Even from this brief survey the reader can intuit the enormous medical and hospital costs incurred each year from this single aspect of the disease called alcoholism.

And, of course, the majority of patients with alcoholism hospitalized for GI disorders are rarely diagnosed as alcoholics . . . so they are treated for symptoms, released and the ugly cycle starts again.

Chapter 6

Cooper Is Not a "Hollywood Drunk"

Now we must look at one of the most fascinating areas of alcoholism—Cooper's behavior in the office, in the home, in the street, in the bars.

Do you remember the old country and western song which contained these lines? . . .

"Cigarettes and whiskey and wild wild women,They drive a
man crazy, they drive him insane."

Wouldn't it be nice if this refrain was a lie?

But the song doesn't lie (except for the 'wild wild women' part since booze is a fake aphrodisiac). Alcohol does make people 'crazy' in many ways.

And alcoholics rarely check themselves into clinics because they have a sudden revelation that they are ill.

They are finally hospitalized *for alcoholism* virtually always because of an ugly incident. Something bad happens to them. Something bad happens because of them.

The alcoholic falls through a plate glass window. He withdraws $3,000 from his savings account and the next morning has only $9 left and can't account for the other $2,991. He is mugged in a motel room after picking up a woman whose face he can't remember in a bar whose name he can't remember. He drives his car into a stopped school bus. After three nights of sleeplessness, he walks out of the house in his underwear on a freezing winter morning and attempts suicide in the garage with his hunting rifle—the bullet misses all vital organs and he is hospitalized for six weeks. He falls off a subway platform. He loses his job because he initiates a ludicrous argument over who neglected to order pickles for the marketing meeting.

The roster of alcoholic disaster is enormous. He causes the firing of two close associates because he totally misinterprets a crucial financial statistic and covers his tracks so that the guilt falls elsewhere. He becomes firmly convinced his wife is having an affair with a neighbor and becomes so abusive that she leaves him. He inexplicably and suddenly decides to move himself and his family to New Orleans because he *knows* things will be better there. He starts to vomit blood, decides he has cancer and goes on a wild three-day gambling binge in Atlantic City. On and on it goes.

In fact, understanding the altered behavior of alcoholics is crucial to understanding the personal and social tragedy of the disease as well as its biochemical configurations—because alcohol is not like other addictions.

Consider for a moment the heroin or morphine addict. It is entirely possible to work in the same office with such an addict and—if he or she has sufficient money and access to the drug—never know that particular individual is addicted because it is the withdrawal situation which induces erratic and/or criminal behavior. But booze is different—very different.

Booze elicits dramatic and often contradictory behavioral changes, continuously and independently of the withdrawal situation in alcoholic and nonalcoholic drinkers alike, although the former, because of the tolerance/addiction mechanism, often exhibits a completely different sequence of changes.

Booze uses the same metabolic pathways that will, say, induce fatty liver to induce changes in all the basic responses of the human organism to the environment—what he or she hears, sees, feels, loves, desires, fears, thinks.

There is no other disease which plays such psychological havoc while being primarily a physical, somatic disorder. There is no other disease which elicits such a mix of psychological and physical symptoms simultaneously and independently of each other.

That is one of the main reasons why a single alcoholic will often undergo a series of (in retrospect) perplexing and consecutive hospital

58

admissions—first for diabetes, then for manic depression, then for intestinal bleeding, then for delusional paranoia—and on and on until half the Merck manual is exhausted, while at no time will he ever be diagnosed as an alcoholic.

Jellinek, whose work was basically responsible for the acceptance of the disease concept of alcoholism, considered it to be a progressive disorder with distinct phases (1952). And within those phases he identified some 43 progressively appearing symptoms—the great majority behavioral in nature, including: guilt feelings, grandiose behavior, marked self-pity, decreased sexual drive, marked aggressive behavior, geographic escape, alcoholic jealousy, psychomotor inhibition, to name just a few.

It is interesting to note that because Jellinek emphasized behavior (the metabolic evidence was not available yet) . . . because alcoholism was accepted as a behavioral/psychiatric disorder by the AMA . . . and because virtually all hospitalized alcoholics shared certain psychological symptoms (passive-dependent, egocentric, sociopathic, lacking in self-esteem, etc.)—it was decided that those symptoms were not secondary to the disorder but the major elements of a premorbid personality profile for alcoholism. This belief still exists in the medical community, although enough evidence has appeared to disallow it and it is, in my opinion, no longer valid at all in the face of overwhelming evidence for a metabolic/genetic etiology for alcoholism.

As Prof. George E. Vaillant of Harvard notes (1983:74): "Not until several prospective studies were available could we seriously entertain the hypothesis that the 'alcoholic personality' might be secondary to the disorder . . . More recent prospective studies by Jones (1968), Kammeier, Hoffmann and Loper (1973) and Vaillant (1980a) all concur that premorbid traits of dependency do not increase the risk of alcoholism."

As a result of his most recent broad-based epidemiological studies, Vaillant confirms that (1983:102) "alcohol abuse was predicted by a set of variables depending on culture and family history of alcohol abuse that were different from those predicting mental health and sociopathy."

Dr. James R. Milam supports that view, indicating that "psychiatric problems are clearly not relevant to the onset of alcoholism." And, as Milam explains, it was Goodwin who provided the most important evidence (Milam & Ketcham 1983:40):

"Goodwin compared the children of alcoholics with the children of nonalcoholics. The two groups were 'virtually indistinguishable' with regard to depression, anxiety neurosis, personality disturbance, psychopathology, criminality and drug abuse."

This evidence now establishes that the addiction comes first and the behavioral changes second and as a result of toxicity and malnutrition of the CNS.

There is a vast literature on the relationship between alcohol and behavior from many vantage points—literally thousands of books and articles and conference proceedings.

But I will limit my discussion to:

- providing the latest experimental and clinical evidence as to how alcohol biochemically alters behavior . . .
- illuminating the statistical correlation between alcohol and known deviant behavior—murder, rape, suicide, etc . . .
- and translating those findings into a coherent picture of how our particular alcoholic, Cooper, is acting, thinking and doing in the world while 'under the influence.'

Our alcoholic case, Cooper, is not a Hollywood drunk. He doesn't spend the day staggering around with a bottle of vodka in his pocket.

In fact, please forget most movies you've ever seen about booze. The popular cinematic conception of alcoholism has little reality.

Let me attempt to graphically lay out the behavioral and underlying biochemical reality of one alcoholic—Cooper—during one particular 24-hour period. This is admittedly a difficult task but really the only way to show the enormous complexity and systemic strength of the disease and to show why it has always been so difficult to diagnose and treat.

Chapter 7

Cooper's Love Life

Our friend Cooper is sitting at a table in his state-of-the-art kitchen, in his beautifully furnished suburban ranch house.

It is 2:45 a.m. on a Thursday morning.

Cooper has just tried to make love to his wife and couldn't function sexually. The desire to make love was there—it is a good marriage—but the ability to perform was simply not there. What really perplexes him as he is sitting there is the fact that at the outset he was very sexually excited—and then the passion had mysteriously vanished as quickly as it came.

Cooper would not be perplexed if he knew that this sequence of events is quite common among alcoholics. Alcohol first increases and then decreases the levels of LH (luteinizing hormone), which stimulates the gonads (Lieber 1982: 65-140) and the effect is dose dependent.

Cooper, of course, has just run into the central sexual contradiction of booze.

Because alcohol is a CNS depressant, it often depresses certain higher brain functions which inhibit sexual behavior. Thus, the alcoholic often feels a heady erotic freedom, divorced from traditional views of fidelity or appropriateness of time and place.

But then the alcoholic, when he tries to act on that freedom, runs smack into the biochemical reality mentioned above.

This contradiction is not confined to male alcoholics. Women alcoholics also experience this dysfunction.

In a recent study, 67% of the alcoholic women in the sample reported their orgasmic experience had deteriorated after their drinking became alcoholic and 47% had become anorgasmic. Like the males, the women reported a subjective experience of increased sexual anticipation while drinking (Covington and Kohen 1984).

But let us return to Cooper, who is not sitting at the kitchen table in what you would call an alert position.

How could he be 'alert'? He's exhausted. He hasn't had a good night's sleep in so long that he no longer even expects it, although he works like a horse all day long and drinks enough to fill a horse.

Cooper, of course, does sleep, but it's in disjointed patterns—a series of bewildering, oddly spaced catnaps throughout the night and sometimes at his desk in the office.

His sleeping behavior is alcohol-induced. This drug, like many others, causes a 'self-sustaining disregulation' of sleep; and the initial alterations of sleep "are probably due to its direct effects on brain systems which are responsible for the states of sleep, mechanisms which control the duration rather than periodicity of sleep stages." (Williams and Salamy 1972:472).

When compared with control individuals matched on age, chronic alcoholics were found to have more stage REM (rapid eye movement) and stage 1 sleep, less SW (slow-wave, 'deep' sleep), more arousals, more frequent changes of sleep stage and more frequent brief disruptions of stage REM than controls. In fact, all these sleep dislocations are remarkably similar to the changes in sleep caused by acute doses of reserpine (Lester et al. 1973), an alkaloid used as an antihypertensive and sedative.

So Cooper sits at the kitchen table at 3 o'clock in the morning, impotent and sleepless.

Now the Hollywood version of alcoholism demands that he go for the vodka—because in Hollywood drinking episodes are always accompanied by or preceded by stress, and surely impotence is stressful.

But Cooper doesn't go for the vodka. Cooper is, in fact, very slightly influenced by outside forces anymore. He is controlled by his homeostatic network of adaptions which we discussed earlier, and his peculiar pattern allows him to temporarily avoid vodka during the early morning hours. He just doesn't drink then. That is part of his pattern. And, if there are, as some people claim, 10 million alcoholics walking around the United States today, there are 10 million homeostatic patterns of alcohol ingestion.

But Cooper does need something. He decides to make himself a cup of instant coffee—believing that a bout with the regular coffee-making machine in his kitchen would be too mechanically complex.

So he boils water and then, into a single cup, he pours two heaping teaspoons of instant expresso coffee. The jar says to use just one teaspoon for each cup of water.

Then he pours into the cup three heaping teaspoons of white sugar and stirs the mess.

He drinks it down slowly, smoking five or six cigarettes along the way.

Poor Cooper: while he is having his few hours respite from booze, his body still craves energy. So Cooper makes a fair (for him) exchange—two high-energy antinutrients (sugar and caffeine) for one (alcohol).

It is virtually impossible for Cooper to do anything other than poison himself continuously. In fact, alcoholism usually encompasses a fourfold addiction—ethanol, caffeine, sucrose, nicotine.

When he finishes the coffee, he thinks he feels a little better. It is now 3:30 a.m. But Cooper doesn't do anything. He just sits there.

And if you, the reader, were in an adjoining house and peering in at him, watching him sit there . . . staring straight ahead apathetically, while, from time to time, agitating the dead cigarette stubs in the ashtray—you would recognize something very familiar in his manner.

In fact, if you were a physician, you would probably say to yourself with absolute clinical certainty: "Ah, this man is by any immediate diagnostic criterion suffering from depression. He is exhibiting both of the classical syndromes. He is swinging between psychomotor retardation and agitation."

Your diagnosis would be correct in one sense. Cooper does show legitimate signs of clinical depression. The problem with the diagnosis is that the depression must be understood as secondary to the disorder. If you don't know that Cooper is an alcoholic and dose him with antidepressant drugs, you are going to get Cooper into a great deal of difficulty. (This unique problem will be discussed later in some depth.)

There is a great deal of data supporting a very strong relationship between alcoholism and depression.

As Solomon notes in his review of the "Psychiatric Characteristics of Alcoholics" (1983:82):

"Shaw et al.(1975). . . found that depression as defined by the Zung Self-Rating Depression Scale, the Beck Depression Inventory and the Minnesota Multiphasic Personality Inventory (MMPI) was present in 98% of male alcoholics on whom these evaluations were performed. Weissman et al. (1977)found that 59% of the alcoholics they interviewed were also depressed and that the symptom patterns of the depressed alcoholics were similar to those of primary depressives . . . Gibson and Becker(1973)also found that there were major similarities between the affect described by alcoholics and that of primarily depressed patients."

There is virtually no disagreement on the fact that alcoholics become depressed. In addition to the clinical evidence the most recent biochemical data for the etiology of depression strongly suggest that it is correlated to some extent with neurotransmitter deficits, and . . .

"Alcohol mimics the effects exerted by other cerebral depressants. These changes in the brain membranes may be related to the observed decrease in the normal Na + [sodium ion] influx into the neuronal membrane and may, in turn, induce a decrease in the action current . . . In addition, alcohol may alter normal Ca + + [calcium ion] homeostasis . . . and this may alter neuronal conductance and release of various neurotransmitters." (Lieber 1982:497).

One of the most significant differences between the syndrome in alcoholics and nonalcoholics is the periodicity factor. A nonalcoholic individual who is clinically depressed will often maintain those symptoms for days, weeks, months.

The alcoholic, however, slips in and out of depression with an often startling rapidity. The alcoholic is, in fact, a living roster of affective disorder symptoms which are constantly shifting. Thus, behaviorally, the alcoholic often mimics the bipolar depressive rather than the unipolar variety and is often mistakenly diagnosed as manic-depressive.

It is this switching of symptoms which often makes the alcoholic such a prime candidate for suicide. HEW estimates that 10,000 known alcoholics kill themselves in every 12-month period and alcoholics constitute 25% of all successful suicide attempts and more than 60% of all failed attempts (everyone who works in the field knows this is a conservative estimate since most alcoholics are not known).

Alcoholic suicide will continue to be a horrendous problem until physicians and administrators accept two simple clinical axioms: 1) depressed individuals should be considered alcoholic until proven otherwise, and 2) all alcoholics should be considered suicidal unless proven otherwise.

Now let me explain the practical import of the constant symptom switching in the suicide statistics. A nonalcoholic individual who is diagnosed for depression is usually watched closely by those who love him or care for him. The possibility of suicide is always present and recognized.

But the alcoholic, who keeps switching his symptoms, is never considered truly in danger by his loved ones because he will always come out of his depression into something else.

There are thousands of horror stories illustrating this phenomenon. I remember one case in particular. An alcoholic killed himself by leaping out of his fourteenth-story office onto Sixth Avenue in New York City, injuring two pedestrians and demolishing a standing vehicle in the process.

His coworkers were astonished and his secretary, when interviewed, noted that for the last two days the suicide had been friendly, happy, and even more communicative than usual. He had even, on the morning of the suicide, brought her a funny newspaper clipping about subtle ways in which a secretary can get back at her boss.

Yes, she said, he did from time to time drink too much, but he could always 'hold' his alcohol. Yes, she said, he was moody. No, she said angrily, he definitely was not an alcoholic.

Let's return to poor Cooper at the kitchen table; he sits there for another half-hour and then decides that maybe a shower will help. He goes to the downstairs bathroom and stands under a cascading stream for a long time, not soaping, just standing there. And suddenly, his body tenses and he shuts the tap off violently. He grows paler than usual. He has remembered that he forgot to do something very important, something crucial. But he can't remember what the hell it was. It was something to do with work, something he forgot to accomplish.

He jumps out of the shower and begins to pace, chain smoking.

As Solomon, in the same review quoted above, notes when discussing the DSM III Field Trial Study of 12,488 psychiatric patients: "Of the patients diagnosed as having a generalized anxiety disorder,21% also had alcoholism." (1983:103).

Yes, Cooper is a very good alcoholic—epidemiologically.

But his neurotic symptom of anxiety soon begins to transform itself into something else . . . what one can call 'biochemical reasoning' or, to steal a phrase, the 'wisdom of the body.'

Here's what happens in sequence.

Cooper decides that what he has forgotten is so important that he must get into the office very early and right what is wrong.

Suddenly suffused with energy and (almost desperate) purpose, Cooper dresses, leaves a note for his wife and drives into the city.

Halfway there, he completely forgets the problem, the reason for getting on the road so early. His anxiety vanishes as quickly as it arrived. In a sense it has done its job.

In its place comes a slight nausea and a generalized systemic discomfort. Cooper is about to start dealing once again with the only thing that really defines him behaviorally and biochemically—the addiction/ tolerance cycle which is alcoholism.

He is about to commence his own unique Byzantine ritual which will bring him his morning drinks and lock him in.

The anxiety attack did its job—it got him into the office by 7 a.m. No one else has arrived for work yet. As he sits there, his physical discomfort starts to increase. He looks out the window and decides it's too early to start work; he should go for a walk.

By now Cooper needs a drink but he never declares that to himself. He does not say: I need a drink. His biochemistry requires it and Cooper, being a moral individual and believing it is somehow wrong to drink in the morning, simply will not honestly articulate his need to himself.

He goes downstairs and takes a long walk. The real purpose of the walk is to search out a less affluent industrial (rather than a service-oriented) area—away from the bars he and his corporate buddies frequent and which are not open in the morning.

And there is another reason for those long morning walks: it's a way to deal with the 'pins and needles' in his legs which have been appearing with increasing frequency.

Like many other alcoholics, Cooper has the beginnings of polyneuropathy, "a nutritional disorder generally associated with deficiencies of the B complex vitamins—including thiamin (B_1), pantothenic acid, nicotinic acid and pyridoxine (B_6) which weaken and eventually damage the peripheral nerves outside the brain and spinal cord . . . [which] . . . carry electrical/chemical impulses which instruct the legs, arms, and torso to lift, move, run, walk, or feel warmth, cold, pain and pressure." (Milam & Ketcham 1983:92).

As the 16th edition of Cecil notes (1982:2046): "This syndrome has been encountered in inmates of prison camps, chronic alcoholics and patients undergoing dialysis for chronic renal failure . . . The salient changes consist of demyelination and axonal destruction of peripheral nerves, involving distal parts more than proximal ones . . . the biochemical lesion antedates clinical manifestations . . . the latter linger on . . . after the metabolic insult has been removed."

Let us return to Cooper who, upon passing an open bar, notices that they are also serving breakfast. He enters, walks to the steam table and orders a buttered roll and container of coffee to go. Then, holding the bag (which will never be opened) he drops all pretense, sits down at the bar and orders a vodka and grapefruit juice—mixed.

Just this one, he says to himself. It tastes very good. It feels very good. He sips it slowly at first but finishes fast.

He's on the cusp of feeling good. His biochemical adaptions are beginning to fall into place like a pinball machine. The cells and organs are getting what they now require after a few hours of deprivation. His blood alcohol homeostatic mechanism is beginning to move.

Cooper stands up to leave—then he sits down again. He orders another drink, only this time he orders the vodka straight up and the grapefruit juice on the side.

He takes just one sip of the juice, then drinks the vodka, not gulping it, just steadily. Then he orders and gulps a double shot of vodka, straight up, doesn't touch any more grapefruit juice, and dumps the roll and coffee into a garbage pail on the way out.

Cooper is now ready for the day. Like all alcoholics, his behavior after 'locking in' is brilliant—he walks straight, he smiles, he can take on the world, he can solve the most difficult problems instantly.

He is back in the office at 8:20 a.m. The place is beginning to hum. He works at peak, almost manic efficiency, clearing up his in-box writing memos, checking figures, formulating long-range plans.

At 10:00 a.m., his secretary, relieved that he's in one of his better moods, gets two cups of coffee from the office pot and brings him one. He thanks her profusely.

When she leaves he takes a sip; grimaces because she didn't put enough sugar in it and places the cup down on the edge of the desk. Alas, he misjudges the distance between the cup and the edge of the desk and as he swings around on his swivel chair—the coffee falls over, onto his shoes and pants cuffs.

A fluke?

No, a persistent symptom of the disease because booze causes all kinds of psychomotor problems—from spilling a cup of coffee to extremely complex accidents which cause injury and death.

The locus of the coffee spilling episode could be the cortex:

"Alcohol hits hardest some parts of the brain required for the most highly integrated actions . . . the functions with largest cortical components seem to be most susceptible . . . A loss of the efficiency of the most complex movements possessing cortical components is apparent." (Himwich and Callison 1972:82)

Or it could have been the musculature (or both):

"It was proposed that alcohol may interact with and/or antagonize calcium at the level of the cell membrane. This theory has been substantiated. Alcohol has been shown to interfere with the movement of calcium ions across the smooth muscle cell membrane . . . Ethanol is inhibitory for both spontaneous and potassium-induced muscle contraction . . . and it is well-documented that it displays a similar effect both in vitro and in vivo." (Lieber 1982)

In other words, Cooper might have misjudged the distance or perceived the distance correctly, but his hand could not complete the complex action correctly.

The coffee foul-up upsets Cooper so much that he increases his smoking. He runs out of cigarettes at 11:00 a.m. and goes downstairs to buy another pack. A newsstand in the building lobby sells cigarettes but Cooper decides to purchase his cigarettes from a vending machine in the bar down the block which is now open.

He gives the bartender a ten-dollar bill, asks for change for the machine, and then automatically orders a vodka and coke with a twist of lemon. He gets the cigarettes and settles in, reminding himself to go back to the office shortly.

One hour and four vodka and cokes later, he realizes he should have something to eat. He orders a London Broil hot plate. When the food comes he decides he is really not hungry because he had the roll for breakfast (he forgets that he threw the roll away) so he just eats some of the mashed potatoes with the heavy gravy, leaving the meat and vegetables.

At around 12:30 he returns to the office and is informed by his secretary that he missed an appointment with one of his associates, Bernini. Cooper shrugs it off. He spends the next hour in his office, half dozing and depressed.

Then Bernini comes into his office, accepts Cooper's lie as to why the appointment was missed and asks Cooper to review an architect's plans to expand and remodel a section of the firm's main store. Bernini asks him to return the plans by 3:00 p.m.

A few minutes later the director of personnel comes in and asks Cooper to fill out and return the biannual evaluation report on his secretary, which will determine the size of her raise, if any.

Cooper finishes the two assignments but sends the architect's plans to the personnel manager and the evaluation of his secretary to Bernini.

Another meaningless, understandable error by Cooper?

On the contrary, a behavioral deficit that is pervasive in the disorder and which often leads to disastrous events.

Why did he make that mistake? He heard the instructions clearly. He understood which package should go to which person: the evaluation report to the personnel director and the architect's plans to his associate, Bernini.

Alas, there are no random events in an alcoholic's life. He acted out of his biochemical reality.

> "Increasing concentrations of alcohol in the blood produce impairment of psychological functions such as perception, discrimination, association and voluntary response." (Begleiter and Platz 1972:338)

Gross (1973b) uses a 'radio' metaphor:

> "Evidence has been obtained which suggested that toxic disturbances of the receptor organs might be the basis for the positive sensory disturbances . . . . Such spontaneous bursts of sensory superactivity could generate 'noise' within the sensory systems, much as a radio would create static . . . "

For Cooper, this small error, this 'static', has more serious ramifications.

The personnel director comes into his office with the architect's plans (which should have been sent to Bernini) and makes a joking reference to Cooper's sanity. It is now 3:30 p.m. By this time Cooper has had the equivalent of 12 shots of 90 proof vodka. He is ethanol drenched but he is not drunk. Cooper reacts suddenly and inappropriately to the harmless joke—with hostility. He curses the personnel director and tells him to get the hell out of the office or he'll throw him out. The personnel director, astonished, leaves quickly. Cooper calms down, realizes what he has done and asks his secretary to write an apologetic memo to clear up the misplaced packages.

Cooper's small act of verbal aggression is, structurally, a model of what is probably the most enormous tragedy in alcoholism—the relationship between booze and violence.

Chapter 8

Cooper Blacks Out

In 1969 MacDonnell and Ehmer performed a famous animal experiment. Aggression was made to occur by extrinsic manipulation—stimulation of the hypothalamus. They found that the time required for all the events in the attack sequence increased as the alcohol dose increased. But the final event in the aggression sequence—the bite—occurred with greater force for the single dose of alcohol at which a direct test was made.

Humans, ingesting alcohol in social groups, do not have to be 'extrinsically manipulated'.

> "When subjects interacted in a group context, aggression appeared or increased after alcohol was consumed . . . the form of beverage, brandy or beer, made a difference in the amount of aggression produced." (Carpenter and Armenti 1972:535)

> "The frequency of aggressive behavior in 149 males in natural settings (party settings) increased with the blood alcohol level of subject both under the beer and distilled spirits conditions, although there was a stronger tendency with the latter." (Boyatzis 1974, cited in Permanen 1976:391)

We have now run smack into the dirty little secret of alcoholism. If, for example, being 'under the influence' were miraculously to become like the 'insanity defense'—more than half the incarcerated felons in the U.S. would be sent to alcohol clinics (and, you must recall, we now have the largest prison population per capita on the planet).

- In a study of 395 criminal homicides in the urban area of Chicago, 'intoxicants' were present in 53.5% of the homicidal scenes (Voss and Hepburn 1968, cited in Permanen 1976:356)
- Janowska (1970) has analyzed data on 279 individuals sentenced for homicide in Poland and she found that 64.5% of the murderers and 49% of the victims were intoxicated at the scene of the crime. (cited in Permanen 1976:357)
- Mayfield (1972) found that in his sample of 307 prisoners in North Carolina convicted of serious assaultive crimes—36% were problem drinkers and these committed the most serious previous assaults. (Cited in Permanen 1975:366)
- Gelfand (1971) investigated 98 native Rhodesians (black) and found that 63% had consumed alcohol prior to the crime. (Cited in Permanen 1976:360)
- Nau (1967) in West Berlin and Grislain & Associates (1968) in France found high proportions of alcoholics in child abusers, 50% and 65% respectively. (Cited in Permanen 1976:365)
- In Rada's (1975) sample of California rapists, 35% of the 77 studied were classified as alcoholics. (Cited in Permanen 1976:365)

So, while Cooper's act of verbal violence was relatively harmless and insignificant, it was, in fact, the paradigm for the alcoholic violence which continues to feed prisons and execution chambers the world over.

As HEW's 1981 report to Congress sums up: alcohol was implicated in 86% of murders, 75% of assaults, 50% of rapes and 60% of robberies.

And the odds are that if Cooper survives a few more years, he will, in spite of his upward mobility and middle-class values, eventually escalate into more significant violence than cursing a fellow vice president.

I am sure the reader will now understand that Cooper, by 3:30 in the afternoon of his typical day has already undergone more stress in 12 hours than a nonalcoholic will endure in a month—and he has undergone it without sleep or significant nutrition. But Cooper has not finished his day yet.

When Cooper finally does leave the office at 6:20 that evening, he has, as we have seen already, experienced anxiety, depression, paranoia, verbal aggression, motor difficulties, sensory deficit, problem-solving errors, sexual impotence (at home) and polyneuropathic 'pins and needles'.

He has already drunk a great deal, but it has been sporadic. In fact, although he is an alcoholic, Cooper got through the day quite well by an alcoholic yardstick. He is still in control.

Now Cooper, however, is ready for more serious drinking because he is truly exhausted and weak.

He makes the obligatory call home, saying he will be late and miss dinner because he has an important meeting to attend.

In one sense Cooper is now more relaxed, because executives are supposed to 'unwind' in bars with booze after work. It is an American custom and there is, unlike morning drinking, absolutely no stigma attached.

Second, he now goes to his regular bar, his home away from home, one that caters to his kind—high priced but very ample drinks, a beautifully appointed interior, nice background music—and where he can 'run a tab' and pay by credit card.

He settles into his high, comfortable mahogany and leather bar stool and orders a vodka martini with a twist.

The bartender greets Cooper warmly, as if he was a returning war hero. On either side of him, other regulars offer their greetings. Conversation ebbs and flows—politics, sports, stocks. Several good-looking, well-dressed women are at the long bar. Cooper smiles flirtatiously at one and she smiles back.

The bartender knows how Cooper likes his vodka martinis and Cooper keeps drinking them, while mulling over certain events of the day. He decides that his impotence was really his wife's fault because she never truly liked sex. His blow up at the personnel director was, he decides, a good thing—it'll keep that idiot off his back for awhile.

Most of the other events of the day are either forgotten or transformed into something else.

At 9:30 p.m., after Cooper has been in the bar drinking steadily for about three hours, something very strange happens.

The bartender notices that Cooper is sitting in front of an empty glass.

He signals wordlessly to Cooper—as he has done thousands of times in the past—to find out if Cooper wants another one right now. The bartender gets no response. Cooper missed the signal.

So the bartender walks over and asks Cooper whether he wants another martini.

Cooper doesn't respond.

The bartender notices that Cooper has fallen into an obvious stupor. He is conscious but stuporous.

The bartender curses his luck. He has been feeding Cooper drinks for years and this is the first time he has ever seen Cooper 'zonked out'—drunk on his feet.

It is customary for bartenders to take care of good customers when said customer has had one too many, so the bartender walks out from behind the bar and with the help of a patron half-carries Cooper to an empty booth and leaves him there.

Is Cooper drunk?

No, he is not drunk.

Cooper has, in fact, after eating virtually nothing for the last 36 hours, lapsed into a condition known as fasting alcoholic hypoglycemia. This condition, surprisingly common among malnourished alcoholics and children who accidentally drink booze, is caused by a multifactorial inhibition of gluconeogenesis by ethanol (Lieber 1982: 107).

It is characterized by a wide range of symptoms, including:

- Conjugate deviation of the eyes
- Extensor rigidity of the extremities
- Unilateral or bilateral Babinski reflexes
- Convulsions
- Transient hemiparesis
- Trismus
- Hypothermia

Cooper, sitting in his booth, stuporous, feeling nothing, experiencing nothing, now has a blood glucose concentration of a little more than 30mg/100ml.

No one in the bar recognizes the condition—for them, Cooper is just drunk: 'zonked'.

One can't blame the bar patrons. In fact, it was not until Salaspurao et al. (1977) showed that this kind of hypoglycemia can be inhibited in man by 4-methylpyrazole, an inhibitor of ethanol metabolism, that the connection was truly accepted. (Cited in Lieber 1982:107)

And even if the patrons know of this syndrome, they are not equipped to do what is necessary to perform a correct diagnosis (accurate history and blood alcohol, blood glucose and plasma insulin determination)—much less treat by administration of 25-30 g glucose by mouth if stuporous and intravenously if comatose.

But don't worry about Cooper.

It is estimated that only about 11% of untreated cases of this syndrome die. The rest recover spontaneously. (Madison 1968, cited in Lieber 1982).

Cooper once again exhibits his survival instincts. He beats the odds (easy to do at approx. 10-1) and recovers spontaneously (the odds of course will go down the next time).

He wonders what the hell he is doing in the booth. He looks at the clock. How could it be 20 minutes before midnight?

He realizes he has to get home—but first he has to remember where his car is. That particular crisis is over and now smaller crises emerge.

There is no rest for the alcoholic.

Chapter 9

The Hypoglycemic Factor

So now we have watched Cooper as he—after a typical day of disordered behavior, constant drinking and no food—lapsed into a well-established life-threatening condition known as Fasting Alcoholic Hypoglycemia.

We described the incidence and course of this condition, the wide range of possible symptoms, the mode of treatment if hospitalized—and then we saw Cooper recover spontaneously.

This was a dramatic, life-threatening episode. Less recognized in Cooper and other chronically malnourished alcoholics is the fact that their lives are constantly impacted by less dramatic hypoglycemic episodes which are not immediately life-threatening.

At the outset we have to remind the reader that here we are not talking about nonalcoholic functional hypoglycemia—an area of persistent and often high-decibel controversy as to its etiology, course, treatment and, for some people, its very existence as a classifiable disorder.

No controversy, however, exists about the symbiotic relationship between alcoholism and hypoglycemia.

"Undoubtedly the commonest cause of hypoglycemia, after overdosage with insulin and the hypoglycemic agents, is overindulgence in alcohol . . . The mechanism of the alcohol effect is related to its metabolism . . . The accumulation of

NADH during the metabolism of alcohol results in the removal of pyruvate (by rapidly reducing it to lactate) and thus interferes with substrate utilization along the gluconeogenic pathway (Brody & Rosenberg, 1980:364).

In fact, if you and I went right out and randomly selected 100 alcoholics—any kind, anywhere—and gave each one a rigorous GTT: between 80 and 90 of these individuals would register an abnormal response to the test using the above criteria—i.e. metabolic dysfunction.

In 1981, for example, L. Ann Mueller surveyed a group of 135 alcoholics, each of whom was given a five or six hour GTT. About 95% showed abnormal peaks and valleys in blood sugar patterns. Two thirds of these suffered both mental and physical symptoms, some at the lowest point of blood sugar and others throughout the test. (Ketcham & Mueller l983: 89)

One cannot get the entire picture of Cooper's deranged behavior during the 24 hour period we have followed him without understanding the brain-disabling consequences of his continuous non-life threatening hypoglycemic episodes.

As one of the 'bibles' constantly reminds us . . .

"Maintenance of the plasma glucose concentration within relatively narrow bounds is a fundamental characteristic of the intact organism. Hypoglycemia represents a high-risk metabolic abnormality . . . because glucose is the primary energy substrate of the brain. Its absence, like that of oxygen, produces deranged function." (Harrison's 1983:682)

To put it simply, hypoglycemia is a homeostatic disorder epidemic among alcoholics.

1. When the chronically malnourished alcoholic attempts to replenish his plasma glucose concentration by increasing liver production of glucose, this usually effective adaption doesn't work . . .
2. It breaks down or is overwhelmed by the metabolic action of ethanol . . .
3. And thus we have the clinical syndrome of hypoglycemia which is always accompanied by behavioral deficits.

While there is unanimity of opinion as to the behavioral consequences of the alcoholism/hypoglycemia relationship—there is a great deal of disunity as to which element in the relation is the chicken and which is the egg.

As far back as 1938, Berman (as cited in Jellinek 1960:86) reported that alcohol acts as a sugar in people who are hypoglycemic.

In 1951, Lovell, and Tintera found that hypoglycemic episodes occur spontaneously in the alcoholic patient particularly when under emotional stress.

Also in 1971 (:175), Abramson & Pezet wrote that: "hyperinsulinism, with its chronic partial blood sugar starvation, is an essential underlying condition of alcoholism."

Palm in 1975 (:54) writes that: "The alcoholic has learned that alcohol depresses the perception of stress even if he does not recognize that alcohol does not supply the brain with the sugar it needs."

Many clinicians have observed that the intake of alcohol will relieve hypoglycemic symptoms. They have also theorized that a preexisting disturbance of the insulin-catecholamine axis may be a contributing factor in alcohol dependence.

Milam said this regarding the perplexing cycle: (Milan & Ketcham 1983:75)

"Alcohol is thus an attractive first aid for hypoglycemia, but it is poor therapy because it triggers a series of chemical changes which soon make the blood sugar level drop like a rock again. As the blood sugar level crashes down, the symptoms of hypoglycemia return with a vengeance—and a reinforcement: the desire for alcohol to relieve the symptoms."

Two important experiments in this general field should be noted.

In 1958 Forsander et al. demonstrated that hormone balance in an organism influences that animal's consumption of alcohol. When insulin production was decreased by administering alloxan, a hyperglycemic agent, the animals stopped drinking alcohol. The alcohol consumption rises once more as soon as the animals are treated with insulin, and increase their intake as the frequency of insulin dose increases.

In 1972 Register et al. fed one group of rats with a typical teen-age 'junk food' diet and another group with a well-balanced control diet. The former continuously increased their alcohol consumption during the study. The latter maintained a low level of alcohol intake. It is interesting to note that both groups significantly increased their alcohol intake when supplemented with either caffeine or coffee. Register and his colleagues concluded that (162)"metabolic controls to drinking exist which are sensitive to dietary factors."

As Ronald A. Arky (1971:220) so aptly sums up:

> "The profound and multiple effects of alcohol on carbohydrate metabolism are merely a reflection of the potent influences of alcoholism and its consequences on intermediary metabolism as a whole. Alcohol by itself or via one of its products causes alterations in transport, metabolism and disposition of carbohydrate substrate . . . In addition, the structural pathology caused by chronic exposure to alcohol, especially in the liver and pancreas, can be an etiological factor in a series of clinical states characterized by abnormal carbohydrate homeostasis."

As for which is the chicken and which is the egg—this becomes important only during the treatment phase where both must be dealt with simultaneously if any 'cure' is to be accomplished.

Right now our task is to show that Cooper's multifaceted and disordered behavior in a single 24-hour period emerges in part from both chronic conditions.

As Brody and Rosenberg point out (1980:357) in their clinical picture of hypoglycemia . . .

> "The neuroglycopenic symptoms consist of headache, mental dullness, fatigue, confusion, hallucinations, bizarre behavior . . . chronic or repeated attacks of hypoglycemia cause loss of intellectual function . . . The adrenergic symptoms consist of palpitations, anxiety, sweating, tremulousness and hunger."

Between 1950 and the present hundreds of clinicians and researchers have worked on the symptom profile of hypoglycemia. Below is a very brief outline.

- Tremor, irritability, numbness and coldness of hands and lips, changes in temperament (Cohen 1950)
- Clouded mental states, negativism, sullen attitude, manic attacks, amnesia, violent behavior (Landmann and Sutherland 1950)
- Headache, visual disturbance, mental confusion, convulsions and coma (Conn & Seltzer 1955)

- Bizarre automatic movements, transient paresis (slight or incomplete paralysis), cardiac arrhythmias (irregular heartbeats) (Kornfeld 1955)
- Vague uneasiness, mask-like facial expression, dilated pupils, headache, vertigo (Gilbertson 1959)
- Apathy, confusion, disturbance in speech and vision, neuromuscular irritability, pallor, tachycardia (rapid heartbeat), apprehension (Peters & Stanten 1965)
- Abdominal pain, mild delirium, night terrors (Patrick 1964)
- Free floating anxiety, dulled affect, impairment of judgment and insight, agitation, disordered perception (Ziven 1970)
- Psychotic behavior (Cecil 1982:1075)

If you've followed Cooper along with me during his 24-hour 'run', a lot of these symptoms look very familiar—don't they?

Once again we have run into one of the central diagnostic problems of alcoholism: identifying the behavioral symptom may be totally meaningless for identifying the underlying disorder.

When you are face to face with an alcoholic—in the office, on the street, in the clinic—what you see is rarely the case.

The almost three million teenagers who regularly use alcohol are a walking compendium of behavioral disorders, among them:

- Impairment
- Slurring of words
- Physically unstable
- Change in behavior
- Belligerence
- Sleeping (nodding)
- Deterioration of appearance
- Absenteeism
- Financial problems
- Unexplained absence from job, home, school
- Poor performance
- Change in performance
- Accident
- Change in peer group

They, above all, must be carefully screened for alcoholism before any diagnosis is made.

The confusion over which is the underlying disorder is rampant in the medical profession and particularly among those psychiatrists who continue to maintain that alcoholism is secondary to mental illness.

This confusion often leads to tragic consequences for individual patients.

Recently, for example, I saw an 18 year old male, the son of an alcoholic father, who had himself been drinking heavily since the age of 13.

He was clinically depressed and suffered recurrent episodes of anxiety and tension along with marked mood swings.

His work-up revealed marked macrocytosis with elevation of his MCV and MCH indicating that he had bone marrow toxicity, secondary to alcoholism.

He also had early alcoholic hepatitis and was malnourished with chronic gastroenteritis.

The patient clearly had the disease of alcoholism and, although he was only 18 years old, was having severe progression of his disease.

He demanded to see a psychiatrist. The psychiatrist told him his drinking problems were primarily due to the aberrations in his childhood heightened by his problems with his alcoholic father.

The young man was assured that a successful psychiatric treatment program would enable him to drink socially without any harmful effects.

The patient promptly checked out of the hospital to seek such treatment and thus was doomed to a further progression of his disease which was not halted until he was led to understand the relationship between his disease and the mental disorders which were secondary to it.

Another case I quickly recall is that of a bright and articulate 34-year-old engineer who also had a family history of alcoholism.

He had been drinking steadily for a period of 12 years with particularly heavy drinking during the past three years—at least a pint of 90 proof alcohol a day.

He became severely depressed and suicidal and was admitted to a psychiatric unit where his alcoholism was simply not addressed.

This individual believed that his drinking was secondary to his depression and that belief was reinforced by those who treated him.

He was given antidepressant medication with little success.

The patient was then subject to 7 series of electroshock therapy.

When he was referred to our service he had residual mental confusion and short memory lapses which concerned him greatly since he had always prided himself on his intellectual ability but now he was unable to remember what he read.

Once this alcoholism was recognized as the primary illness, his malnutrition was corrected; and the patient was rendered alcohol free for a period of time—his depression and insomnia lifted and he is currently in a stable situation without psychotropic medication.

I can cite hundreds of such current cases but I would also like to deal right now with another kind of case—where psychiatrists attempt to diagnose a 'notorious' individual retrospectively.

William B. Ober's justly famous case study, *Swinburne's Masochism; Neuropathy and Psychopathology* (1975) attempts such a reconstruction of the medical disorders of the late 19th century British poet, Algernon Charles Swinburne.

Swinburne, from adolescence, exhibited depression, mania, sadomasochistic fantasies and activities, alcoholism, fainting spells, tics, hyperkinetic behavior—to name just a few. Acknowledged as a great poet, he was also acknowledged as a thoroughly deranged individual by any standard.

Searching for the primary disorder which explains his mental derangement, Ober speculates that it must be "anoxic brain damage incurred at birth" with resulting minimal cerebral dysfunction.

In his article, Ober describes Swinburne's long-standing alcoholism. (:540)

> "During his years in London Swinburne became more and more addicted to alcohol. The legend is that Richard Burton . . . introduced him to brandy in the early 1860s and it became his favorite drink . . . Swinburne continued to drink heavily . . . Munby (Hudson 1972) cites no fewer than six occasions when he saw him drunk at the Arts Club in the early 1870s. . . . During these years Swinburne's letters are filled with apologies for being unable to fulfill engagements because of a 'bilious attack' or unable to write because of a 'wretched influenze'; transparent disguises for chronic gastritis and the malaise of a continuing hangover. He suffered many painful accidents when he would stumble and fall while drunk. By 1879, when Theodore Watts rescued him from his

filthy disordered quarters on Guilford Street near Russell Square and moved him to The Pines, he was probably on the verge of delirium tremens."

There can be no doubt from the above passage that Swinburne was an alcoholic. But because Ober considers alcohol to be a secondary disorder, he ignored it in his attempted diagnosis and, as we have seen, speculates that it was infant brain damage.

To explain the alcoholism, he states:

"That he was sensitive to small quantities of alcohol, consistent with brain damage, is shown on one occasion when he became intoxicated after only a pint of wine."

What Ober was not aware of is that alcoholics vary greatly in their daily intake of alcohol—it affects each person differently and is only consistent with that individual's biological and metabolic individuality. There are many alcoholics who maintain themselves on a pint of wine or so for a period of time.

Secondly, and more importantly, Ober was not aware of the fact that drunkenness after a pint of wine might signify a late stage of alcoholism in an individual where the toxicity has overwhelmed the tolerance/addiction cycle. For example, skid row derelicts will often become roaring drunk on one shot of whiskey if they have abstained and fasted for several hours.

Maybe Ober is correct and it was infant brain damage. We will never know. But there is an equal chance that twenty years of deranged behavior in the poet was secondary to his alcoholism and nothing else. It is interesting to note that after Swinburne broke his addiction to alcohol, in his late 40's, most of the behavioral disorders vanished.

Now let's broaden our inquiry into the history of medical practice.

No one knows how many thousands of individuals were placed in asylums until it was discovered that their psychotic behavior was merely a common symptom of the deficiency (niacin) disease called Pellagra.

Medical history is filled with those long-forgotten tragedies where nutritionally-based disorders were classified and diagnosed as 'forms of madness.' Alcoholism, like all other medical fields, has its own ghosts—one of which is Wernicke-Korsakoff Syndrome.

As *Cecil* (1982:2046) notes . . .

"Of all the disorders of the central nervous system associated with the protracted and abusive intake of alcohol and nutritional depletion, Wernicke's disease and Korsakoff's psychosis are the most frequent. The term 'cerebral beriberi' has sometimes been applied to these conditions."

This is usually a 2-stage disorder. Wernicke's disease appears first and is characterized by disturbed ocular motility, ataxia, impaired mentation. The patient then displays a characteristic amnesic syndrome known as Korsakoff's psychosis along with many abnormalities of cognitive function.

A thiamin deficiency is the main factor in the pathogenesis of the disorder and thiamin alone, given orally or parenterally, can dramatically reverse many of the symptoms and signs.

While all the pathogenic mechanisms underlying thiamin deficiency in the human nervous system are still not completely understood, experimental evidence suggests that the cerebellar dysfunctions may be due to failure of serotonergic neurons (decrease in the uptake of serotonin) and decreased glucose utilization in discrete anatomical areas of the brain. (*Cecil* 1982:2047)

The onset of this disorder may be quite abrupt but it is seen primarily in the very late stages of alcoholism—and our particular alcoholic, Cooper, while always at risk, is not yet a candidate.

But the mechanisms involved in the pathogenesis of Wernicke-Korsakoff Syndrome are always at work in Cooper in many transmutations, eliciting behavioral symptoms of all kinds—tremors, perceptual derangement, memory loss and even full-blown psychotic language and acts.

In fact, all the clinical and pathological evidence suggests that (Dreyfus 1974) . . .

1. nutritional deficiency is the major etiological factor in most neurological diseases associated with chronic alcoholism

and, more specifically . . .

2. hypovitaminosis—particularly of the B group—plays a primary role in the genesis of alcohol induced neurological syndromes.

I have already identified Cooper's (and all other alcoholics') chronic, systemic malnutrition.

And I presented a model of the wide-ranging, integrated adaption formation which characterizes the diseases and which renders Cooper biochemically unable to eat properly or to metabolize, utilize and store nutrients when he does eat.

When I characterized Cooper's malnourishment as systemic—I meant just that: it is evident in all of his body's systems—central nervous system, respiratory system, cardiovascular system, digestive system, skeletal-muscular system, blood, skin, endocrine system, immune system.

But now I want to pay a little closer attention to the relationship between Cooper's nutritional and behavioral deficits.

I want to answer three specific, important questions.

1. Which nutrients are associated with the proper functioning of the central nervous system, the endocrine system and the immune system?

2. How and why does Cooper deplete these nutrients?

3. What behavioral symptoms are associated with nutrient depletion and subsequent deficiencies in these symptoms?

Chapter 10

Disordered Minds and Disordered Metabolisms

Today, the study of the relationship between nutrition and behavior is a major area of scientific inquiry.

The scope of the inquiry is in fact enormous: from sophisticated fifth generation experiments into the classical deficiency diseases (which were responsible for the original disclosure of the relationship) to UN population studies in the Third World tracing the correlation between malnutrition and retardation . . . from studies of the behavioral consequences of immunosuppressant therapy to challenge testing of schizophrenics for allergies . . . from studies of how ascorbate blocks amphetamine induced behaviors in rats to experiments dealing with the effects of folic acid deficiency on antibody production . . . from individual nutritional intervention for children with severe learning disorders to large scale dietary experiments involving populations of maximum security prisons.

Alcoholism has always played an important role in this field because alcoholics are uniquely disordered—both behaviorally and nutritionally.

And, because all evidence so far continues to point out that the major nutritional elements in behavioral disorders of all kinds are deficiencies in vitamins, major minerals and trace elements—the alcoholic becomes even more important. Our alcoholic, Cooper, for example, is a walking lexicon of these deficiencies.

Consider phosphorus—a major mineral, but one we don't pay much attention to, except in regard to bone metabolism.

Approximately 85% of the 11 to 14 g of phosphorus per kg fat-free tissue in the normal adult is in the skeleton. The rest is distributed between tissue and membrane components of skeletal muscle, skin, nervous tissue and other organs.

Phosphate in the past has not been considered a nutrient which elicits major behavioral consequences when there is a deficiency—but that may be because only recently have scientists discovered that it is one of the most synergistic nutrients in the body.

"The phosphate ion is essential for the metabolism of carbohydrate, lipids and protein, functioning as a cofactor in a multitude of enzyme systems and contributing to the metabolic potential in the form of 'high-energy-phosphate' compounds. Phosphate functions to modify acid-base equilibrium in plasma and within cells and plays fundamental roles in modifying the development and maturation of bone, in the renal excretion of hydrogen ions and in modifying the effects of the B vitamins." (Avioli 1980:305).

The main sources of phosphorus in the American diet are milk, poultry, fish and meat.

Is Cooper deficient in this mineral? Are alcoholics in general deficient in phosphorus?

Yes, dramatically so. Hypophosphatemia occurs in approximately one-half of patients hospitalized for treatment of alcoholism. (Knochel 1979)

Knochel (1979) found that hospitalized alcoholics had, on average, a total muscle phosphorus content of 1,000 mmols. Normal total content should be approximately 1,450. This is a significant deficit.

Knochel lists six factors which may be responsible for this deficiency:

- Inadequate dietary intake
- Vomiting and diarrhea
- Magnesium deficiency
- Deranged Vitamin D Metabolism
- Calcitonin
- Acidosis

Knochel notes (:184) also that disorders of the central nervous system have been well documented in hypophosphatemic patients, including . . .

"... irritability, apprehension, muscular weakness, numbness, parethesias, dysarthria, confusion, obtundation, convulsive seizures, coma and death."

Phosphorus deficiency in alcoholics is in a sense a profound example of the insidious malnutrition of alcoholics as it often appears in the face of adequate intake since, oddly enough, there is a great deal of this mineral in soda pop (Cooper, if you recall, is addicted to soda pop . . . it sweetens his vodka). The deficiency is a result of multivariable aspects of malnutrition and toxicity in alcoholism.

But Cooper has much more immediately dangerous deficiencies vis-à-vis his mind than phosphorus, although it is a significant deficit and may be implicated in many behavioral disorders.

Before I deal with the broad behavioral implications of the major vitamin deficiencies in alcoholics, I want to recall for the reader the two most important tenets of alcoholic malnutrition.

First, it is essentially a subclinical panmalnutrition which systemically weakens all the body's homeostatic mechanisms and which interacts with the profound, continuing toxicity of ethanol on all the cells of the body.

Second, this systemic malnutrition is the stage on which each alcoholic plays out his or her biochemical individuality. Each alcoholic has a unique, inherited pattern of susceptibilities and resistances . . . deals with essential nutrients differently . . . has different nutritional needs. That is why a physician may look at seven individuals with the same measurable thiamin intake, and only one or two may show deficiency symptoms.

As Professor William Shive of the University of Texas noted in his important paper, "Development of Lymphocyte Culture Methods for Assessment of the Nutritional and Metabolic Status of Individuals" (1984: 15):

"Survival on existing dietary habits places limits on extremes of quantitative nutritional requirements of individuals, but within these limits there exist broad variations which are primarily the result of genetic differences."

Dreyfus applies the general concept of biological individuality to the clinical problems associated with alcoholic malnutrition (1974:266):

"The various alcoholic nutritional syndromes may be present separately in relatively pure form, but more frequently they occur together in varying combinations, some being decidedly more prevalent than others. It is not known why, under seemingly identical circumstances, one nutritionally depleted patient develops one or several neurological syndromes while another seems to emerge essentially unscathed. Basic constitutional and genetic differences combined with as yet unknown metabolic factors may underlie the individual response of patients to the chronic ingestion of alcohol . . . The chronic alcoholic patient not infrequently presents symptoms and signs of withdrawal which may mask in part those attributed to nutritional depletion. The relatively frequent coexistence of these two alcoholic complications should be kept in mind when therapeutic measures are instituted. In a marginally depleted patient, a full-blown nutritional syndrome can be precipitated by the injudicious use of calorie-rich parenteral fluids for withdrawal symptoms. Therefore adequate doses of B vitamins should always be administered despite the fact that the withdrawal symptoms are not caused by vitamin deficiency."

But the most important insight the physician needs when facing an individual behaviorally-disordered alcoholic, even before any tests are administered, is an understanding of the biochemical certainty of alcohol malnourishment—the alteration in metabolism of nutrients as a result of chronic alcohol ingestion.

Smith's summary (1979) is most helpful here because it provides a 'map' of what is happening metabolically in most alcoholics at any one time.

- a decrease in plasma or serum zinc
- a decrease in plasma or serum calcium (transient)
- a decrease in plasma or serum vitamin A and retinol binding protein
- a decrease in plasma or serum glucose
- an increase in plasma or serum cholesterol, phospholipids and triglycerides

- a decrease in plasma or serum thiamin
- a decrease in the absorption of thiamin
- a decrease in the absorption of B_{12}
- a decrease in the absorption of folic acid
- a decrease in the absorption of glucose
- an increase in the absorption of iron
- an increase in the urinary excretion of Mg
- an increase in the urinary excretion of K
- an increase in the urinary excretion of Zn

This capsule chart shows the wide-ranging alterations in the plasma, urinary excretion and absorption of the key nutrients as a result of chronic alcohol ingestion.

Obviously, a lot is going on in the alcoholic and all of it is bad from the standpoint of any pathway from metabolism to behavior as mediated by the endocrine and the CNS—the systems which are most associated with nutrient deficiency—and related behavioral disorders such as reduced sexual function, depression, insomnia, anxiety, mental confusion (Cooper is exhibiting all of these but the changes in his perception of reality preclude him from realizing it). And of course this metabolic dysfunction is in addition to the appetitive derangements which always accompany the disease.

When I described a typical 24 hours in our alcoholic case Cooper's life, punctuated by a series of bewildering behavior patterns—that ensemble of disordered behavior must always trigger in the physician who treats an alcoholic patient this question: How severe are his or her nutrient deficits?

That question must always be asked (and answered) because the statistical probability of key nutrient deficiencies is overwhelming.

The magnitude of significant B vitamin deficiencies in alcoholics—the vitamins most implicated in CNS and endocrine dysfunction both singularly and synergistically—is highlighted by Thompson (1979:405-428) who found the following in a cohort of chronic alcoholics . . .

—B_6 deficiencies in 75% of tested alcoholics
—folic acid deficiencies in 65% of tested alcoholics
—B_1 deficiencies in 60% of tested alcoholics
—B_2 deficiencies in 52% of tested alcoholics
—B_{12} deficiencies in 15% of tested alcoholics

Sherlock (1984:437) speculates that the low serum levels of B_6 (pyridoxine) are "probably due to ethanol and its metabolite acetaldehyde acting on hepatic storage and metabolism of the vitamin."

B_6 is an extremely interesting nutrient, a deficiency of which has been implicated in maladaptive reactions to foods and chemicals and infectious disease. It is, in fact, immunosuppressive:

> "Marked decreases in the activity of serum antibody were observed in rats with pyridoxine and pantothenic acid deficiencies. Thus, in these deficiency states, there was a qualitative difference in the type of antibody formed as well as a diminution in the total quantity of antibodies produced. This qualitative change is manifested by a lowered ability of the antibody to combine with the antigen . . . deficiencies of pantothenic acid, biotin, pyridoxine and tryptophan produced marked inhibition of the secondary (booster) as well as of the primary response to this antigen . . . Repeated injections of diphtheria toxoid were unable to overcome the inhibitory effect of a pyridoxine deficiency induced by dietary means or by the administration of the pyridoxine antagonist." (Axelrod 1980:579)

It is also interesting to note that the nutrients which have been characterized as synergistically important to the proper functioning of B_6—Vitamin C and Magnesium—are chronically depleted in alcoholics.

Smith's chart we presented confirmed the findings of McCollister et al.(1958) that acute ethanol administration increased urinary magnesium excretion 2-3 fold—and the similarity in the neuromuscular excitability of hypomagnesemia and acute alcohol withdrawal has long been noted. (cited in Lieber 1982:561)

Vitamin C, of course, is deficient in alcoholics with or without liver disease (O'Keane et al. 1972: 6-11) and its behavioral implications stem from its vital role in adrenal metabolism and the reaction of the body to stress.

Sherlock, in her Lancet review (1984:436), however, reminds us that most specific nutritional deficiencies in alcoholics have their roots in ethanol toxicity—alcohol-induced organ damage . . .

> "Alcoholic gastritis causes anorexia, retching and vomiting. The small-intestinal disease leads to diarrhea with electrolyte

loss and to difficulties in absorption of specific nutrients, including thiamine, folate, vitamin B_{12}, glucose and amino acids. Pancreatic disease leads to steatorrhoea with malabsorption of essential fatty acids, fat-soluble vitamins and calcium."

"Alcoholic liver disease among other things leads to failure of protein synthesis, amino acid imbalance, reduced zinc storage, enhanced metabolism of and failure to store Vitamin A, and failure to store Vitamin B_6. Accumulation of triglyceride fat is associated with fatty-acid accumulation in the hepatocytes, which may contribute to the functional and morphological changes."

I will deal with the actual management of these deficiencies in a later section but right now I wish to make one very important point. Alcoholics in general usually present with a variety of neurotic and even psychotic behavior secondary to the malnutrition and toxification of the cells of their CNS. Only after these factors are corrected can the true mental status of the individual alcoholic patient be ascertained. It is imperative that this be done prior to attempting to make a definitive psychiatric diagnosis.

Once this principle is followed one finds that the incidence of underlying serious psychiatric pathology is about the same as in the general population - 5 to 7%.

Chapter 11

Cooper and the "Brown Trout"

Now I want to take this nutrition/behavior/ethanol relationship a bit further—into an area which is one of the most exciting new fields of medical inquiry and one which may have an enormous impact on the management of the alcoholic in the future. I am talking about Behavioral Immunology, or, to put it in concrete terms, about Cooper's continuous self-administered immunosuppressant therapy.

What, you may be asking yourself, does immunosuppressant therapy, associated with transplant surgery, have to do with alcoholism and behavior?

A great deal. Many of its insights have been crucial in the development of the field called behavioral immunology which is now becoming very important to alcoholism because it deals with the relationship between the CNS and the immune system.

When a patient undergoes immunosuppressant therapy to decrease the hostility of the immune system to a 'foreign' organ transplant, said patient also develops a dangerously increased susceptibility to infectious disease and often severe behavioral disorders including a disabling depression.

Cooper and all alcoholics have a great deal in common with the transplant patient in regards to immune response. In fact, no other group in American society has such a high rate of fatalities from both pneumonia and suicidal depression as alcoholics—to mention just two possible consequences of chronic ethanol toxicity vis-à-vis the immune system.

"Cell-mediated immunity is depressed in alcoholic patients, as shown by in-vitro tests of suppressor-cell function and by helper/suppressor-cell ratios. These abnormalities are probably reflections of protein malnutrition, since triceps skin-fold thickness and hypoalbuminaemia correlate with skin-test anergy. Alcoholics of good nutritional status also show poor responses to tetanus toxoid and to hepatitis B vaccine, indicating a reduced humoral response." (Sherlock 1984:437)

Lieber (1983) reviewing several studies in this area concludes that they have "clearly shown an association between heavy drinking and decreased immune responsiveness" and adds that "regardless of the exact cause of the immunosuppressed state that is associated with alcohol abuse, it should be considered as a potential contributory factor to the increased cancer incidence seen in heavy drinkers."

But other developments have been equally important in the growth of the field called behavioral immunology. Let me deal with them briefly.

First, evidence now exists that there is a crucial relationship between nutrition and the immune system. We have already discussed one of those deficiency/immunosuppressive states as it relates to pyridoxine. One of the most fascinating new research vectors in this area is the relationship between nutrition, aging and the immune system. This can be significant because alcoholics experience severe memory loss which often mimics, in fact, a geriatric population.

"A considerable body of evidence indicates that the aging process can be influenced by a variety of dietary modifications. A deterioration of various immunologic systems also occurs with aging. The possibility that modifications in the metabolic activity of certain nutrients occurring with advancing age produce immunologic changes associated with or influencing the phenomenon of aging is an interesting speculation." (Axelrod 1980:588)

Second, the allergy paradigm has been substantially broadened.

"Although the symptoms produced by inhalation of pollen are localized in the mucosa with which it comes in contact, the sensitization is systemic . . . Similarly, the normal effects of emotional states upon the nasal mucosa are often exaggerated in the allergic patient." (Cecil 1982:1801)

There are a great many studies which now show that allergic-hypersensitive reactions to foods, chemicals, tobacco, etc. include a wide repertoire of behavioral disorders. Only recently millions of Americans watched a PBS/McNeil-Lehrer documentary on the juvenile penal system in California where significant decreases in fights, assaults and other infractions have been achieved through the removal of white sugar and certain 'junk foods' from the inmate diet.

Third, the new findings of Behavioral Immunology itself, among them the studies of hospitalized patients which suggest that cell-mediated immune processes may be involved in brain mechanisms, underlying cerebral atrophy, depression, dementia, schizophrenia and mental retardation. (Jankovic et al. 1982:687-697)

But, of all these developments, it is the field of Immunology-Allergy-Hypersensitivity which is most immediately relevant for Cooper because like many individuals with alcoholism he has a 'leaky gut' and it is this organ damage which may create the first link between his panmalnutrition, his immune system and his CNS. Let us deal with that first.

I am not ordinarily a betting man but I will wager any of my readers ten dollars to one dollar that if Cooper was given a series of twenty allergen tests now (your choice of food, chemicals, etc.) he would test positive on at least ten of them.

Actually—the bet is 'fixed' because all physicians who perform allergen tests on alcoholics know that their patients show an unprecedented and unexplained hypersensitivity to a bewildering variety of substances.

But is it really unexplained?

And what does this have to do with Cooper's behavior and the course of the disease itself?

Let us start at the beginning—at the phenomenon of the 'leaky gut'—a near universal phenomenon in chronic alcoholism.

In a recent study of 36 alcoholic patients without liver cirrhosis, it was shown that they . . .

> "almost invariably had higher intestinal permeability than controls . . . The site of altered intestinal permeability was shown by an invitro permeability test to be the small bowel." (Bjarnason et al. 1984:179)

Summarizing their important study, the authors note (:181):

"This study shows that moderate alcohol abuse is associated with a striking change in intestinal permeability . . . independent of gastric inflammation and the nutritional state of the patient. In many cases the raised permeability was evident up to 2 weeks after cessation of drinking."

The implications are important: (179, 181)

"It has been suggested that changes in intestinal permeability may be important in the pathophysiology of various gastrointestinal diseases and that increased permeability to antigens may account for some of the extra intestinal manifestations seen in these disorders . . . Moreover, it is interesting that patients with Crohn's disease and coeliac disease, like alcoholics, are at risk of malignant disease and a common denominator in these disorders is a disturbance of intestinal permeability."

In other words, substances that in the nonalcoholic would be totally digested are, in the alcoholic, passing through the gut wall into the general circulation because ethanol "has been found to damage the lining of the small intestine . . . and enhance the permeability of the gut wall." (Lieber 1983)

Does this seepage of imperfectly digested matter into the blood stream trigger an antigenic response? It does in gluten-sensitive enteropathy.

"The damaged mucosal epithelium is rendered permeable to wheat glycopeptides and other soluble wheat and milk proteins, which may be antigenic. Participation of these proteins in antigen-antibody reactions might thus account for high antibody titers to food proteins in the sera of coeliac patients. Transmucosal passage of food antigens across a damaged small bowel mucosa has also been suggested to account for high titers of antibodies to milk proteins and gluten fractions in the serum found in a patient with systemic mast cell disease studied in this laboratory." (Broitman & Zamcheck 1980:922)

It used to be assumed that the gastrointestinal tract was an impenetrable barrier to the uptake of intraluminal antigens—but starting with Alpers & Isselbacher's 1967 study on protein synthesis by rat intestinal mucosa that view has changed. More and more evidence is

98

coming to light that under certain conditions, relatively large amounts of immunologically significant protein in the diet may pass through the gut wall into the blood stream with resulting sensitivities.

Is this the reason why alcoholics test positive on so many different allergen tests? Do they have a chronic, systemic hypersensitivity to substances because of their 'leaky gut' and deranged immune response? We don't know all the answers yet. We do know that the gut wall of the patient with alcoholism allows partially digested substances to pass through.

Allergy and adverse food reactions occur to a greater degree in patients with alcoholism than in the general population. Whether the allergic patient has an increased risk of developing the disease or whether the disease increases the number of allergic problems is a "chicken and egg" question we have not yet answered. Much research on this correlation is needed. What we do know is that it is very important to identify allergic and adverse food reactions and correct for these in the overall management of the alcoholic patient.

Allow me now to introduce a rather jarring metaphor—Cooper's relationship to a fish called the brown trout.

Let me explain.

As we have seen, the toxicity of alcohol and its inevitable derangement of Cooper's nutrition and metabolism has also deranged his immune system. We also saw that Cooper, like many alcoholics, has developed a 'leaky gut' and fairly large amounts of immunologically significant partially digested protein are passing through the intestinal wall into the blood stream with resulting sensitivities that will show up on allergen tests.

Is Cooper's deranged behavior tied to his deranged immunocompetence as well as his nutrient deficits and the direct toxicity of ethanol on his CNS?

To understand this very important question we first have to understand that the overwhelming factor in Cooper's life as an alcoholic is stress.

There is the stress that comes from needing a drink; the stress that comes from hiding the fact that he needs a drink; the stress that comes from the constant alcohol-induced anxiety, depression, malnutrition and toxicity; the stress that comes from his fear that he will say the wrong thing and do the wrong thing; the stress that comes from his inability to sleep and make love and just to understand what the hell is wrong with himself. And, of course, adding significantly to his problem are his dependence on sugar, caffeine and nicotine.

Cooper, in fact, is very similar to the famous brown trout that have been the focus of a recent series of brilliant experiments in England by A.D. Pickering and his colleagues ("Why"1985).

They found that slight changes of temperature, water quality and disturbances from handling can spark off a wave of illness among brown trout on fish farms.

They next discovered that these stressed fish react to the outside stimuli by dramatically increasing the amount of circulating steroids in their blood.

They then showed that the steroids (cortisol) impact on the white blood cells lessen their ability to recognize and fight invading organisms.

But what about humans?

"In our laboratory, we have studied prospectively and longitudinally the husbands of women with advanced carcinoma of the breast at approximately monthly intervals up to and following the death of spouse, assessing immunologic function . . . the response of purified lymphocytes to the T cell mitogen PHA and to the B cell mitogen (pokeweed mitogen) were significantly depressed after bereavement . . . it is of note that a similar depression of lymphocyte stimulation occurred as early as 2 to 3 weeks following loss of spouse . . ."

"An extensive network of central nervous system, neurotransmitter, endocrine and other biological processes may be involved in the modulation of the immune system. In addition considerable evidence demonstrating a relationship between psychosocial factors and immune function is accumulating. Psychosocial processes may be reflected in changes in central nervous system activity and pathways linking limbic and higher cortical areas in the hypothalamus may be involved in the effects of psychosocial processes on visceral, endocrine and immune functions. The interaction of biopsychosocial phenomena with the immune system may, in turn, alter the development, onset and course of a range of medical disorders." (Stein 1981: 203, 216)

But the relationship between the CNS, the immune system and behavior is more sharply drawn in recent experiments with psychiatric patients and other severely disordered individuals. Cooper, you must always remember, has, like all chronic alcoholics, wide oscillations in behavior from benign to blatantly psychotic, which is why, up to about the 1940's, alcoholics were often hospitalized along with psychotics as a matter of course—including, by the way, in Bellevue. (This practice, unfortunately, essentially continues because of misdiagnosis rather than ignorance. Patients with alcoholism continue to occupy a disproportionate number of beds in psychiatric hospitals.)

Jankovic and coworkers (1980:515-522) studied 208 psychiatric patients with cerebral atrophy, 46 with dementia, 82 with depression and 481 with schizophrenia. The control group consisted of 56 normal individuals and patients with neurosis.

All were skin-tested with human S-100 brain protein, soluble fraction from the brain and liver protein. The local Arthus and delayed hypersensitivity reactions were read at 4-6 hr and at 24 hr respectively.

The great majority of tested psychiatric patients developed positive Arthus and delayed skin reactions to S-100 protein and soluble brain protein fraction.

A small number of control subjects responded to those antigens. The authors note:

> "The results obtained suggest that there is a correlation between local cutaneous sensitivity to neurotissue antigens and psychiatric disease, and that both humoral and cell-mediated immunity are involved in the pathogenesis and development of cerebral atrophy, dementia, depression and schizophrenia."

We have gone from brown trout to widowers to hospitalized schizophrenics but it will take even more than these disparate examples to find out whether there actually are quantifiable behavioral pathways between Cooper's immune system, his CNS and the world which is always ten seconds away from falling down on him.

Cooper is continuously and precariously balanced on the behavioral/immunological frontier.

Since Cooper is now, because of his ethanol-induced increased intestinal permeability "leaking" partially digested matter into his general circulation and thereby suffering from systemic allergenic sensitivities—enhanced by constant stress—can we tie those sensitivities to his behavior?

Once again we have a chicken and an egg problem—like we had in the relationship between alcoholism and hypoglycemia.

The epidemiological and statistical correlations between CNS and immune disorders are on their way to becoming well-established. Some mechanisms of action have been identified. But no one has yet answered definitively the question: Do the immunological variances result from an individual's alcoholic depression or does the immunological problem preexist and act as a contributing factor to the development of alcoholism?

As I noted earlier, the field of Behavioral Immunology is new, exploding and characterized by a very wide range of inquiry.

- Sugerman and associates (1982) studied antibody levels in adult alcoholic, depressive and schizophrenic patients with healthy adult controls using 33 allergen tests—12 inhalants and 21 foods. Positive test results were most significant for allergen specific IgE with the highest totals achieved by the depressives, then the alcoholics, then the schizophrenics. The allergens most often positive were those from the perennial/mold group, although the most frequently positive single allergen was egg white and 100% of the depressives were sensitive to it.
- Bardos et al. (1981:609-611) investigated the neocortical lateralization of NK activity in mice and their finding "strongly suggests direct relationships between the central nervous system and the immune system, both involved in biological adaption for the maintenance of homeostasis and body integrity in relation to the external environment."
- Abramsky & Litvin (1978:104-114) note that "the recent discovery that several autoimmune diseases, such as myasthenia gravis, are the result of an immunopharmacological block at receptor sites, together with several observations of immunological disorders in Parkinson's disease and schizophrenia, suggests the possibility that certain types of Parkinson's disease and schizophrenia might be the consequence of an autoimmune blockade of striatal or limbic dopamine-receptors, respectively."

Hundreds of articles and reports like these are constantly appearing; each one making a small advance in our understanding of that very perplexing but very important relationship between the immune system and the CNS.

But perhaps one of the most relevant recent experiments pertaining to the question of behavior and immunity was recently performed by John Crayton, M.D., Associate Professor of Psychiatry, University of Chicago, and reported on during a professional society meeting he attended in Seattle in 1984.

Crayton recounted the origins of his involvement. A colleague of his told him he had treated a patient in whom the eating of meat (beef specifically) would induce epileptic attacks.

Crayton did not believe his colleague until he participated in challenge testings which corroborated his colleague's findings by clinical observation and tests: the ingestion of beef was followed by seizures. The patient was fed a variety of substances and experienced seizures with blind ingestion of beef and not any other substance.

Crayton then gathered 56 subjects—each one of whom claimed to have a history of behavioral disorders induced by food sensitivities.

He isolated them in an environmental unit for eight days where they fasted for the first four days, drinking only spring water.

Then each subject was given 8 specific food and substance tests— administered in 15 gram capsules and accompanied by a battery of psychological, physiological and blood tests to quantify their reactions: anger, anxiety, depression, etc.

Crayton found that in two thirds of the subjects—their self diagnoses had been correct.

These two-thirds had statistically significant behavioral symptoms induced by the substance sensitivities in double blind cross-over testing.

I think it is now evident that anyone concerned with the diagnosis and treatment of patients with alcoholism must deal with the CNS/ Immune System relationship.

In other words, we need a coherent clinical view of the relationship.

Chapter 12

How to Recognize an Alcoholic Marriage

We have been exploring and documenting the many possible path-ways of alcoholic behavior itself. We saw that, in a single alcoholic such as Cooper, the repertoire of disordered behavior can be enormous and the pathways of that (ultimately ethanol induced) behavior may be . . .

- the direct effect of alcohol on the CNS (acute and chronic toxicity)
- panmalnutrition
- specific nutrient deficiencies
- alcoholic hypoglycemia
- allergies and immune hypersensitivities
- an antecedent behavioral disorder accentuated and complicated by ethanol toxicity
- or any combination of the above

How then can any diagnosis be made? How, in fact, does one approach an individual who is exhibiting severe paranoid behavior, for example, and whom you suspect of drinking too much too often—so that he may have already triggered the tolerance/addiction syndrome which points to alcoholism.

Well, first you have to be able to recognize the disease. But even if you are not capable of recognizing the disease you have to be careful of making a firm and irrevocable psychiatric diagnosis that discounts alcoholism.

As T.C. Manschreck, Associate Professor of Psychiatry at Massachusetts General Hospital puts it in his overview of Paranoid Behavior 1981b:67): "studies have indicated that a significant percentage of paranoid patients admitted to U.S. state mental hospitals suffer from alcohol-induced paranoid psychoses."

In fact, the incidence of hospitalization (and ensuing costs) for mental disorders secondary to alcoholism—*but not recognized as such*—are probably as great as the scandal of tens of thousands of untreated and undiagnosed alcoholics who fill the beds of general hospitals each year for everything from aspirative pneumonia to G.I. bleeding.

To give you just one example of this phenomenon—last month a 57-year old individual was admitted to our clinic for alcoholism. He—let's call him Larry—had been an alcoholic for 16 years but this was his first admission for alcoholism per se. However, during that 16-year span, Larry had 17 admissions to general hospitals (and at least two admissions to psychiatric hospitals) and at no time during those years was this unfortunate man ever treated for alcoholism or recognized as an alcoholic.

The misdiagnosis of alcoholism is endemic in the medical community—and it has enormous ramifications both individually and societally.

Alcoholism is, in a sense, a 'communicable' disease. But what is communicated is not the disease itself—rather the disordered behavior of the alcoholic spreads out in circles—like tentacles—to close family, to associates, to the community at large.

And those tentacles are violent, disruptive and lethal.

A recent study by Abel and Zeidenberg (1985) looked at 3,374 deaths investigated and considered to be violence-related by the medical examiner's office in upstate New York's Erie County between 1973 and 1983. They include traffic and other accidents, homicides and suicides.

In 42.5% of the total cases, the victim had been drinking (BAL of 10 mg/dl or higher).

No one has ever measured the impact of the violent deaths (in this or any other study) on non-alcoholics as the death was occurring (i.e. injuries to passengers in the 'other car'; emotional trauma to bystanders viewing the carnage, etc.) or, even more important, during all the years of heavy drinking and disordered behavior that characterizes these individuals before their disease became fatal.

So, now I must begin to deal with the first and most important reach of the alcoholic tentacles: the family of the alcoholic. And, more specifically, the wife.

Or, to put it another way—during all this daily turmoil . . . during all this impotence and paranoia and anxiety and depression which is Cooper's daily lot as an alcoholic trying to survive in the world — *what is happening to Mrs. Cooper?*

I want to deal with Mr. and Mrs. Cooper and the 'folie à deux' of the alcoholic marriage.

But first consider this scenario.

A husband and wife live in a small apartment on the 16th floor. The husband develops a persecutory delusional system which includes the belief that the tenant beneath him on the 15th floor is continually moving furniture in order to drive him crazy.

His wife does not share the delusion at first because she doesn't hear any furniture being moved (none is) but she eventually comes to believe it to the extent that she goes downstairs, bangs on the door and demands that the moving of furniture be stopped.

This is, of course, just one example of the classical 'folie à deux' associated with some forms of paranoid psychoses.

This phenomenon is, to some extent, a model which provides insight into the alcoholic marriage and family.

It is now believed that . . .

"The family often facilitates alcoholism, that the family frequently presents obstacles to the alcoholic's recovery and that the family is as much a victim of alcoholism as the alcoholic himself." (Mapes et al. 1984:67)

And there is now evidence of the existence of a unique entity called the 'alcoholic marriage.' Steinglass (1977:260) explains that this term implies "that both members of the marriage had an equal stake in the perpetuation of the alcoholic symptoms" even though the symptoms were limited to one partner.

Just as, until recently, it was believed that there was a distinct premorbid personality profile for alcoholism—so it was believed that there was a premorbid personality profile for non-alcoholic wives (and husbands) of alcoholics.

"Initial clinically-oriented studies pictured the wife as a disturbed pathological personality with dependency conflicts and complex needs that directed her to choose as a husband an alcoholic . . . It was suggested that if the husband began to improve, many wives exhibited their own form of emotional disorder." (Ablon 1976:211)

This was eventually shown to have as little validity as the existence of a specific premorbid personality profile for alcoholism per se.

In its place came the concept of the family as a homeostatic mechanism similar to physiological mechanisms.

"The notion is that families tend to establish a sense of balance or stability, and have built-in mechanisms to resist any change from that predetermined level of stability. This stability does not necessarily imply a healthy state of affairs. The family, for example, might include as part of this stabilization pattern a piece of chronic psychopathology, such as chronic alcohol abuse." (Steinglass 1977:264)

When that concept is understood, many behavior patterns of the nonalcoholic wife can no longer be viewed as primarily pathological—but simply 'feedback' loops which the wife uses to restore stability. An example of this is the wife who demands to be taken to a restaurant where booze is served every time her alcoholic husband promises abstinence.

These strategies for coping, for stability, exhibited by the wives of alcoholics fall into quickly recognizable patterns which have been named and described.(Mapes et al. 1984)

Among them are . . .

The 'enabler'—who will make excuses to family, friends, relatives and employers in order to help the alcoholic conceal his drinking and rescue him from the consequences of his behavior.

The 'scapegoat'—who the alcoholic blames for his drinking, who accepts that blame, who is the target of the alcoholic's projections, who bears the brunt of the alcoholic's criticisms but who continually tries to please the alcoholic.

The 'compensator'—who attempts to overshadow the alcoholic's failures and unacceptable behavior through overachievement and efforts toward perfection.

The 'opportunist'—who does not want the alcoholic to recover because it provides her (or him) with acceptable justification to do what she wants to do—i.e. have an affair.

But the most dangerous basic strategy of all is the one which wives of alcoholic husbands exhibit almost universally: the refusal to believe that their husband is suffering from a metabolic disease. It is this belief which, if not changed, dooms the alcoholic and all possibilities for a successful long-term treatment.

In the next few pages I wish to explore two alcoholic marriages.

The first is the marriage of Malcolm and Margerie Lowry. This marriage ended in the death (by suicide or accident—no determination was ever made) of the alcoholic Malcolm, author of *Under The Volcano* and one of the greatest novelists of the 20th century.

And then I will proceed to a different kind of alcoholic marriage —our own Mr. & Mrs. Cooper.

Chapter 13

Death from Misdiagnosis

On the evening of July 5th, 1957, in a small cottage in a village called Ripe, in East Sussex (England), the 47-year-old novelist Malcolm Lowry and his wife, Margerie, had a fight. Lowry was sprawled on his chair holding a half-empty gin bottle. He refused to respond to any of his wife's comments. She put on his favorite record. He still didn't respond. She tried to take the gin bottle away from him. He punched her, then smashed the bottle and came after her with the jagged bottle neck. She fled from the house and spent the night with a neighbor.

The next morning she returned to the cottage and found her husband dead, along with the smashed gin bottle, a smashed orange squash bottle and an empty vial which had contained 20 of her sodium amytal sleeping tablets.

The medical report stated the cause of death as "acute barbiturate poisoning associated with a state of chronic alcoholism." (Day 1973:17)

No one said it was suicide. No one said it was not suicide. It is difficult to make a decision when a man had been an alcoholic for more than twenty years.

Lowry was the very model of a chronic alcoholic. He moved constantly: Liverpool, Cambridge, London, Paris, New York, Hollywood, Mexico, Vancouver, Haiti, The Western Pacific, the Mediterranean and dozens of points in between.

In his last ten years or so he drank himself unconscious every day. He was, ultimately, an impotent, bedwetting, insomniac alcoholic— swinging wildly between mania and depression. If he couldn't get gin, he

111

drank anything from shaving lotion to cooking sherry in enormous gulps. He was physically powerful, imaginative and devious, and, in an odd way—like many other alcoholics—lovable, particularly to those who saw him only briefly at parties or in bars or on the street.

Because he was a famous writer, we have an enormous amount of information on his marriage. In fact, through biographies of Lowry by Douglas Day and others, and through critical studies of his works which use letters from people who knew the couple (and treated them)—we have perhaps what is the only heavily documented look at the full range of pathos, lunacy and error that is shared by millions of other people caught in alcoholic marriages.

Margerie Lowry was, in fact, the classical example of the nonalcoholic wife who used the strategy we identified as "the enabler."

The "enabler", if you recall, is a husband or wife who, in order to maintain the stability (homeostasis) of the marriage, tries to rescue the alcoholic from the consequences of his behavior.

Margerie rescued Malcolm from a tree he had climbed during the ferocious Hurricane Edna. She apologized for him when he called the police and claimed his house had been robbed because his favorite magazine had vanished from the kitchen table where he always left it, and with good alcoholic reasoning concluded only a robber would dare move it (Lowry had actually left it in the bathroom).

She helped him home from pubs. She borrowed money to repay his bad debts. She smoothed over the hurt feelings his comments often elicited among their friends. She spent, in fact, her whole married life cleaning up after him.

In addition to her "enabling" strategy, she also began to 'mother' him, which, of course, Lowry (and many other alcoholics) thoroughly enjoyed. She dressed his wounds when he bumped into doors. She helped him to the typewriter and prepared his materials. She took him where he wanted to go.

Her strategy was expensive. In her case she did not exhibit a clear mental pathology which is so common among the wives of alcoholics and which is one of the main reasons it was believed (falsely) that there was a premorbid personality profile for the wife in an alcoholic marriage—i.e. that she could not help but choose an alcoholic husband.

But Margerie did begin to exhibit a wide range of physical symptoms that forced her to continually visit doctors.

And, no matter how many physicians she consulted (there were many) or how many tests she underwent—no illness was ever diagnosed.

Margerie became a walking psychosomatic casualty so that once in a while, when he was capable, Malcolm could 'mother' her.

So the scene was set. Her strategy locked them into a difficult, stormy, exhausting, sexless and sometimes hellish marriage. But the marriage was stable—it survived.

Margerie knew that her husband was an alcoholic. She also believed that she knew what alcoholism was: an addiction which is caused and reinforced by some kind of mental anguish or trauma or psychological impairment. She believed that Malcolm drank because he was unhappy, a bit deranged, a bit unbalanced—but the moment his mind was put straight he would no longer need a drink.

Not only did she believe this—but she acted upon it. And she thereby set into motion the events which necessitated his death. I will show how this particular alcoholic marriage played out its fatal course for the simple reason that Margerie had no inkling whatsoever that the alcoholism which afflicted her husband was basically a genetically predisposed, metabolic, biochemical disease entity.

Margerie, as the marriage progressed, continued to protect her husband from the consequences of his increasingly harmful behavior. She continued to help him get from point A to point B. She continued to 'mother' him.

And, above all, she maintained the optimistic belief that once Malcolm was psychologically sound, sobriety would follow, or, as she put it in a letter to a friend . . .

> "They say he's only a 'secondary alcoholic' which I could have told them and the trouble is actually his mind—which of course I've known for years . . . But he's written nothing for over a year, can't even write letters, as you see, and was losing all contact with reality." (Day 1973: 29)

The seeds of Lowry's death were irrevocably sown when Margerie decided to act on her belief and initiate a series of 'therapeutic' steps— *all of which were opposed to what we now know about alcoholism and its biochemical/metabolic mechanism.*

Malcolm was particularly morose and difficult during his constant morning drinking (gin and water).

To relieve him and herself of this morning anguish and to help him 'cope'—Margerie began the following regimen.

At night she would dose him liberally with good brandy and Nembutal.

The 'morning drinking' problem was solved because Malcolm would not awaken until about noon of the next day in a somewhat corpselike state. Whereupon, Malcolm was then given his daytime dose—a stiff brandy and 2 more Nembutal.

Obviously, Malcolm's behavior became less 'difficult.' Margerie considered this a definite improvement—and from her standpoint, from the standpoint of the stabilization of the marriage, it definitely was. From the standpoint of Malcolm's survival, it was not.

After a short period of time, however, Margerie thought better of her 'therapy' because Malcolm started to develop new and even strange behavior patterns—and he started to prefer brandy to gin which, when drunk to excess in the late afternoon seemed to make him more violent.

She started to make inquiries at psychiatric hospitals. She consulted friends. She read. She searched for the therapy that would ease his psychological burdens and then—poof—the dragon would vanish.

She even went so far as to contemplate lobotomy and discuss it with Malcolm. He cheerfully agreed—like many alcoholics he would often agree immediately to the most outlandish suggestions to please someone.

She gave up that idea and sent him to a psychiatric hospital where, as part of his psychotherapy, he was given sodium pentothal during psychiatric sessions.

This did not help Malcolm. He began to suffer severe hallucinations and paranoid symptoms.

The sodium pentothal experiment was dropped and the physicians decided that they should first deal with his addiction. They opted for a very 'heroic' therapy.

"Accordingly he was now subjected to . . . apomorphine aversion treatment. Lowry was to be totally isolated, placed in a tiny cell illuminated only by a small red bulb for ten days, during which time he would be given injections of apomorphine and allowed to drink as much alcohol as he wished. The apomorphine was to induce nausea and vomiting which, in theory, Lowry was then to associate with the experience of

114

drinking alcohol, creating in him a conditioned aversion to drinking. Very little food was to be given to him, and very little water; the emphasis was to be on alcohol, whenever he wanted it." (Day 1973:29)

After ten days he was pulled out, given 48 hours to rest, saline solution, glucose, tomato juice and a little food. Then he was sent back for another 11 days of 'treatment'.

When he finally emerged, he was pronounced cured.

Three days later Lowry climbed the wall, escaped the grounds and went on a violent 2 day bender.

He was brought back to the hospital by the police totally exhausted and for the next few weeks he was quiet and cooperative. He entered a new cycle of psychotherapeutic treatment and was discharged in January 1957.

Once home everyone agreed that it was a new Malcolm. He was writing, not drinking a lot, happy, curious. Everyone was delighted—most of all Margerie.

Six months later he was dead.

An extreme case of mutual pathology in an alcoholic family?

On the contrary, a common case, as the reader will see as we now deal with the alcoholic marriage of Mr. & Mrs. Cooper—keeping the Lowrys as a reference point.

Chapter 14

Mrs. Cooper's Ultimatum

There are many varieties of alcoholic marriages. The Cooper's marriage, for example, is quite different from the Lowry marriage which we have just described. What their marriages share in common is the mutually reinforcing pathology fueled by the husband's alcoholism.

Lowry, you will recall, was home all the time and his wife was therefore always experiencing and being victimized by his alcoholic behavior.

Cooper, on the contrary, is never home. He leaves early in the morning and comes home late at night.

Mrs. Lowry used an "enabling" strategy to preserve the marriage—continually rescuing her husband from the consequences of his actions. Mrs. Cooper uses a different strategy—one that deals with her husband's most glaring fault (according to her): his absence from the marriage. She has become what is called a 'compensator.' She tries to overcome his unacceptable behavior by her overachievement and efforts towards perfection. And Mrs. Cooper is quite good at it. She is president of the PTA at her younger child's school. She is active in dozens of community organizations. She is loved and respected.

Astonishing as it may seem, Mrs. Cooper does not know her husband is an alcoholic.

She knows he drinks too much when he's away from home, which is now always.

And though we are in the 1980's and Mrs. Cooper is an intelligent and sophisticated woman (with a B.A. in Economics from the University of Michigan where she met her husband)—she has only one concept of alcoholism: an alcoholic is an individual who is constantly and publicly drunk. But her husband never is.

Of course, Cooper has really given her enough evidence—but what good is evidence if the detective is not on the case?

Mrs. Cooper knows that her husband never eats home any more except the cakes and cookies she constantly buys for the children and which her husband cadges. But this too is meaningless to her. Food tastes change, she reasons.

Mrs. Cooper knows that her husband often comes home looking ill and feeling ill, and impotence is now a constant problem.

And Mrs. Cooper sees that her husband has begun to forget things, garble messages, trip over obstacles that aren't there.

But she does not add it all up to alcoholism.

What she does believe is that her husband is cracking under the stress of his job.

She knows intuitively that there is something wrong with her husband—systemically—with his behavior, his health, his thought processes, his eros—but that can't be alcoholism.

Mrs. Cooper does not know that alcoholism is a systemic malnourishment/toxicity syndrome triggered metabolically (tolerance-addiction cycle) in genetically predisposed individuals.

And if you told her, she would just smile, agree and not believe a word of it.

She has made her own analysis. It's simple. His job is killing him, she concludes, and he will either have to quit his pressure cooker job or seek help from a professional who can help him cope.

He cannot quit his job, she realizes. They have two children, two cars, a large house and a larger mortgage, two aged relatives they partially support and little money in the bank.

So, five months after Cooper's lapse into more or less continual sexual impotence, she waits up for him one night at the kitchen table.

She holds in her hand a small slip of paper and on the paper is the name and phone number of a psychiatrist.

Cooper arrives home at twenty minutes past midnight. He walks into the kitchen to get a cold soft drink from the refrigerator to 'settle his stomach.' He is exhausted and vodka drenched. The only thing he feels other than a queasy stomach from the car ride home is a tightening of the back of his neck and pins and needles in the foot that was on the accelerator.

When he sees his wife waiting for him in the kitchen, he grimaces, hoping it is not another interminable lecture on why he should start spending more time with his family, etc.

Mrs. Cooper, in fact, starts out that way but when her husband refuses to make any intelligible response—she gets right to the point: she is not interested in preserving the marriage if he can't even make love.

Cooper is hit hard. He doesn't say a word.

She pushes the piece of paper across the table and tells him to call the psychiatrist and make an appointment.

Cooper tries to wriggle out. He tells his wife he can't afford any extra expenses right now, particularly not to the tune of about $300 a week for a psychiatrist—what with orthodontist bills for the kids, etc.

She tells him it is a community service program where psychiatrists contribute a few hours a week for individuals who can't afford the normal fees.

Cooper says he's making more than $60,000 a year and he'll be damned if he'll take charity.

She tells him you pay what you can afford: there is no set fee—it is negotiated.

Then she tells him that this time she is serious. She wants a change. She wants her husband back. She pushes the piece of paper closer to him and goes to bed.

Cooper studies it, folds it and places it in his wallet. It has dawned on him that she is serious and the idea of losing his wife and kids sends him into a panic. He will call the next morning.

He does call. And so begins a series of events which will eventually put me in touch with Cooper, even though at that time I am thousands of miles away.

It is not a happy story, as you will see, but it is a classic example of what happens to an individual when those who love him and treat him do not understand the parameters of the disease called alcoholism. And I assure you Cooper's subsequent history will illuminate many of the central problems of managing the alcoholic in American society.

As we have seen, Mrs. Cooper gave her husband, finally, an either/or choice. Either seek help to diminish the behavioral ramifications of his pressure cooker job (she, if you recall, does not believe that Cooper is an alcoholic) or face the possible dissolution of their marriage.

Cooper agrees to seek help and calls the psychiatrist whom his wife has contacted. He makes an appointment.

And, he shows up for that appointment, attesting to the gravity of the marital situation that Cooper now sees himself in.

It is not easy for him because an early evening appointment means he cannot do his serious drinking until much later. It means he'll have to on certain evenings forego his regular place in the bar in which he lives.

To get himself in metabolic synch he has three quick shots of vodka forty minutes before his appointment and then eats two chocolate bars to get the smell away and reinforce his energy levels.

He does not lie to the psychiatrist about why he is there. He tells him his wife has demanded he seek treatment. He happily embraces the wife's theory as to his deteriorating condition—that his job is literally killing him.

The psychiatrist takes a brief case history. Does he abuse alcohol or drugs? Cooper raises his eyes in astonishment: "Of course not. Drugs, never. Booze, once in a while when on a business lunch I have a few martinis."

Cooper *never* discloses the extent of his drinking patterns to anyone. He considers vodka his best and only friend and "knows" that a vast conspiracy is "out there"—somewhere—waiting to pounce, to remove his 'friend', to place a barrier between them, to prevent him from feeling good.

The psychiatrist has no reason to believe that Cooper is lying. He sees in front of him a forty-four year old man, well-dressed, well-groomed, well-built (a bit overweight and out of shape), holding a very responsible job and seemingly in control of himself, intellectually and physically—although obviously stressed.

In addition, he sees a man who has the good sense to realize that his wife's analysis of his behavior was correct—it is destroying their marriage.

Cooper then goes into the specifics of his case. He tells the psychiatrist about his constant anxiety, his panic attacks and his morose states.

He describes the many pressures of his job and his responses to them. He openly and frankly deals with his newly-emerged sexual problem: where he desires his wife but is unable to function.

Under expert questioning by the psychiatrist, more specific symptoms of his condition emerge. Among them are:

- shakiness, jitteriness, trembling, muscle aches, fatigability
- sweating, dry mouth, dizziness, cold clammy hands, frequent urination, diarrhea, paresthesias
- worrying, ruminating, anticipating that something bad will happen to him and his loved ones
- insomnia, difficulty in concentrating, impatience, irritability

After the third session the psychiatrist knows what he is facing because he has seen it hundreds of times before—it is the classic, upwardly mobile, middle-class neurosis: a general anxiety disorder with depression.

The psychiatrist is absolutely correct according to DSM-III. And he would probably be clinically correct if Cooper was not an alcoholic.

But we have seen that virtually all of the symptoms associated with a general anxiety disorder (with depression) are also indicative of chronic alcohol abuse and its subsequent toxicity and malnutrition.

Just as the psychiatrist has made a classical diagnosis based on Cooper's lie (the psychiatrist is essentially blameless; it takes a different kind of training to uncover such a lie)—now he takes a classical therapeutic step.

In conjunction with a twice-weekly schedule of psychotherapy, he prescribes diazepam for Cooper—5 mgs four times a day, because it (and other benzodiazepines) is still "preferred for treatment of anxiety with depression" (Mansky & Neu 1981:63).

Cooper is delighted. Here is something that he can swallow (just like vodka); that will clear up all the problems and allow him to get back to trouble-free drinking (so he thinks).

Here is the kind of hard-nosed treatment that a fast-track merchandiser like Cooper can understand and appreciate.

Poor Cooper. He will pay dearly for his lie when he begins taking diazepam *and* when he ceases taking it.

Poor Cooper. He doesn't understand that the lie is going to come home to roost. After all—nothing much has happened: he simply lied to his psychiatrist about his drinking, was diagnosed for a general anxiety disorder with depression—and, as part of his therapeutic regimen, was given 5 mgs of diazepam four times a day.

After all, diazepam is, of course, one of the most prescribed substances in America (at least 45 million prescriptions for Valium and other brand incarnations are filled each year (Breggin 1983:85)) and it has proven its worth in many circumstances—from the treatment of anxiety disorders to the alleviation of withdrawal symptoms in the recovering alcoholic to postoperative care.

But it is very, very dangerous when used in conjunction with alcohol and only now are we beginning to understand both the dangers and the extent of the dual abuse/addiction.

In 1977 Alcoholics Anonymous surveyed its then 1 million members.

They discovered that 18 percent of them admitted to having been dual-addicted, with the great majority of these combining alcohol and diazepam. (Hughes & Brewin 1980: 36)

So Cooper is not unique at all. His situation, in fact, is quite common.

It is so common that I and many of my colleagues now believe that thousands of deaths occur each year that can be directly attributed to dual addictions but are misdiagnosed as something else.

Why are diazepam and similar substances so dangerous when used with alcohol?

"Adverse reactions from ethanol-drug interactions may result from the additive or synergistic effects of ethanol and the other drugs on the target organ such as the brain. This is particularly true of certain drugs with sedative properties (meprobamate, benzodiazepines). Apart from this effect, ethanol may also interfere with the metabolism of other drugs and produce toxic reactions that may be important clinically." (Muhoberac et al. 1984:589)

But it is much more complex than just one drug over-potentiating another. As Muhoberac and his colleagues explain . . .

"The development of toxic manifestations depends on the type of ethanol exposure and on whether the injurious agent is the parent drug or its metabolites). In general . . . acute ethanol administration depresses the biotransformation of other drugs by cytochrome P-450-dependent hepatic microsomal enzymes. Thus, the decreased elimination of certain benzodiazepines, meprobamate and pentobarbital may result in more profound sedation; that of warfarin in greater anticoagulation and bleeding; and that of tolbutamide in possible hypoglycemia."

Dozens of experiments in both animals and humans have shown the additive and synergistic effects of ethanol on other drugs.

> "When alcohol or other sedatives is combined with diazepam, a particularly potent synergistic effect may be generated which—even with low doses of each drug—can result in extreme or even fatal central nervous system depression . . . Since individual tolerances and rates of metabolism for sedatives vary widely, no precise level of dose or duration of use can be reliably predicted as consistently problematic." (Kauffman et al. 1984:11)

But an even more dangerous effect is now recognized and being studied—one in which there are no answers yet.

And this is where the reverse happens—instead of ethanol increasing, for example, the sedative properties of sedative drugs—the drug 'flips over' and produces the opposite effect.

Hundreds of reports on the so-called 'paradoxical rage reaction' in individuals combining alcohol and diazepam are now on file with the FDA. (Hughes & Brewin 1980:57)

In other words, when combined with alcohol, diazepam, in many individuals, becomes a rage-producing substance eliciting anger and hostility that is totally uncommon to the individual even when drinking.

This well-documented and often seen phenomenon is particularly perplexing because we have known for a long time that "diazepam caused a significant increase in the duration of sleep caused by ethanol." (French 1971:468)

And, because we now know that diazepam causes 'true pharmacological dependence' after 6 weeks (Murphy et al.1984) of daily use (we will discuss this shortly)—we know why a chronic drinker who withdraws from diazepam suffers greater withdrawal symptoms than a non-drinking individual: he or she is dual-addicted and is withdrawing from both at the same time.

But now let us see and try to understand exactly what happens to Cooper.

Cooper begins his diazepam regimen (part of a total psychotherapeutic package) correctly. He follows instructions: 5 mgs four times a day.

During the first week of his diazepam maintenance he experiences a profound change.

The synergistic and additive interaction of ethanol and diazepam (the scope and possible mechanics of which we have already documented) 'dampens' down his CNS dramatically.

Everything becomes slow motion.

Most nonalcoholic individuals would not really consider this an improvement. But for Cooper (and other alcoholics) it is a profound relief.

The desperate mood swings, anxiety, panic, and other behavioral disorders that characterize the pressurized existence of an alcoholic trying to maintain job and family—vanish.

For the alcoholic, slow motion is better than the exhausting, never ending whirlwind.

That first week on diazepam, everything slows down. Cooper can even smile. He can carry on a long, dull, but essentially logical conversation. He can study objects for an extended period of time.

At the beginning of the second week, this welcome slowdown vanishes. Cooper immediately begins to increase his diazepam dosage without informing his psychiatrist.

Cooper, in fact, has embarked on a deadly phenomenon that is quite common when alcoholics begin taking tranquilizers, sedatives and all other drugs which act as central nervous system depressants.

Milam & Ketcham (1983:172) perfectly describe the phenomenon:

"When the alcoholic takes these prescription drugs, he experiences an unusual effect—the prescribed drug dose is simply not strong enough. The alcoholic is instantly tolerant to central nervous system depressants because his central nervous system cells are already tolerant to alcohol. Having adapted to one drug, his cells are also adapted to similar drugs, and in order to get the intended effect, he must take more pills than prescribed.

This instantaneous ability to withstand the effects of drugs pharmacologically similar to alcohol is termed cross-tolerance. It accounts for the alcoholic's ability to continue to function with tranquilizer or sedative doses, for example, which would be incapacitating or even lethal for nonalcoholics."

Cross-tolerance is inexorably and progressively risk producing. As Milam & Ketcham explain:

"The dangers of cross-tolerance are obvious. Because of his increased tolerance, the alcoholic has to drink more to experience the desired effects of alcohol; if he is taking prescription pills, he will also have to increase the dosage to get the intended effect."

Cooper continues to increase both his diazepam and alcohol intake but that first flush of slow-motion well-being never, in fact, returns.

What he gets instead is a renewal of his clinical symptoms of depression along with a great deal of trembling and motor difficulties.

By the seventh week, still lying to his psychiatrist about his alcohol intake and about his increase of diazepam ingestion (his psychiatrist still thinks he is on 5 mgs four times a day), Cooper is just swallowing bizarre amounts of the drug and drinking in even more random and voracious patterns.

Cooper, in order to get more of the drug and continue to deceive the psychiatrist, simply contacts another physician and repeats his original lie. He get another prescription which he fills at a different pharmacy. Cooper has now discovered pharmacy roulette.

Cooper, if you have been following him, has led a sort of charmed existence.

He has beaten all the odds so far. He recovered, if you recall, from his hypoglycemic stupor (11% mortality probability).He has avoided a serious vehicular accident (his alcoholic father, if you recall, was killed in one). He has not been hospitalized for any of the 'masked' disorders secondary to alcoholism. He still has his high paying job. His family life is precarious but still intact.

Yes, he has been doing o.k.—given his chronic condition.

But now the odds begin to even out.

The diazepam 'flips over' and Cooper experiences that strange, quite common, but still unexplained phenomenon of the 'paradoxical rage reaction' which we have already identified.

It is, as you will see, a minor aberration, but it will have wide ramifications.

Chapter 15

From Single to Dual Addiction

After nine weeks of therapy, Cooper has become a walking time bomb.

He swallows diazepam indiscriminately but no matter how many pills he pops he cannot (except for fleeting instances) bring back that very nice 'slow down' he experienced during that first week of his regimen before the cross-tolerance took hold.

He is drinking even more. He is confused. And he is very tired.

One evening after work he goes into his usual bar and begins his vodka martini regimen. He drinks and smokes quietly.

Cooper has run a three day tab in the bar. Around ten o'clock the bartender totals the three-day bill and, as he has done a hundred times before, brings it over to Cooper and asks if Cooper wishes to settle it.

Cooper, for some odd reason, becomes enraged at the perfectly sensible request.

He begins to curse the bartender for not trusting him, curse the bar for cheating him on drinks, curse his fellow drinkers for being so stupid as to continue to drink in the bar.

The bartender steps back, astonished, never having seen Cooper like that before. He walks away—waiting for Cooper to calm down.

But Cooper doesn't calm down. He throws some cash on the bar and storms out, yelling that he'll never come back again.

Once out on the street, Cooper is trembling. His fury rises. He hates the bar and the bartender. He feels sick. He feels crazy. He decides that the psychiatrist and his wife have gotten him into this mess.

He goes to a pay phone and dials his psychiatrist. He gets an answering machine. He waits for the beep and then leaves a message that he is terminating the therapy and adds a goodbye stream of invective.

He starts walking, clearing his pockets of all the diazepam containers and flinging them down the nearest drain.

Twenty minutes later Cooper is sitting in another bar, having a vodka martini. The rage has vanished.

Cooper has just exhibited a 'paradoxical rage' episode which is ubiquitous among alcoholics who ingest diazepam.

It is so widely reported in fact that:

> "Many researchers . . . are starting to think rage is a true reaction to (diazepam), especially in combination with alcohol, not a paradoxical one. The price many people pay in anger and hostility when they combine such . . . substances . . . can be high indeed. One of the more chilling examples of this adverse reaction in the FDA files is of a woman who had several drinks and then engaged in an argument with her husband. When he left the house she took several (diazepam) tablets to calm down. She went to sleep but woke up when her husband returned, took out a pistol and shot him dead. The FDA file tersely refers to the incident as 'an obvious paradoxical rage reaction'". (Hughes & Brewin 1980:57)

When Cooper finally gets home that evening he thinks that the worst is behind him. He has gotten rid of the psychiatrist and the pills and things will be better.

What Cooper doesn't know is that things are about to get much worse because he is now addicted to diazepam even though he can't even conceive that such an addiction can occur, particularly since he has been on the regimen only about nine weeks.

But, of course, Cooper does not have access to the medical journals.

> "Our study suggests that withdrawal reactions occur after as little as 6 weeks' treatment with diazepam . . . Withdrawal of diazepam at 6 weeks from a mean daily dose of 11.4

mg produced a marked increase in symptoms . . . Our findings suggest that the symptoms exhibited after stopping benzodiazepines constitute *true pharmacological dependence* as they are absent after withdrawal from buspirone . . . " (Murphy et al. 1984:1389)

It is interesting to note that the study quoted above utilized 5l patients—none of whom were alcoholics.

But Cooper is an alcoholic and the individual cross-addicted to alcohol and diazepam is, as we shall see, a bit more potent.

Cooper doesn't have the slightest inkling that diazepam can produce true pharmacological dependence after only six weeks in some individuals—and he is one of those individuals. He doesn't understand that he has become cross-addicted.

"Once addicted to both alcohol and prescription drugs, the alcoholic experiences a complex combination of withdrawal symptoms, and his mental and physical torment multiplies. The dual or multiply addicted alcoholic is caught in a brutal cycle of increasing pain and decreasing benefits, as he must step up his use of alcohol or pills to medicate himself against the ever-impending and increasingly severe withdrawal symptoms. Blackouts, mental confusion and suicidal depressions intensify with multiple addictions, and the possibility of overdose dramatically increases."

"A critical and dangerously overlooked aspect of addiction to alcohol and/or drugs is its permanence. Once established, the addiction can be reactivated by using either alcohol or prescription drugs, even after prolonged periods of abstinence. Tranquilizers and sedatives, for example, . . . can reactivate the physical addiction to alcohol, causing a craving for alcohol which leads to a return to drinking. Many sober alcoholics given medication for tension, pain, or insomnia have relapsed and started drinking again." (Milam and Ketcham 1983:175)

I wish to make three points about cross-addiction right now—while leaving an indepth discussion of the matter to a future time.

First, cross-addiction is common. As you recall, we noted that about 20% of AA membership (one million individuals) states that they combined alcohol and drugs.

Second, cross-addiction is one of the most serious unrecognized health problems in the U.S. and is responsible for thousands of deaths each year. (In younger age groups cross-addiction may run 40-50% among those who are in treatment facilities.)

Third, diazepam, lorazepam and chlordiazepoxide are not the only drugs which cross-addict with alcohol. All the major and minor tranquilizers are implicated, as well as the hypnotics, hallucinogens, narcotics and amphetamines. Cocaine, particularly, has become a major new threat. Alcohol is very hospitable.

Now let us return to Cooper.

Thirty-six hours after his final diazepam ingestion, he begins to suffer withdrawal symptoms. And they continue.

They are not the usual behavioral problems which Cooper always exhibits and has learned to live with as an alcoholic: anxiety, depression, motor difficulties, etc.

These are serious, and, in a sense, disabling symptoms: "tremors, nausea, abdominal and muscular cramping, profuse sweating." ("Tranquilizer" 1985)

Cooper needs relief from these mysterious (to him) new developments. He cannot function unless he gets relief.

So, he treats himself the only way he knows how—with more alcohol.

Cooper, of course, drinks heavily each and every day, but now he substantially increases the amount of alcohol he ingests in order to remove the diazepam withdrawal symptoms.

This dramatic and sudden increase in consumption breaks down Cooper's homeostatic mechanism of tolerance.

So, for the first time, our alcoholic Cooper begins to act like a Hollywood drunk.

He walks out of bars unsteady. He vomits. He talks stupid. He looks stupid.

And, for the first time, he begins to exhibit aspects of drunkenness at work.

Two weeks into his withdrawal stage, Cooper is evaluated for a promotion to Group Vice President—a job that Cooper has sought for a long time.

He is passed over. (Cooper's increasingly degenerative performance and behavior does not signal to his company that he is in trouble—only that he did not fulfill his corporate promise.)

This decision sends Cooper into a very deep depression. It is, for him, the most profound disappointment of his life. The Group Vice President promotion would have changed his life—a great deal more money, a great deal more prestige, and most important of all, a shot at the really big plums in the corporate structure.

Cooper tries to understand what happened. And, for the first time he clearly sees what is happening—he finally understands that he cannot live without a great deal of alcohol each day and that alcohol is making him sicker and crazier.

He contemplates going to AA and then quickly rejects the idea. In that rejection is hidden a very fascinating story which must next be told.

Chapter 16

Why Is Cooper Afraid of A.A.?

Cooper has, as we have seen, accelerated his decline. This came about, if you recall, through a well-meaning decision by his wife to force him to enter psychotherapy—one component of which was the regular ingestion of diazepam.

Cooper became addicted to that substance and suffered severe withdrawal symptoms after ceasing ingestion as a result of a violent episode: a 'paradoxical rage reaction' which is endemic among alcoholics who use diazepam. (Remember—for an alcoholic to use diazepam is automatically to abuse diazepam. There is no other way to look at it.)

The diazepam withdrawal symptoms forced him to dramatically increase his alcohol intake thus breaking his 'steady state' tolerance/addiction formation. The result was public drunkenness and extremely bizarre behavior which cost him the most important thing in his life—the promotion that he had worked for, angled for, hustled for.

The shock at being passed over was so great, in fact, that Cooper is forced to implicate his drinking as a causal agent in the disaster—and to contemplate Alcoholics Anonymous.

He rejects the idea after contemplating it briefly. He does not articulate to himself the reasons why he rejects A.A.—it's just, upon reflection, 'not for him'.

But let us dig a little deeper into Cooper's decision—using as a focal point an extremely important and illuminating new study reported by LeClair Bissell and Paul W. Haberman (1984:5).

407 subjects were in this study—all of them professionals who described themselves as alcoholics and A.A. members who had maintained sobriety for at least a year.The total sample consisted of 214 men and 193 women.

The 97 physicians and 49 dentists were all male; the 100 nurses and 56 college women were all female; and 49 of 55 attorneys and 19 of 50 social workers were men.

The median ages of men and women were 51 and 46 respectively.

The respondents attended their first A.A. meeting at the median age of 40, about eleven years after drinking started to interfere with their lives and they had their last drink two years later at the median age of 42.

Approximately two-fifths of both men and women had received psychiatric treatment for their alcoholism before achieving sobriety in A.A.

Thirty-six percent of all subjects reported being addicted to drugs other than (or in addition to) alcohol at one time or another.

As you can see, Cooper is very close to this group in many respects—length of time drinking, age, professional and education status, dual-addiction, etc.—and would have fit cleanly into a composite profile. Except, of course, that the participants in this study, unlike Cooper, did not reject A.A.

But, in fact, many of them did at first, and in their tentative rejections we can understand the reasons for Cooper's rejection.

Bissell and Haberman analyze this rather unique contradiction: (:89)

> "Very few of our subjects had first heard of A.A. as part of their professional training . . . Many of those who had heard of it were poorly informed or even misinformed. Some had been led to believe that it represents a somewhat suspect variety of folk medicine, while others gathered that it was a group of people who now substituted for the dependence on alcohol an equally unhealthy dependence on A.A. Some were wary of involvement with what they feared was a fanatic religious group or a group whose members were of a much lower social class than their own."

It is time for us to dig a little deeper into the A.A. phenomenon. Hundreds of books, magazine articles, movies, TV serials have brought A.A. into the popular consciousness but what they have to say about this truly unique therapeutic community is always romanticized and never analytical—and of little value to the physicians or the interested layperson.

I want to identify why A.A. has been so successful while the great majority of other programs fail. I want to analyze those aspects of A.A. which should be integrated into all existing programs for alcoholism and other addictions . . . and want to bury forever the still widespread belief among physicians and scientists that A.A. is a variety of folk medicine practiced by defrocked preachers.

Isn't it strange that right now there are millions of alcoholics scattered throughout the world who are sober because they belong to a loosely structured organization called Alcoholics Anonymous?

It is strange. It is remarkable. And this fact is extremely perplexing to many people. The success of AA has seemed to defy analysis for surely no scientist could believe that its success lies in the simple fact that an alcoholic stands up in front of his peers and states he is an alcoholic, whereupon his peers applaud and welcome him warmly; then said alcoholic is assigned a sponsor and begins to attend weekly meetings.

Surely this kind of simple process cannot be what is working, for we are dealing with chronic, disordered alcoholics—individuals with one of the most intractable of diseases.

Of course there is a lot more.

AA encompasses an extremely sophisticated methodology hidden behind often simplistic formulas and rituals such as "the12steps" and the "12 traditions" and the "last house on the street."

First and foremost AA pioneered the concept of alcoholism as a disease two decades before the concept was accepted by the medical profession.

Second AA encompasses a multifactorial concept of the disease and its treatment.

As AA puts it in many booklets, alcoholism is "a physical compulsion, coupled with a mental obsession." And, of course, the physical and mental are combined with the spiritual . . . "We came to believe that a Power greater than ourselves could restore us to sanity." Body, mind, and spirit.

Third, AA deals day by day with alcoholics. No long term pledges are made. AA supports each alcoholic's goal of making it though the next 24 hours sober. And this is of crucial importance.

As Zinberg and Fraser put it: (1979:377)

"A . . . tenet of AA, basic but little understood, is the view that an alcoholic is always recovering, never recovered. One is sober from minute to minute, from day to day; and because the next drink is always imminent, overconfidence is dangerous. An AA member may stay sober, but by his awareness of what he must overcome he is always potentially a drinker."

This simple belief is actually a remarkable and very sophisticated insight into the pathology of alcoholism.

"It rests upon the recognition that the alcoholic has two fears which are so strong as to be phobic: the fear of drunkenness and the fear of sobriety. These phobias continue to appear all the way from detoxification to the last stage of recovery. The alcoholic, despite his pleas that he likes to drink, that drinking makes him feel better and more able to exist in his own skin as well as with other people, comes to loathe and fear his drunkenness. Will he once more be compelled to defile and degrade himself physically, emotionally and socially by getting and staying drunk? But even in the depths of alcoholic torment in a detoxification ward, he will insist that some day he can become a controlled drinker. Whatever drink supplies, it is much prized; to an alcoholic the prospect of a life without drink is terrifying, even phobic . . . In time, however, the social and psychological advantages of sobriety tip the balance toward abstinence; the experience of being in control of oneself and able to interact with people directly rather than through a boozy haze becomes reinforcing. Unlike the members of the straight world, to whom the advantages of sobriety are self-evident, AA does not underestimate the alcoholic's fear of being sober. Instead, by insisting that the alcoholic is always recovering, never recovered, it keeps the possibility of drinking always at hand but still a hand's breadth away."

The fourth pillar of complexity supporting AA's seemingly simplistic slogans is the anonymity of the organization and its members.

As AA wisely puts it: "anonymity is the spiritual foundation of all our traditions, ever reminding us to place principles before personalities."

Coupled with that anonymity is the refusal of AA to support, endorse, criticize any outside facility, movement, theory, ideology, person, etc.

This focus on the anonymous alcoholic is a continuous confirmation that the organization exists only for the management of the disease. All statements, all meetings, all camaraderie, all cups of coffee are there for only one reason—to help an alcoholic make it sober through the next 24 hours.

So, it appears that physicians and medical scientists who scorn AA because of a perceived "simplistic and pietist" approach, are all wrong.

I think I have showed that the AA slogans, in fact, rest on a very sophisticated and rigorous bedrock of concepts.

Let me recapitulate just briefly.

First there is the AA belief that alcoholism is a disease.

Second, the belief that the disease is multifactorial—encompassing body, mind and spirit.

Third, the belief that alcoholics are never fully recovered; they keep recovering day by day so that the emphasis must be on 24 hours of sobriety.

And fourth, the belief in anonymity in order to focus all the strengths of the organization on the management of the disease.

All of these have been crucial to AA's acknowledged success.

But there is a fifth factor which is even of more importance and to understand this we have to go back to the origins of AA.

We have to go back in time to 1935 when William Griffith Wilson went to Akron to lead a proxy fight for control of a small machine tool company.

Bill W. (as he came to be known) was an alcoholic who had been dry for six months since he had been released from his 4th detox at Towns Hospital in Manhattan in 1934.

Upon his release Wilson had become active in a church related group and he was preaching enlightenment and sobriety to Big Apple alcoholics from all walks of life with no success at all.

This trip to Akron was, he hoped, a way to recoup his financial fortunes.

The trip, alas, was a failure. He lost the proxy fight and found himself marooned and alone in a hotel in Akron a day before Mother's Day.

He suddenly realized that he needed a drink desperately—and that he was going to drink.

The realization that the cycle was about to start again induced a terrifying panic in him.

He called long distance to New York to find out if his church group could give him the name of someone to talk to in Akron. What he really wanted was another drunk to be with.

He found one: Dr. Robert Holbrook Smith (later called Dr. Bob) who, when he telephoned, was lying passed out under the kitchen table.

This time Bill didn't preach. He was too scared he was going to drink again. He just told his own story as an alcoholic to his newfound friend. He told Smith what he had learned in Towns Hospital about alcoholism as a disease. He told Smith that he never would have been able to maintain sobriety this long if he hadn't been able to grasp a spiritual truth for the first time in his life.

And, he sobered Smith up so that three days later he could perform an operation.

That, in essence, was the beginning of the phenomenon called AA.

Do you understand what happened?

For the first time, one alcoholic, in a strange town, realized that the only way he was going to maintain sobriety during the next 24 hours was if he could help another alcoholic stay sober.

And it was that enormously powerful insight which triggered the world wide AA phenomenon and, in fact, was the model of thousands of self-help groups—from schizophrenics to battered wives to ex-cons—in which individuals who share a common illness, history, or disability come together because only they can understand and help each other.

The AA insight in fact has had a profound impact on the entire social landscape of American life.

Is there, however, any scientific validity to a concept which states that only an alcoholic can understand and help another alcoholic?

None whatsoever. Obviously, every day, physicians without pneumonia treat and cure individuals with pneumonia.

But there is an enormous emotional validity in this concept for the practicing alcoholic because no single segment of the health care system in its widest sense (hospital, police, church, family, etc.) understands the systemic toxicity that alcohol induces.

Each segment of society sees a different aspect of the alcoholic: his depression, his violence, his lack of will, his intestinal problems, his malnutrition, his public drunkenness.

Each segment of society sees and deals with what it is capable of seeing . . . what it is trained to see.

But all of that is happening simultaneously in the alcoholic and the only one who can perceive that immediately is another alcoholic. That is the fellowship of AA.

Alas, AA has not always been immune to the tendency of all successful organizations to build a fence around themselves in order to make sure that new truths will not hurt them. And we must deal with the price AA in the past—and our society in the present has paid and is paying because of that fence.

Chapter 17

Natural Allies

AA, at one time, built a fence around itself to protect its successful ideology, and in doing so essentially changed the thrust of the organization without even being aware of it.

By building this fence AA removed one of the three legs of its original triad—the 'body' had been removed from 'body, mind and spirit.'

Happily, AA has recently begun to dismantle the fence because it understood that the fence was keeping it from helping literally millions of alcoholics who simply cannot be helped by any kind of behavioral therapy, alone.

Let me show you why.

Consider Mr. O. He is a 55-year-old gentleman with a long drinking history. He decompensated between 1972 and 1974 and in 1974 was admitted to the hospital—had DT's and a suicide attempt.

He stopped drinking from 1974 to 1981. He resumed drinking in 1981, had progression with several 5-day detoxs during that period.

He presented to the hospital on January 9, 1986 with the following findings . . .

- Alcohol Dependence Syndrome
- Alcohol Withdrawal—Severe
- Blood Pressure—180/100
- Pulse-140
- Extremely tremulous—high risk for recurrent seizure
- Alcohol Liver Disease
- Possible Liver Failure (proper studies ordered)
- Chronic Obstructive Lung Disease
- Emphysema—probably secondary to smoking (patient currently smoking when interviewed)
- Malnutrition—severe, gums are hypotrophied and bleeding, tongue is flat, nail change is compatible with Zinc deficiency, skin changes compatible with Vitamin A deficiency
- Alcohol Peripheral Neuritis—the patient has a broad-based gait and difficulty walking. He has a positive Romberg and cannot stand stable if he closes his eyes
- Electrolyte Imbalance

Alone, no type or amount of behavioral therapy—past, present, or future—can truly help this man.

He is severely ill. He is a metabolic cripple. He must be reconstituted metabolically and nutritionally in order to survive. Detox is only the first step and an insignificant one if the other elements—his systemic malnourishment for one—are not given top priority.

Alone, no amount of AA 12-step work . . no amount of dedicated AA sponsors . . . no amount of meetings with coffee and donuts will help this man (in fact he has to stop overconsuming coffee and sugar donuts and AA, now, as part of its fence dismantling efforts is starting to replace this traditional meeting fare with more nutritious snacks).

AA can only help him if it lets the new evidence on alcoholism enter and influence its programs.

By dismantling the fence AA has started to return to one of the most basic, important and pioneering concepts of its creed—that alcoholism is a three-pronged disease: body, mind and spirit.

The reader will recall that Bill W.—the cofounder of AA—was a fervent believer in the disease concept of alcoholism even prior to the historical founding of AA. He had learned this concept from his scientific 'guru'—Dr. Silkworth of Towns Hospital in Manhattan who had detoxed him.

Over the years, Bill W., in fact, raised money outside of AA to support distinguished researchers who conducted often landmark biochemical, nutritional and metabolic research on patients with mental disease and alcoholism . . . research which Bill W. believed was of crucial importance to alcoholics.

He fought, often without success, to introduce these kinds of broader-based programs in general hospitals with psychiatric departments, mental hospitals, alcoholic rehab centers, veterans facilities, and AA sponsored 'drying out' tanks, as a way to reintroduce the 'body.'

But when he died in 1971, the fence had already been built too high and too strong by some members of AA. AA was, at that time, committed to its unique and relatively successful form of behavioral therapy no matter how much new evidence was uncovered that showed alcoholism to be closer to diabetes and atherosclerosis than personality disorders . . . and no matter how much new research showed that long-term recovery from alcoholism must be accompanied by a serious, individually tailored medical program which includes nutritional, immunological and metabolic considerations.

The fence began to crumble as more and more AA members—accepting the new metabolic data—realized the importance of the body in the equation and reaffirmed the wisdom of the original AA adage: 'bring the body along, and the mind will follow.'

But, while most AA members have seen the light, the fence is still an insidious factor in other segments of today's tragic picture of alcoholism and its victims.

And the continuing refusal by the wider health world to accept the new alcoholism findings has helped drive the nails in the coffin of needed alcohol funding of all kinds.

There are enormous practical consequences of ignoring the new metabolic and nutritional findings re alcoholism because the behavioral mode of treatment alone simply will not work over the long term with the majority of alcoholics in this country whether that treatment is sponsored by AA or the AMA or any other organization or 'school.'

Remember Mr. O? What were the practical consequences to his life and health?

If you recall, this 55 year old individual presented with the following: alcohol dependence syndrome, alcohol withdrawal, severe; blood pressure, 180/100; pulse, 140; extrememly tremulous with high risk for recurrent seizures; alcohol liver disease; possible liver failure; chronic obstructive lung disease; emphysema; malnutrition; alcohol peripheral neuritis; electrolyte imbalance.

It is important for our discussion that you know what happened next in this case . . . that you know the nitty gritty everyday tragedy of trying to treat sick individuals in a world that simply refuses to accept these individuals for what they are.

After I had worked Mr. O. up, he said he was now willing to try to get full treatment. I proceeded to develop a comprehensive plan for him.

Our business office then told me to call the 800 number of Mr. O's insurance firm for treatment approval.

After several ludicrous telephone misadventures with secretaries, I finally was transferred to an individual who could, so I was told, resolve my problem immediately.

I explained the case to her. She said the Medical Officer involved was not available. The woman refused to identify whether she was an RN. She implied that she was a social work counselor. I asked to speak to the Medical Director. She said no. I asked for his name. She refused to provide it.

I explained the whole case to her and she said that regardless of the individual's condition, he could only have 7-10 days total treatment.

My recommendation to her was full detox, rehab for three weeks and then possibly some sort of half-way house for at least another four weeks.

I carefully and fully explained to her the nature of the complications of his illness, the fact that he must have full rehabilitation and the fact that only full rehabilitation will be cost-effective in the long run.

The person at the other end of the line obviously did not know what I was talking about. She told me it did not matter what the condition was—they would not support any type of inpatient rehab or any treatment beyond ten days at the most and she would have to call me in 7 days to see if he needed the other 3 days.

I explained to her that it would be very dangerous and not cost-effective to treat this individual in such an arbitrary manner. She said I had the right to appeal.

She then proceeded to request a detailed account of the medications he was on: she wanted the exact nature of the drugs he was being detoxed with and the dosages, including his respiratory therapy.

I read all this off in terms of tranquilizing agents, nutrient supplements, respiratory therapy, etc. and I asked why this was necessary.

She said she wanted to make sure I knew what I was doing.

I asked her whether she felt she was equipped to judge my competency. She said the information would be put into the computer and that she, herself, has had a great deal of experience in the field. Our conversation finally ended with a totally capricious decision that this man would be given 7-10 days treatment.

In short, the insurance company is writing this 55 year old man off in spite of the fact that there is a real potential for him to get well.

But they can't really write him off because sooner or later, as a result of their decision now, he is going to come back into the hospital with liver disease or broken hip or bleeding from a gastrointestinal attack or a paralysis from his neuritis or mental incompetence from a wet brain syndrome.

All this will cost hundreds of times more than treating him adequately to start with, not to mention the gross disregard for human dignity.

So you see, the insurance is just one more structure (Medicare's current alcoholism policy is even more irrational and less cost-effective) which exhibits no understanding at all of the nature of the disease of alcoholism. They, too, have built a fence around themselves to keep out the new research . . . the new findings . . . the new therapies.

Insurance companies, of course, are not the culprits. In back of their decisions are the government decisions . . . the corporate decisions . . . or the union decisions not to provide adequate treatment of alcoholism. The poor woman I talked with was merely blindly carrying out the mandate of a computer programmed to reflect those tragic decisions.

Well, I have spent a lot of pages discussing the very many strengths of Alcoholics Anonymous and its very few weaknesses.

You the reader may be wondering why I have been deviating from the main thrust of the book to spend so much time on AA.

There are many reasons.

First, AA is the most prestigious organization in the world of alcoholism and if the medical profession is to mount a successful campaign against the increasing constriction for funding for alcohol programs of all kinds—AA must somehow, even though it rightly refuses to support any position, join that fight.

Secondly, AA, in spite of being a lay organization, is the only institution in the United States that has any inkling whatsoever of the medical problems involved in alcoholism and the enormous human and economic costs of alcoholism in our society.

Only AA really understands that there are literally millions of undeclared alcoholics walking around, checking in and out of hospitals for masked disorders, killing themselves and others in a daily ritual of mayhem.

Third—no physician can or should treat an alcoholic unless he truly understands AA's philosophical premises which are applicable to all alcoholics for all time—i.e. that an alcoholic is never 'cured' . . . that an alcoholic fears both sobriety and drunkenness, etc.

Physicians have much to learn from AA.

Fourth—and most important—is the fact that until members of AA, working together with the medical profession, go even further in accepting the new metabolic model of alcoholism and incorporate that model into all their programs, the world will continue to ignore the new evidence and the medical profession will continue to treat alcoholism behaviorally and thus doom alcoholics to continuous hospitalization and an early death.

I, personally, depend on AA, consult AA, learn from AA.

And, I continually remind them that it was their co-founder, Bill W., who once tried unsuccessfully to get rid of coffee and donuts and other sweets at AA meetings because he was one of the first to accept the controversial new evidence that there was a strong correlation between alcoholism and hypoglycemia.

Bill W. wrote in his famous *The Vitamin B-3 Therapy: A Second Communication to AA Physicians* (1968:32):

> "Knowing that Dr. M.H. an A.A. physician has had extensive experience in treating alcoholics, I recently asked him to estimate the incidence of hypoglycemia among alcoholics, as a class. He replied that 'the incidence is certainly not lower than 70% and may amount to 90%; the conditions ranging from very mild to very serious.'"

Bill W. quotes two other physicians in his pamphlet: (33)

One says:

> "Several months ago I had twenty consecutive alcoholic patients of mine tested on a six-hour glucose tolerance basis. Every single one of them turned out to be hypoglycemic in some degree or another."

And another notes: (33)

"The main features of the hypoglycemic condition are easily understood. When the hypoglycemic takes sugar, his blood sugar curve rises rapidly to an abnormal height. In order to control this situation, the pancreas excretes a heavy charge of insulin, enough to rapidly force the blood sugar level far below normal. In the effort to remedy this condition, the adrenals then come into play, thus creating a state of hyperadrenalism which in turn adds to the tension and discomfort. In short, the victim is alternately whipsawed between too much insulin and too much adrenalin."

Bill W. was one of the first to understand that alcoholics are often self-treating their hypoglycemia without knowing it (:33).

"Unconsciously, we alcoholics try to cure these conditions—first by sweets, and then by coffee. The sweets temporarily raise our blood sugar and we feel better. Coffee also gives us a temporary boost because it lessens the shock of the blood sugar drop. In exactly the wrong way, we are unconsciously trying to treat ourselves for hypoglycemia."

No one who knows the early history of Bill W. and AA should be surprised by his insight because the cofounder of AA knew before anyone (as we have already shown) that alcoholism was a disease of the body which then manifested itself as well into 'mind' and 'spirit'. Now, after his death, AA is returning slowly to that original premise.

Yes, AA and all physicians who treat patients with alcoholism are natural allies. But our alliance is only strong if we can constructively engage each other through learning, criticism and exploration. Nothing else ever works.

Chapter 18

Cooper's "Heart Attack"

Everything has changed for Cooper since we last met him and nothing has changed.

He is still vice president of the large retail firm but he has lost that key promotion and he knows that his days at the firm are numbered.

While for a brief moment he seriously contemplated AA as a result of the lost promotion and the disastrous end of his encounter with the well-meaning psychiatrist who prescribed diazepam (without knowing Cooper was an alcoholic)—he now has returned without qualms to his daily drinking schedule; morning, afternoon and evening.

His wife, while still worried and perplexed by his drinking, his sexual estrangement, his potential for violence and his total alienation from a normal existence—has decided in the interim to just quietly support him in whatever he does.

It has been an exhausting year so far for Cooper but now he achieves a kind of sodden acceptance; he achieves a level of existence built around a constant but shallow depression—and not the manic highs and deep lows which usually characterized his alcoholic personality in the past.

Weeks slip by into months. He finds a new bar and spends his evenings there, very quickly becoming that most desired of social graces— "a regular." (The reader will remember that Cooper alienated his old bar by a violent outburst while on diazepam therapy.)

This level of life, this quietude that Cooper slips into is to a great extent merely fatigue brought about by his panmalnutrition.

He now does everything, it seems, in a sort of slow motion.

And, insidiously, he is progressively increasing his alcohol intake (the tolerance is 'expanding') because it takes a great deal of booze to induce in him even the slightest glow: the price for feeling good is becoming more and more costly each day and on many days there is no hope at all.

One Thursday night in January, Cooper arrives home at about three o'clock in the morning.

This is late, even for him, but during the evening of drinking he had the sudden idea to stay home the next day and take the entire family out. It simply didn't occur to him that his family might have had other plans— like school.

Anyway, by the time he arrives home he has completely forgotten his plan. He just sits, as is his practice, at the kitchen table drinking heavily sugared instant black coffee and smoking cigarette after cigarette while he stares outside at the snow banks.

Cooper turns and looks at the wall clock. It is now 3:25. Very late.

He crushes out the cigarette and stretches.

Suddenly he feels something very strange.

Something is going on inside of him.

Something seems to have come loose, to have gone crazy. In his chest.

He breaks out into a sweat. He feels weak. He feels more frightened than he has ever felt in his life.

Poor Cooper has, for the first time, begun to experience his own heartbeat—but the beat seems to have gone mad in his chest.

It goes faster and faster. It seems to skip beats and then double beats.

And then as quickly as it came—the irregularity and the speedup vanishes.

Hands trembling, Cooper reaches for and lights another cigarette.

Two puffs and it starts again.

"I'm going to die," he says, "I'm going to die."

For some reason he doesn't want to die in the house, in the kitchen, in front of his family.

He staggers out the door and into the freezing night. It is getting worse and worse inside of him—the beat goes faster and faster and more erratically.

He falls into a snowbank and buries his face in the snow.

But Cooper doesn't die. What he has experienced passes. He gets back into the house wet and dirty and frightened.

He believes dimly that he has suffered a heart attack even though there was little or no pain.

What Cooper, of course, has experienced was paroxysmal atrial fibrillation, the only common arrhythmia in which the ventricular rate is rapid and the rhythm irregular.

The toxicity and malnutrition of alcoholism are beginning to take effect. As Sokolow notes:

> "Infection, trauma, surgery, poisoning or excessive alcohol intake may cause attacks of atrial fibrillation in patients with normal hearts." (1982:214)

Cooper's atrial fibrillation episode did not result in hospitalization but it is in fact one of the more common events in alcoholic pathology and is responsible for thousands of hospital admissions each year (and I may add, for a great deal of confusion and misdiagnosis).

We must look at it briefly because it provides a logical introduction to the entire field of alcoholism and cardiovascular disorders.

An important new study of this phenomenon has just been reported by Rich (1985:30).

As the authors note:

> "An association between alcohol use and atrial fibrillation has long been suspected. Ettinger et al. reported 32 disrhythmic episodes (including 12 with atrial fibrillation) in patients who were drinking heavily and found a disproportionate number of the hospitalizations for these episodes to follow weekends and holidays. Other investigators have induced atrial irritability and arrhythmia by administering alcohol to patients with a history of this 'Holiday Heart' phenomenon. Furthermore, Lowenstein et al. recently reported that 35% of patients presenting with new-onset atrial fibrillation at their public hospital were intoxicated with alcohol. Alcoholism and binge drinking are therefore included among potential etiologies for acute atrial fibrillation."

In their study, Rich and his colleagues retrospectively reviewed 64 cases with idiopathic acute atrial fibrillation and 64 age- and sex-matched controls, randomly selected from among general hospital admissions.

"Sixty-two percent of cases and 33% of controls had documentation as heavy users of alcohol. Furthermore, patients with alcohol-related atrial fibrillation were significantly more likely to manifest alcohol withdrawal syndromes than were other inpatients with heavy alcohol use.

Patients with alcohol-related acute atrial fibrillation were not different from other patients with acute atrial fibrillation with respect to clinical evidence of congestive heart failure, electrocardiographic abnormalities, cardiomegaly, electrolyte disturbance, or response to therapy."

The authors speculate that (:832):

"Alcohol-related atrial fibrillation might be induced by an arrhythmogenic effect of alcohol on the myocardium. Greenspon reported atrial or ventricular tachyarrhythmias induced by whiskey consumption in ten of 14 patients with a history of chronic alcohol use and heart disease. In another study, Engel and Luck reported on ten patients with alcohol use but no evident heart disease other than a history of arrhythmia; these patients were given alcohol and five developed atrial fibrillation or flutter with atrial extrastimultion. Changes in atrial myocardial refractory period have been observed in animal models after massive exposure to alcohol . . . "

This 'Holiday Heart' phenomenon is cross cultural and worldwide in its incidence.

"After any weekend, not just special occasions like May Day or Midsummer, Finnish casualty physicians know that the wards will contain at least one patient in whom acute atrial fibrillation developed after drinking. Such patients usually do not have heart disease or any history of heart diseases. Sinus rhythm usually returns as the alcohol intoxication subsides. However, it is customary to administer intravenous digoxin and oral quinidine sulphate, which almost invariably restores the sinus rhythm . . . Atrial fibrillation apart, the electrocardiogram is almost always normal. Unfortunately, perhaps because of the great number of such patients, thorough cardiological tests are seldom done and the patients are not followed up." (Spilla . . . 1985:391)

The reader will notice that in all of the sources quoted, it is taken for granted from the evidence that atrial fibrillation among heavy drinkers is always alcohol dose specific rather than symptomatic of a broader cardiovascular problem secondary to alcoholism. In fact, we know very little about this phenomenon, particularly as to what happens to these individuals down the road, even if they embrace sobriety. No long term studies have been done.

Atrial fibrillation in terms of mortality is a minor problem among the more serious cardiovascular disorders that we see in patients with alcoholism. A great deal of new information has emerged implicating ethanol as a causal factor in many cardiovascular problems of alcoholics—but not necessarily in nonalcoholic drinkers. This research and this paradox are of great interest.

In the 19th and early 20th centuries several clinicians and pathologists uncovered an association between nonspecific heart disease and large amounts of alcohol, ingested regularly.

Heart enlargement associated with alcoholism was described by the German neurologist Friedreich in 1861. Walsche, an English physician, described a pathology common among alcoholics as "patchy cirrhosis of the heart" in 1873. After reporting on 25 cases of alcohol-induced heart disease in 1893, the famous English physician Graham Steell said, "Not only do I recognize the alcoholism as one of the causes of muscle failure of the heart but I find it a comparatively common one."

Through the mid-1950's in the U.S. the medical profession pursued the entity 'beriberi heart disease' (Thiamine deficiency.) Then the inquiry shifted to concentrate more on the direct effects of alcohol on the heart muscle and the term 'alcoholic cardiomyopathy' came into general use.

Arthur L. Klatsky provides the most useful historical and current review of the entity in his masterful *The Relationship of Alcohol and the Cardiovascular System* (NIAAA 1982).

151

Klatsky codifies (:183) the experimental and clinical evidence in support of the entity . . .

1. Association of drinking and heart muscle disease noted by numerous authorities
2. High proportion of chronic users of large amounts of alcohol among patients with congestive cardiomyopathy
3. Cases that show convincing evidence of heart muscle dysfunction in relation to episodic drinking
4. Acute impairment of heart muscle contractility due to alcohol in humans and animals
5. Acute rhythm disturbances related to alcohol in humans ('holiday heart' syndrome)
6. Impaired heart function in alcoholics without acute alcohol load
7. Heart muscle metabolic dysfunction in animals related to acute alcohol load
8. Alcohol-produced heart muscle cellular abnormalities in animals
9. Autopsy evidence of heart muscle damage in alcoholics with no history of clinical heart disease
10. Well-documented acute and chronic skeletal muscle syndromes due to alcohol

In spite of all this evidence the field is now in the midst of full-blown controversy because several recent studies have shown that small amounts of alcohol not only do not contribute to cardiovascular disorders but may help to prevent them—in nonalcoholics.

For example, it has been found that there is no relationship or an inverse relationship between small amounts of alcohol and hypertension—while there is a direct relationship when large amounts are ingested.

Another example is Arsenic (As) beer drinkers disease where there is no relationship when alcohol is ingested in small amounts but with large amounts there is synergistic myocardial toxicity of Arsenic and alcohol.

Similar paradoxes seem to have emerged in relation to atherosclerotic coronary disease, stroke and venous conditions. And, several population studies showed that social drinkers suffer fewer major coronary events than the general population but alcoholics have a higher frequency.

I find this to be no paradox at all. Anyone who has ever dealt with alcoholics knows that what makes them so vulnerable to so many disorders is that they contain within themselves so many proven risk factors.

They smoke very heavily (heavier than any other quantifiable group—alcoholics are the last of the 'chain smokers' in the U. S.). They drink enormous amounts of coffee. They do no exercise. They depend on sugar for energy in the form of candy bars, etc. They use too much salt. They continuously suffer the stress of anxiety and depression. They are massively malnourished.

And their dual-addictions run often to more exotic realms.

A recent study showed (Lesiuer et al. 1986) that 152 out of 395 individuals being treated for alcoholism were also addicted to one or more of the following substances: Librium or Valium, barbiturates, amphetamines, hallucinogens, cocaine, heroin, marijuana.

A brandy after dinner for a healthy, well-fed, nonalcoholic, nonsmoking, reasonably adjusted individual is no risk at all—and probably, as several studies have shown (as well as everybody's grandmother) kind to the organism.

But the alcoholic has a totally different relationship to the brandy he or she ingests—and that's why he or she has a far greater chance to develop (and they do) cardiovascular disorders. If you do not understand this, I have failed so far in this book.

It is very similar to what they found out during the golden age of polar exploration (late 19th century).

Marooned explorers near the North or South poles who developed severe protein deficiencies often developed scurvy even though they ate foods which were brought along just to prevent that condition.

While, on the other hand, many explorers survived quite well without those special foods if they were able to kill and eat seals and other animals.

In other words, it is not the substance alone which determines the relationship—it is the metabolism, health and biological individuality of the person.

The disease called alcoholism is above all a massive dysfunction in an individual's ability to process alcohol while maintaining an ability to avoid it.

And all these biochemical transformations are taking place in a body and mind that is dual-addicted, malnourished and constantly stressed. The social drinker has no such problems. We are talking about apples and oranges.

Chapter 19

Cooper Becomes a Statistic

As you are aware by now, I have been balancing two kinds of information.

On the one hand I have attempted a detailed, analytical profile of a single alcoholic (Cooper) in his attempt to survive and function in the world.

And, on the other hand, I have used that individual as the basis of a more generalized medical/scientific inquiry into the various aspects of the disease called alcoholism.

Now I intend to join those two strands together.

In the following pages I will concentrate on the events which led Cooper to seek my help; and describe the actual processes and programs (and the rationale for each) which I used to manage his illness, successfully.

If you recall, Cooper had experienced an episode of atrial fibrillation. At the time he thought he was experiencing a heart attack and was near death.

In the weeks that followed, Cooper maintained a belief in his coming demise even though there were no other episodes—and this sent him deeper and deeper into his depression and drinking cycle.

He can no longer do a day's work. He has difficulty moving easily from point A to point B. He is really unable to carry on anything other than the most rudimentary conversation. He is weak, exhausted, confused.

And then, suddenly, Cooper has one of those delusional 'insights' which so often characterize alcoholics . . . which often seem to the alcoholic to be absolutely true beyond any shadow of doubt but which usually have no bearing on reality at all.

Cooper comes to the conclusion that all his troubles stem from one source—the area he lives and works in, the place in which he exists, the character of the geography in which he is trapped.

He suddenly 'knows' that if he could get away . . . if he could move . . . if he could flee and go somewhere else where no one knows him—everything bad will become good. Everything!

The 'truth' of his delusion hits him hard. His fatigue, nausea, depression instantly vanish. He feels powerful and intelligent.

He feels that he has finally found the key to a life for him and his family that will enable him to escape the trap—and all he has to do is pack up and leave.

Cooper leaves work in the middle of the day and rushes home. His wife is astonished to see him at that hour. She is even more astonished at his remarkable transformation.

He acts like the old Cooper. He is alive, articulate, persuasive.

He tells her what he has discovered. At first she doesn't understand. And when she does, the idea of suddenly uprooting the entire family makes her sit down in shock. It is a very radical move. She says they have to think about it.

Mrs. Cooper does not know that 'geographic flight' (AA calls it the 'geographic cure') is a very common delusion among alcoholics who refuse to deal with the source of their relentless unwinding—physically, intellectually, emotionally.

And, in fact, she cannot withstand her husband's delusion.

He is like many alcoholics, extremely persuasive and seemingly logical on random occasions.

In addition, the sudden change in his personality under the momentary impact of the delusion has been such a welcome change that she is loath to 'bring him back down.'

He counters every one of her objections with impeccable but delusional logic. He paints a glorious picture of a new life in the East where their marriage will be good again. He formulates an elaborate plan for quickly selling the house and liquidating their assets.

He tells her about all the opportunities waiting for him in New York. He says he can make a fortune there as a retailing consultant, as his own boss. He describes the beauty of Long Island's North Shore where they can find a house.

I have in previous sections dealt with the pathology of the alcoholic marriage, and how the nonalcoholic spouse, in a form of folie à deux, will often participate in and enhance alcoholic behavior.

So it is no surprise that Mrs. Cooper folds. She agrees.

Cooper is so happy he spends the afternoon drinking in a suburban bar near their house—something he has been careful not to do before. He knows it is going to be very good for him in the Big Apple. Poor Cooper!

Once Cooper convinces his wife of the efficacy of the 'geographic cure' (i.e. a new place and new people will insure a healthy new lifestyle for him and his family)—events move in a manic blur.

The house is sold for cash ten days after it is put on the market at a price far below its true value.

Cooper gives two weeks notice on his job and signs all the necessary papers to cash in on his corporate profit sharing and stocks.

Their furniture is put into storage. He calls a real estate agent on Long Island and over the phone takes a six month rental on a house, wiring the agent references, two months security, and three months rent. The agent describes the house as a nine room colonial (three bedrooms) and the rent is $1,700 a month with an option to renew at the end of the 6 month period for $1,950 per month.

Cooper calls the relevant school district on Long Island to get transfer instructions. He calls two old friends who now work at large buying offices in Manhattan and tells them he will be coming to see them shortly.

He studies the New York papers to check out the latest monthly car rental rates because he decides to sell both family cars before leaving.

He begins to make elaborate lists on possible work opportunities; typing out dozens of resumes, proposals, schemes.

His wife is totally astonished at Cooper's nonstop physical and intellectual energy.

She doesn't understand that Cooper is paying for it. Along with the quantitative increase of velocity in movement and thought comes an increase in his motor instability.

He moves much quicker but he drops more things. He thinks quicker but his logical connections are often absurd.

And, above all, his chronic malnourishment forces him to seek out more and more sugar. In addition to constantly eating junk, he switches his drink from vodka to blackberry brandy on the rocks with a twist of lemon. This very sweet booze with a touch of sour 'does the trick' although he begins to experience splitting headaches.

Astonishing as it may seem to those who are not familiar with the manic resolve of delusional alcoholics, six weeks and five days after Cooper's illumination of the geographic source of his misery—the Cooper family is sitting in a rented house on Long Island—dazed, exhausted, but together.

The next morning Cooper takes the train into Manhattan.

He visits one of his old friends. They chat and Cooper leaves his resume.

Cooper makes no other visits that day. He spends two hours in a bar and then goes to a movie.

The next day he goes to an agency that specializes in placing retailing executives. He is interviewed and leaves his resume. He completely discards his original plan to become an independent consultant in his field.

Three weeks pass, during which time Cooper establishes his pattern.

Each morning he commutes into Manhattan. Upon leaving the train station he goes to a bar and drinks until the library opens at ten o'clock. Then he sits in the library, takes out a yellow pad and plots his employment strategy. That's all he does—plots.

At noon he goes into a bar and drinks until about three. Then he goes to a movie, goes to another bar, and gets home about ten—lying to his wife about the day's activities, telling her he has made several important contacts.

By now all the delusional energy has been expended. The geographic cure has not worked. He is in a new place and things seem to have gotten worse, not better.

On the third Monday of April, Cooper spends his usual day of drinking in Manhattan.

However, on that particular day he stays in Manhattan later than usual and does not arrive at the train station until about ten in the evening.

He buys a ticket and then asks the ticket seller when his train leaves. The ticket seller tells Cooper to go to the Information Booth for train information.

Cooper demands an answer. The ticket seller tells him to move away. Cooper curses the man. The ticket seller curses him back. Cooper starts to raise his voice. The ticket seller turns his back and walks away.

This act enrages Cooper even more. He loses all control and begins to smash his attaché case against the ticket booth's shatter-proof glass.

It takes three police officers to overpower him even though they probably have spent one third of their working lives dealing with alcohol related violence.

A half hour later Cooper is in the holding pen of a nearby police precinct house surrounded by junkies, hookers, and muggers.

He has lost one shoe. His suit is ripped to shreds. He is bleeding sporadically from the nose. Two teeth are loose. He has urinated down his pants' leg.

Leaning against the wall, eyes closed, he has only one thought in his bruised head—he wants to die.

Two days later Mrs. Cooper calls and makes an appointment with me for her and her husband.

So Cooper has finally come 'home.'

For him and hundreds of thousands of alcoholics in America each year, 'home' is that place they reach when, as a result of a violent life-denying episode, they finally realize that they are very ill and that they need help immediately to survive, if they want to survive.

For countless other thousands each year—that 'home' becomes suicide. So Cooper is lucky.

Chapter 20

Getting Cooper Sober and Keeping Him Sober

When Cooper arrives at my office we are actually at cross purposes. For Cooper really thinks that all he has to do is 'dry out' and leave, healthy, in control, ready to resume his life.

I know better. Detox is not treatment. It is the necessary preliminary to enable the patient to commence therapy. I am after his long-term health and thus I must have information.

Watching Cooper during our first meeting, I, of course, can see dozens of small signs of his disease—his flaccidity, his skin tone, his tremulousness, his aversion to certain questions, his obvious agitated depression. But a physician's anecdotal experience does not a therapy make.

The information I need to treat Cooper will come to me in only three ways.

First—a detailed medical history/biography of Cooper obtained from him personally, which includes a general history, a nutritional history, a toxicological history, an occupational history (*see appendix for actual questionnaire*).

Second—a rigorous, comprehensive physical examination picturing his current state vis-à-vis ethanol toxicity and malnutrition—from calf tenderness to oral hygiene to testicular atrophy (*see appendix for the actual physical examination conducted*).

Third—a roster of laboratory tests covering every aspect of his person—from protein metabolism to Pyridoxine status to Alb/Glob ratio (*see appendix for roster of tests*). Not all patients need all of the laboratory evaluations indicated. Diagnostic testing should be based on individual evaluations.

And Cooper, for his long-term health, must obtain certain information from me: the nature, origins and course of the disease which afflicts him.

Until all these conditions are met there will be no chance for Cooper—and I tell him this. He really doesn't believe me, but getting him to believe is part of the process.

What was the actual state of Cooper's health at about the time he entered the clinic (of course he was experiencing the alcohol withdrawal syndrome)?

The examination and tests (see appendix) yielded a great deal of data which can be summarized by the following:
Cooper was—

- hypertensive
- hypoglycemic (with hyperinsulinism)
- malnourished (with generalized toxicity)
- probably afflicted with alcoholic hepatitis

He exhibited—

- impaired immune response with multiple environmental allergies and adverse food reactions
- major deficiencies in folic acid and pantothenic acid
- minor deficiencies in Niacin and Vitamin C and Thiamine
- hypoproteinemia
- hypophosphatemia, hypomagnesemia and hypokalemia

Cooper was —

- tremulous
- suffering persistent loss of balance and exhibiting several other neurological symptoms
- suffering from a general anxiety disorder with depression

Cooper, luckily, exhibited no apparent permanent derangement of liver, kidney, central nervous system or pancreatic function at the time of his admission to the clinic.

Each of Cooper's symptoms—metabolic, cardiovascular, neurological, psychological, etc.—would alone qualify a nonalcoholic to be considered worthy of extended treatment.

Yet—hundreds of thousands of alcoholics leave detox clinics each year with no follow-up designated as if the alcohol withdrawal symptom was the central fact of their illness.

Of course, in many clinics, the testing procedures are so inadequate that the majority of Cooper's problems would never be noticed or measured—particularly his vitamin deficiencies.

After the initial history, physical and appraisal I knew that Cooper was in the late stages of alcoholism and it was imperative that he should seek inpatient treatment. I presented this to Cooper and he refused because he was still in a state of denial of the fact that he had the disease.

Denial is one of the cardinal symptoms of alcoholism. Once a patient reaches the late stages of alcoholism with its attendant malnutrition and toxification, the physician often finds it difficult to impress upon the patient the critical nature of the situation. This is, of course, understandable, given the accompanying mental deterioration.

I reiterated this in a calm, quiet manner. Cooper again refused. I came on even stronger, giving him an analogy that he was like a person bleeding to death and this was a severe emergency.

Cooper again held onto his denial. Now I was in a dilemma because although Mrs. Cooper had called and made the appointment, and her life was vitally involved in this—I could not legally communicate with her without his permission.

Cooper, again off the hook, readily agreed to do this. At that point, Cooper signed a release allowing me to contact his wife. I then called Mrs. Cooper and told her that I thought her husband was seriously ill and I arranged an appointment for the following day for them to appear together. I had Cooper sign a form releasing me from responsibility for his case based on his refusal to enter the hospital and I watched sadly as Cooper left the clinic. I was extremely skeptical that Cooper would show up the following day.

However, the next afternoon he appeared in our clinic with his wife. All the lab results were now available. I turned on a tape recorder so that Cooper and his wife would have a record of the meeting.

Then I slowly and carefully reviewed all the results of Cooper's history, including the genetic background of his alcoholism, his physical appraisal and all the laboratory tests in detail.

I spread the tests out in front of them and explained what each one meant, and how together, they were incontrovertible diagnostic proof that he had alcoholism and was in the late stages of the disease.

I assured him that the disease was highly treatable and that although he could never be totally cured, he could get into a recovered stage where, without alcohol and following a specific protocol, he could live an alcohol-free life and regain and maintain his physical and mental competency.

This type of confrontation and information is frequently very helpful in helping to break a person's denial and bringing them to a rational assessment of their situation.

When the patient sees elevated liver functions; when they see the devastated picture of their metabolism laid out before them—it is very hard for them to deny that they are seriously ill from the disease of alcoholism.

I reiterated to Cooper that this does not mean he is good or bad, or smart or dumb, or weak or strong. There are no moral categories involved. It just means he has a disease and that disease has caused him to become very toxic and malnourished and has literally affected all the cells of his body.

If allowed to continue, this process would kill him. I explained to him the medical ramifications of this highly fatal disease.

Then, with kindness, I asked him to consider the devastation it has caused his family, piecing together the information I gleaned from Mrs. Cooper and Cooper himself. He was young, I told him, and he had his whole life in front of him and he could become well just as many others before him had done.

I recommended strongly that we immediately admit him to our inpatient medically oriented alcohol treatment hospital.

Cooper's response to all of this was initially to light up another cigarette and commence a monologue to the effect that I really was exaggerating the situation and all he really needed was detox. It was not a major problem he said and he could easily cut down on his drinking.

At this point Mrs. Cooper broke down and started crying and through her sobs said that if he did not seek treatment she was going to take the children and go back to her parents, because she could no longer stand the situation. She realized that she had, in the past, been enabling him in his alcoholism and she had made the decision that she would no longer participate in his destruction.

Cooper clumsily tried to comfort her, then put his cigarette out and said to me: "O.K. Doc, I'll go."

I experienced an enormous sense of relief because I knew if we could get Cooper into treatment and keep him there for even a brief period of time, we had a high probability of saving his life. In fact, the probability of a patient with Cooper's condition getting into a recovering state from his alcoholism and drug addiction and maintaining it is quite high if he receives adequate treatment. And this percentage is enlarging daily as we gather new information and learn how to incorporate it into alcohol and drug treatment programs. In my opinion it is now possible to get 85% of patients into a recovery state within a 12-month period.

So now the odds had changed for Cooper and were beginning to work in his favor. Unfortunately, this is not so for millions of other alcoholics.

First, we know that at least 60% of alcoholics are never diagnosed as having the disease of alcoholism and never receive treatment for it.

Second, we know that many of those who do receive treatment are not receiving the proper kind of treatment. They are not in a facility with a comprehensive program involving body, mind and soul with full application of all new developments that relate to the biochemical, nutritional, metabolic and immunological aspects of the disease. Therefore the outlook for their recovery is very poor.

More important, I have seen hundreds of individuals who, when confronted with the severity of their problem, as Cooper was confronted, were able to maintain their denial in order to avoid dealing with the reality of their situation. They merely survive until the inevitable disaster actually does happen.

And when it does happen they end up incarcerated or institutionalized or so impaired or disabled that it is very difficult for them to ever be reconstructed.

The overwhelming problem in alcoholism is that it is a disease that tells you—you do not have it. It is the disease that impairs the functioning of the brain so severely that the individual one is trying to coax into treatment simply is no longer functioning on a rational level due to the toxicity, malnutrition and metabolic changes. The great challenge in the treatment of alcoholism and drug addiction is that one is dealing with a broken brain at the same time one is trying to fix that broken brain.

Cooper, by his decision to enter treatment and to be adequately detoxed, also changed the odds for himself in preventing another major and very common disaster that befalls alcoholics.

Sometimes this disaster occurs as a result of their own resolution to stop drinking alone, and at other times it occurs as a result of well-meaning friends and pseudo-experts who give 'deadly' advice to the patient with alcoholism.

Let me illustrate this with an actual case.

Recently, a prominent architect was summering in the Berkshires. His drinking was out of control and he was becoming severely impaired.

The family summoned a strong willed and well-meaning friend to give them counsel. He instructed the patient that what he needed to do was just stay in the house and quit drinking; and to treat his withdrawal symptoms with large doses of caffeine, nicotine and sugar (in the form of coffee, cigarettes and candy bars).

This advice was followed. About 50 hours after the architect stopped drinking he had a grand mal seizure.

This is a type of seizure in which the effects of the withdrawal of the alcohol on the brain are such that it causes massive unprogrammable electrical discharges from the brain. These discharges caused him to go into a series of jerking, tonic, clonic movements in which his muscles paradoxically contracted vigorously and then relaxed. It caused him to involuntarily pass his feces and urine and to have difficulty in breathing. The situation was compounded by his involuntary vomiting and the partial aspiration of some of this into his lungs.

The patient continued to seize and was rushed to a local hospital. Unfortunately, there was a problem of communication with the hospital staff in that his family withheld the full history of what happened to him in terms of his alcoholism.

His seizures continued unabated and were rapidly joined by the onset of delirium tremens. This is a condition where the patient's mid-brain functions go totally awry. This individual's temperature went up to around 104. His pulse went up in the area of 160-170. His blood pressure went up precipitously. In between episodes he was having wild hallucinations which apparently were nightmarish in content. He became totally disoriented, confused and began to act and react to his hallucinations. He had to be restrained by four attendants and put into total body restraints or what we call 'full sheet restraint' so that he could not hurt himself or others.

The patient was finally transferred to our center by ambulance. When I saw him, he was at the point of death. He was placed in the intensive care unit and over an heroic five day period his life was spared.

As he began to come around, I recognized that he was one of the most charming, witty and intelligent of human beings. The only problem was he had completely lost a key memory mode as a result of the brain damage ensuing from a detoxification in which there was inadequate sedation given, inadequate nutritional replacement (particularly the B complex vitamins and electrolytes and other metabolites which have to be rapidly replaced) and inadequate control of the other side effects or complications of withdrawal, DT's or seizures.

The tragedy of this man still haunts me because even now he will walk into a room, have the most sophisticated type of conversation, and put you totally at ease. But if you remove him from the room and then bring him back again in fifteen minutes he will do the same thing all over again without any memory that he has ever seen you before in his life.

This condition has now persisted in him for a period of over two years and it appears to be permanent.

He now travels the world with a companion, going through it like a motion picture camera without film. However, his wit and charm have at least allowed him to enjoy the conversations of those about him.

The whole point here is simply that a patient who is addicted must be detoxified in a hospital with a staff that is specifically prepared and knowledgeable in how to carry out a proper detoxification. Any other route can be extremely life threatening to the patient. Now let me get back to Cooper.

He was immediately admitted into our alcohol treatment hospital, which is fully set up and organized as a *medical* facility and which treats alcoholism in a comprehensive manner as a *medical* disease.

The highly trained multi-disciplinary staff immediately focused on Cooper. He was brought to the ward along with his records and test results.

The nurse supervisor reviewed everything again, checking to make sure he did not have problems with allergies; then she assigned Cooper a room in the detox unit.

His vital signs were taken on a four hour basis for the first twenty-four hours. He was immediately assessed as starting to go into withdrawal by monitoring his pulse and blood pressure and by his increasing agitation and hyperactivity.

The nature of the detox protocol was explained carefully to Cooper. He was told we had to medicate him to cover the receptor sites in his brain which were withdrawing from alcohol and that he would be on this medication for only a few days. It was explained that he had to work with us as a team in order to bring him down very slowly with as little discomfort as possible. He was cautioned to notify the unit staff if any untoward symptoms arose or if the discomfort became severe. Every attempt was made to allay his anxiety and to treat him in the same calm manner that one would treat someone in severe complications from diabetes or someone with an impending heart attack.

Any approach to patients other than understanding and kindness (with firm hard love) is not acceptable in this disease, and personnel who bring blame or hostility to patients suffering from the disease of alcoholism should do something else. This behavior is not to be tolerated.

Cooper was immediately placed on chlordiazepoxide HLC (Librium) 100 mg STAT and 50 mg every four hours times 6 doses. He was given a PRN dose of Librium 50 mg Q 2 to 3 hours in between the above doses, with a gradual reduction of dosages over the next four days. Other facilities use phenobarbital or another long-acting diazepam-type drug. This is perfectly acceptable. Rarely is there any indication for the use of sedative-hypnotic drugs other than the acute phase of detox. In addition other support measures were initiated immediately including oral and intramuscular multivitamin therapy. Cooper's anxiety began to lessen and he relaxed and fell into a deep sleep.

The staff made contact with Mrs. Cooper right away and the social service workers encouraged her to meet twice a week (along with her children if possible) with the people treating her husband. She was told that Cooper's progress will be quicker if she understands and participates in the program. The purpose of this is the clear cut recognition that alcoholism is a family disease and that the nonalcoholic members of the family often become as sick as the alcoholic, suffering confusion, anger, depression, hopelessness, frustration.

Cooper was lucky. He still had a wife who loved him and, after an initial reluctance to involve the children, she agreed. She had reached that important point where nothing is to be swept under the rug anymore and the entire family must be cognizant of everything.

The next morning on rounds Cooper was appraised again. His blood pressure was still elevated and his pulse was still rapid in spite of very heavy sedation during the prior 18 hours.

However, he was beginning to sense that people were there to help him and they would try to minimize his suffering to the best of their abilities. He showed no signs at this point of impending DT's or other severe complications. His thinking remained confused and distorted.

At the end of the first 24 hours as his brain began to clear somewhat from alcohol, he began to be severely depressed. We expected this since more than 90% of all patients exhibit severe depression. Cooper was carefully watched in order to make sure that he did not manifest any evidence of suicidal intent.

By the third day, Cooper was down to a markedly decreased level of Librium and by the end of the fourth day the Librium was discontinued.

At this point Cooper was beginning to feel much better indeed. Some of his laboratory figures were beginning to come back to normal and his mind was beginning to function more normally although he still exhibited some fragmented thinking and depression. The latter, however, was beginning to lift.

We then recommended to Cooper that he go into a rehabilitation program for 28 days. Here Cooper raised many objections. His family was here; his funds were running out; he did not have a job; he had to rush to make up for the lost time; his cat ate only a certain kind of food and he was the only one who knew where to buy it.

The team, consisting of the social worker, the nurse and myself countered all these objections by explaining to him that he was just beginning to recover and that his alcoholism must be his first priority. Cooper said he would think about it for a while. Another meeting was held with Cooper and his wife and the team and I again reiterated the importance of his immediately entering a rehabilitation program . . . and I again explained that detox is only a first step in his recovery.

With strong urging from his wife, Cooper finally agreed.

On the fifth day Cooper was stable enough in detox to transfer him to rehab. At that point Cooper was out of immediate physical trouble and was sent to the AA meetings which occur nightly on our wards. Initially he was reluctant to attend these meetings but we explained to him the importance of the AA step process to the balance of the treatment program. At the end of the treatment program he could decide for himself whether or not he wanted to continue in AA outside our facility. However, while here, it was stressed that he must go to AA.

Cooper and his wife went through a parallel integrated program in which they began to be educated about every facet of the disease of alcoholism.

Cooper had individual counseling from a staff psychologist to help work on his denial.

Sophisticated behavior modification techniques were applied in order to help him begin to change his ways of handling stress and adapt to an alcohol-free life.

In a series of sessions the entire area of alcoholism and sexuality was explained to Cooper. He was led to understand that it was not unusual for sexual desire and the ability to perform sexually to diminish and even vanish in the late stages of alcoholism. He was told that in the majority of cases a healthy sexuality returns within the first three months of sobriety.

1. He was seen by a physician on a regular basis with constant follow-ups on lab tests until they returned to normal.

2. A major emphasis was placed on nutrition. A broad spectrum nutrient supplement as well as calcium and phosphorus and a gram of ascorbic acid were given daily to Cooper throughout the rehab period. The foods which were giving him the greatest trouble in terms of adverse reactions were removed from his diet. He was set up with a regimen of green vegetables, fresh fruits and protein. Cooper, like so many other alcoholic patients, was highly allergic to molds, wheat, corn and potatoes—which are the major ingredients of alcoholic beverages.

His weight began to change very markedly; he went through a period of diuresis and urinating out fluids. Cooper was also detoxed during this period from caffeine, sugar, food additives, chemicals and 'junk' foods. The dietitian worked carefully with him and his wife explaining to them the necessity of eating a greater variety of whole foods in a less frequent manner and reemerging and getting used to a rotational diet in order to keep his adverse food reactions down to a minimum.

At the end of the first ten days Cooper was allowed to go outside to the gym. The activity director formulated a progressive program for him based on instructions from the medical director which was designed to get his endorphins and other neurotransmitters regulated again. Thus, the long path to bringing him back in shape again was begun.

After 28 days of rehab, most of Cooper's symptoms had vanished. He had lost 20 pounds, his body was beginning to firm up, the bloat and pallor that had accompanied him on admission had gone away. His energy was returning; his sleep pattern was approaching a normal level; he was even beginning to experience morning erections which signaled a returning sex drive.

It was explained to Cooper over and over again that he had to switch totally to a life style which was characterized by its health in all aspects of life and that he had to maintain that life style rigorously after he left the institution. Only such a life style would prevent a return to the high stress levels he exhibited upon admission and which would guarantee a craving for alcohol.

Cooper was one of the lucky ones. His liver disease was resolving and it was apparent there would be no severe residual impairments from his alcoholism. The dramatic changes in his physical and laboratory findings were reviewed with him in a team conference including the nurse, social worker, physician and activity person. Cooper's engaging personality began to return and he actively entered into this as a critical member of the team—which met weekly.

He was beginning to have hope. By the third week his depression had lifted almost entirely although he still suffered bouts of anxiety as he contemplated the tremendous shattering that he had carried out on his career. He was reassured that with a clear head and a sound body and mind he could rapidly regain this lost territory.

An important transition took place in Cooper's family. As they engaged in the treatment together and began truly to understand the nature of the disease, they started to share their hurt, their anger and their confusion with each other. They began to knit as a unit again, something that was absent for a long time because alcoholism isolates individuals, radically.

It was explained to Cooper, however, that inhospital treatment was only Spring Training and that he had still to play the game afterwards—in the real world. Therefore, the following type of continuing care was set up for Cooper at his discharge.

He was scheduled to attend a weekly after-care meeting held at the hospital with the same people who had gone through the program with him. Under the guidance of an experienced counselor, they help each other through the re-entry and in maintaining sobriety.

Cooper readily agreed. First, because he knew and liked his fellow patients—executives, lawyers, engineers, truck drivers, police officers, individuals who had gone through what he went through. And, even more important, he was now aware of the ravages of the disease. He had seen people who were in the late stages of liver disease from alcoholism. He had seen people with irreparable brain damage. He had seen people severely injured from alcohol related accidents or violence. He now knew what he had temporarily escaped from, and what awaited him if he couldn't maintain sobriety.

In addition, Cooper's temporary sponsor in AA while in the hospital worked out a schedule of AA meetings for him near Cooper's home on the North Shore of Long Island. Cooper was advised to attend daily meetings for the first 90 days and the importance of this was stressed to Mrs. Cooper.

Cooper was shown how to maintain his diet after he left the hospital and placed on a broad spectrum of nutrient supplements as well as calcium and phosphorus, including essential fatty acid compounds containing high levels of linoleic acid as well as the amino acids —L-Glutamine, DL-Phenylalanine, L-Tryptophan and pyridoxal 5-Phosphate. He was asked to refrain from caffeine and refined sugar and adhere to his diet of frequent feedings of fresh vegetables, fresh fruit, fish and lean meat, complex carbohydrates, etc.

He was to take all these nutrients for the first year after leaving the hospital.

In addition, he was scheduled to be seen in our clinic two weeks after his discharge and on a monthly basis subsequently until he had maintained the first year of sobriety. He was given the phone numbers of one staff person and one physician that would be available to him on a 24-hour 7-day-a-week basis. He was told to use those numbers the moment he felt he was slipping in any fashion. It was also explained to Cooper in great detail how to protect himself from anyone attempting to medicate him. Detailed lists of all medications, tranquilizers and other psychotropic drugs which would cause addiction and cross addition were given to him; and their actions explained to him. He was also told which products on the market contain alcohol, such as cough medicines.

The importance of the need for a structured, monitored and exact life style change to insure Cooper's continued sobriety is illustrated by the actual texts of instructions given to him and reproduced below. This format and its importance to patient care was pioneered by Geraldine Owen Delaney, Chief Executive Officer, Little Hill - Alina Lodge — one of the most perceptive, creative and experienced individuals now working in the field of alcoholism.

- Keep all liquor and mood-changing substances out of your home.
- Stay away from liquor stores and any exposure to alcohol and chemicals.
- Avoid liquor like the plague.
- Maintain absolute abstinence.
- Attend a minimum of ninety AA meetings in ninety days.
- Mix your AA meetings up with open, closed discussion and step meetings.
- When comfortable in an AA group, join the group.
- Get active and involved in your "home" group as well as in AA as a whole.
- Be on the lookout for a strong male AA sponsor.
- Meanwhile, follow any suggestions your contact may have.
- Stick with the winners in the fellowship.
- Share more with those you trust.
- Watch the "13th step stuff."
- Do not reactivate any old emotional entanglements until after you have been sober a year.
- Always remember that your sobriety is your #1 priority.
- Make an appointment with your personal physician for a follow-up physical checkup; have your medical record sent to him.
- Continue your vitamin therapy for at least one year.
- Adhere to your high protein, low carbohydrate and low fat diet.
- Avoid sugar, excess salt and caffeine.
- Continue your attempt to cut down smoking.
- Postpone elective dental work for as long as you can unless an emergency arises.
- Stick to your structured living.
- Plan your day.
- Pace yourself.
- Steer clear of becoming a "workaholic" again.

- Bear in mind the word "HALT". (Hungry, Angry, Lonely, Tired)
- Start your day by reading your 24 hour a day book.
- Keep some AA literature around to read in your spare time.
- Take your 1st three steps of the AA program each morning.
- Strengthen your commitment to your sobriety.
- Make some time each day for your personal prayers and meditation.
- Take a daily "mini" inventory.
- Work on your self-honesty.
- Watch your anger.
- Nip your resentments and self-pity in the bud.
- Discipline yourself.
- Curb your tendency to procrastinate and to be lazy.
- Aim to be less critical, less judgmental and more tolerant and patient.
- Keep an open mind as well as a positive attitude.
- Gradually resume your personal and professional responsibilities.
- Be more flexible.
- Try to develop a sense of humor and balance.
- Tone down the envy and jealousy.
- Don't have your eye on the "dollar" so much.
- Make out a budget.
- Arrange with your creditors a system for repaying slowly what you owe them.
- Live within your means.
- Seek professional help as needed.
- Set some realistic goals for yourself.
- Try to develop more self-respect and self-confidence.
- Write your attitudes and your feelings in your journal.
- Gradually incorporate the twelve suggested steps into your life-style.
- Keep in touch with your own feelings but be sensitive to the feelings of those closest to you.
- Play all family relationships by ear.
- Be as good a husband, father, son and brother sober as you can be.
- Ever so slowly, try to reestablish your relationship with your children.
- Spend time with your wife and children individually.
- Do some things with each one of them that they would like to do.
- Continue your communication with them and be open.
- Practice caring, consideration and consistency in your dealings with all your children. By your example, they will begin to trust and realize that their father is okay now.

- Resume your personal responsibilities at home but do not drift into dependence again.
- Strive to be more open and more communicative with your family members, particularly with your mother, your aunt and your sister.
- Gradually deepen your lines of communication with all your loved ones.
- Do some brisk walking daily and gradually work into an exercise program.
- Go bowling with non-drinking friends.
- Take in a movie once in a while.
- Tinker with your own computer.
- Read for your own pleasure.
- Balance your lifestyle with AA, work, family, friends, rest and recreation.
- Call your counselor (name, phone number) once a week and let him know how you're doing.
- Lots of luck and may God be with you.

Once out in the world, Cooper did quite well. A major problem surfaced after three months when he once again exhibited severe hay-fever and allergic rhinitis, along with episodes of depression associated with some craving for alcohol.

He was retested again with skin testing and found to be highly allergic to the molds. As desensitization proceeded, these episodes of depressions and other problems did not recur. Management of the allergic reactions of alcoholics is crucial to relieve craving and to restore the integrity of the immune system.

Cooper followed his diet, kept to his nutrient supplements, avoided substances which he now knew caused adverse reactions and allergic responses.

At the end of 12 months Cooper was without craving, all the laboratory tests were within the normal range, his health was largely restored, and his family even more intact. He landed a job as a sales representative for a hi-tech company on Long Island. He and his family, in short, were beginning to flourish again—physically, emotionally and economically.

The Cooper story is a success story. But Cooper was very lucky. He did not kill himself before he obtained treatment and the treatment he did obtain was the best possible. And he was fully supported by his family once they understood the nature of his disorder.

Charting Cooper's Recovery

The following data in chart form show the wide-ranging therapeutic intervention that is required to get Cooper sober and keep him sober.

Medical Phenomenon	Treatment Response
1. Acute withdrawal from Alcoholism/Drugs with systemic toxicity	Safe detoxification as painless as possible; relieve symptoms, prevent progression of withdrawal, prevent complications; prepare for rehabilitation.
2. Malnourishment	Immediate intramuscular or intravenous nutrient replacement for first five days. A broad-based and comprehensive nutrient replacement by mouth starting on day one and continuing for one year.
3. Malabsorption	Digestive enzymes.
4. Abnormal carbohydrate metabolism with hyperinsulinism and reflex hyperadrenalism with production of excessive steroids, adrenalin and noradrenalin.	Personalized high protein, low carbohydrate diet with broad-based nutrient supplementation.
5. Impairment of Essential Fatty Acid with consequent impairment of Prostaglandin metabolism.	GLA or DGLA supplementation: fatty acids which by-pass the alcohol-blocked step (Horrobin DF, *Medical Hypotheses* 6: 929-942, 1980)
6. Neurotransmitter Imbalance	Amino Acid Supplementation.

Ingredient	Restored Brain Chemical	Mechanism	Expected Behavioral Change
D-Phenylalanine	Enkephalins	enzyme inhibition	Anti-craving; anti-depression
L-Phenylalanine	Dopamine; Norepinephrine	precursor loading	Reward Anti-depression
L-Glutamine	GABA	precursor loading	Anti-craving; Anti-stress
L-Tryptophan	Serotonin	precursor loading	Anti-craving; Anti-depression; Anti-insomnia
Pyridoxal-5 phospate	Vitamin B6 Active Metabolite	co-factor in aminoacid synthesis	All of above Also promotes GI absorption of amino acids.

Blum K & Trachtenberg MC, *News* Vol. 13, No. 2; Calif. Soc. for Treatment of Alc. & Other Drug Dependencies

7. Environmental and Allergenic Adverse Food Reactions and Impaired Immune Response Entrenched.	Allergy testing including testing for Adverse Food Reactions, chemical reactions and high suspicion as to chemical toxicology.
8. Addictive Diathesis: refined sugar; refined carbohydrates; caffeine; junk foods; nicotine.	Detoxification from sugar immediately. Elimination of refined carbohydrates from diet. Detox from caffeine from admission. Detox from junk foods. Begin education on danger of smoking for complete cessation after one year of sobriety.
9. Long period of not eating.	Frequent small feedings.
10. Absence from regular meals.	Regular three meals each day with snacks in between breakfast and lunch, lunch and dinner, and before bedtime.
11. Sleep disturbances.	Regular bedtime, regular waking time and reassurances that sleep will return.
12. Impaired sexual function.	Counseling and repair of the damage. Special measures indicated if sexual function does not return within the first twelve months of abstinence from alcohol and drugs.
13. Lack of exercise and muscle atrophy.	Supervised progressive exercise program within cardiac and physical limitations.
14. Alcohol liver damage with probable alcohol hepatitis.	All of above.
15. Hypertension secondary to alcohol toxicity.	Vanishes as treatment progresses. May need active control during the acute phase.
16. Central nervous system impairment of cognitive functions (memory loss, inability to concentrate, confusion, confabulation) and peripheral neuritis.	All of above plus a detailed neurological evaluation with special attention to ruling out possible injury during blackout or unconscious state.
17. Impaired relationship with wife and children.	Family counseling involving intensive education on the disease; individual follow-ups and contacts. Spouses, loved ones and children should be involved in this process.
18. Unemployed but employable.	Problem will heal itself if alcoholism is corrected.
19. Major ignorance of the disease of alcoholism.	Intensive, persistent education analyzing alcoholism as a metabolic disorder of genetically predisposed individuals which wreaks enormous damage to body, mind and soul.

177

20. Major denial of the severity of his illness and what it has done to his life.	Patient, constant, kind, never relenting pressure and confrontation.
21. High stress state. Poor or absent mechanism for dealing with stress. Major isolation from family, friends, and society at large.	Sophisticated stress modification techniques, counseling, group therapy, AA and aftercare.
22. Cooper did not manifest any basic underlying psychiatric problem. About ten percent of patients will have alcoholism plus mental problems.	Psychiatric problems should not be diagnosed before the first month of sobriety attained unless an emergency. Addictive psychotropic drugs should not be used. Bi-polar mood swing treated with Lithium. Other problems treated as indicated.

It is important to remember that the great majority of alcoholics never receive any treatment whatsoever for alcoholism.

And it is equally important to understand that given what we now know, Cooper's problems could have been avoided:

1. Cooper, because of a family history of alcoholism, could have been informed about the genetic basis of the disease and educated about his high susceptibility.

2. With better education, Cooper could have known that the symptoms which appeared early in his drinking career were pointing to his alcoholism.

3. If the psychiatrist who initially saw Cooper had carried out a few simple tests and was more alert to the diagnosis of the disease of alcoholism—intervention could have happened much earlier and the dangers of a drug-supported therapy would have been avoided.

4. If Cooper's company had been more alert to his increasingly bizarre behavior .. if the company had an aggressive and cost effective program to help the 10% or more of their employees who are suffering from the disorder (indeed, the inability of the company to diagnose Cooper's disability early and put him into treatment cost it a ten-fold loss compared to the expense of his treatment). . . . if. . . . if. . .

But these 'ifs' are what this book is all about—to help turn them into reality.

Only a correct diagnosis based on testing and a correct treatment based on the metabolic/genetic model of alcoholism can break the spiral of alcoholic tragedy in this country. For it really is the most treatable of all the chronic diseases.

A Lay Person's Guide To
Diagnosing Alcoholism Correctly

IS YOUR HUSBAND, WIFE, LOVER, SON, DAUGHTER, MOTHER, FATHER OR FRIEND AN ALCOHOLIC?

In this section I am going to deal with that most perplexing and important of all alcohol related matters: How does the lay person know that an individual is suffering from the disease of alcoholism without the benefit of a battery of laboratory tests or the advice of an experienced physician.

I am going to give you a simple question and answer list which will enable you to quickly diagnose alcoholism if it is there without interrogating the subject. All it requires of you is a fairly intimate knowledge of the individual's affairs.

But before I present that diagnostic aid to you it is important that you understand that several diagnostic 'maps' are now widely available, each one looking at the disease through a different lens.

For example, the American Psychiatric Association in its *Diagnostic and Statistical Manual of Mental Disorders,* 3rd edition states (1980:169):

"The essential features of Alcohol Dependence are either a pattern of pathological alcohol use or impairment in social or occupational functioning due to alcohol and either tolerance or withdrawal. Alcohol Dependence has also been called Alcoholism."

It defines Tolerance as (:163):

". . . markedly increased amounts of the substance are required to achieve the desired effect or there is a markedly diminished effect with regular use of the same dose."

It defines Withdrawal as (:165):

"... a substance-specific syndrome follows cessation or reduction in intake of a substance that was previously regularly used by the individual to induce a physiological state of intoxication."

The World Health Organization publishes their own diagnostic manual called the *International Classification of Diseases* (1978). It diagnoses the 'Alcohol Dependence Syndrome' thusly (:1080):

"A state, psychic and usually also physical, resulting from taking alcohol, characterized by behavioral and other responses that always include a compulsion to take alcohol on a continuous or periodic basis in order to experience psychic effects, and sometimes to avoid the discomfort of its absence; tolerance may or may not be present . . ."

These diagnostic descriptions are elegant and there is little to argue with them. But they are, obviously, totally irrelevant to the wife who must face a husband acting very peculiarly and drinking a great deal. They are broad configurations, good for books.

On the other hand, there are much more specific diagnostic clues— clinical evidence of alcoholism which includes:

• Fatty degeneration in absence of other known causes
• Alcoholic hepatitis
• Laennec's cirrhosis
• Pancreatitis in the absence of cholelithiasis
• Chronic gastritis
• Hematological disorders: Anemia: hypochromic, normocytic, macrocytic, hemolytic with stomatocytosis, low folic acid; clotting disorders—prothrombin elevation or thrombocytopenia
• Wernicke-Korsakoff syndrome
• Alcoholic cerebellar degeneration
• Cerebral degeneration in absence of Alzheimer's disease or arteriosclerosis
• Peripheral neuropathy
• Toxic amblyopia

- Alcohol myopathy
- Alcoholic cardiomyopathy
- Beriberi
- Pellagra

Any individual who drinks and exhibits any complex of symptoms from this list (it is a very abbreviated list) can be considered to be alcoholic. But none of this makes any sense outside a clinical setting. An individual must be tested to find these entities.

So, we have seen a very general and a very specific diagnostic map of alcoholism—neither of which help a wife discover whether the husband she is domiciled with is an alcoholic.

Many efforts have been made to bridge the gap—to bring the 'macro' and 'micro'—the epidemiological and the clinical—the behavioral and the organic . . . together in a single intelligible and practical synthesis that can be used by both the physician and the lay person.

The Medical Book of Lists: A Primer of Differential Diagnosis in Internal Medicine (Greenberger et al. 1983:74) presents the following Diagnosis of Chronic Alcoholism:

- Evidence of alcohol withdrawal syndromes
  - Tremulousness
  - Alcoholic hallucinosis
  - Withdrawal seizures or 'rum fits'
  - Delirium tremens
- Evidence of tolerance to alcohol
  - Ingestion of fifth or more of whiskey per day
  - No gross evidence of intoxication with blood alcohol level at more than 150 mg/100 ml
  - Random blood alcohol level more than 300 mg/100 ml
  - Accelerated clearance of blood alcohol at or in excess of 25 mg/100 ml per hour
- Psychosociologic factors
  - Continued ingestion of alcohol despite strong contraindication to do so; threatened loss of job; threatened loss of spouse and/or family; medical contraindication known to patient
  - Admission of inability to discontinue use of alcohol
- Presence of alcohol-associated disorders
  - Erosive gastritis with upper gastrointestinal bleeding

- Pancreatitis, acute and chronic, in the absence of cholelithiasis
- Alcoholic liver disease (fatty liver, alcoholic hepatitis, cirrhosis)
- Alcoholic diseases of the nervous system:peripheral neuropathy; cerebellar degeneration; Wernicke-Korsakoff syndrome;Beriberi; Alcoholic myopathy; Alcoholic cardiomyopathy

This is an excellent 'map' but it is still essentially a guide for physicians requiring lab tests to verify. And, more important, it presents a picture of late alcoholism. We are interested in identifying the alcoholic who is still functioning quite well.

A more recent effort by Vaillant(1983:331)uses the Cahalan scale among others, with a numerical grade for each of the following:

1. *Frequent intoxication*: 5 or more drinks once a week; or 8 or more drinks on 1 of the most recent 2 drinking occasions and twice in the last 2 months; or12 or more drinks on one of the last 2 occasions and twice in the last year; or currently getting high or tight at least once a week.

2. *Binge drinking*: being intoxicated for at least several days at one time or for 2 days or more on more than one occasion.

3. *Symptomatic drinking*: more than one of the following: drinking to get rid of a hangover; having difficulty in stopping drinking; blackouts or lapses of memory; skipping meals while on a drinking bout; tossing down drinks for quicker effect; sneaking drinks; taking quick drinks in advance of a party to make sure one gets enough.

4. *Psychological dependence*: drinking to alleviate depression or nervousness or to escape from the problems of everyday living . . .; a drink is needed when one is tense or nervous.

5. *Problems with spouse or relatives*: spouse leaves or threatens to leave the respondent or is chronically angry or concerned over the respondent's drinking; spouse or

relative asks the respondent to cut down on drinking; the respondent himself feels his drinking has had a harmful effect on his home life.

6. *Problems with friends or neighbors*: friends or neighbors had suggested cutting down on drinking; respondent feels that drinking has been harmful to friendships and social life.

7. *Job problems*: respondent lost or nearly lost a job because of drinking; people at work suggest that he cut down on drinking; drinking has been harmful to work and employment opportunities.

8. *Problems with law, police, accidents*: trouble with law over driving after drinking; drunkenness; drinking contributed to an accident in which there is a personal injury.

9. *Health*: respondent feels that drinking is harmful to health and doctor advised cutting down.

10. *Financial problems*.

11. *Belligerence*: felt aggressive or cross after drinking; got into a fight or a heated argument.

This is an interesting and practical method to help in making a tentative diagnosis of alcoholism.

However, there are several problems with it that would make it less than ideal for a nonalcoholic wife dealing with a husband she suspects may be alcoholic.

First, it requires a very willing respondent; someone who already knows essentially that he or she has a severe drinking problem. But most alcoholics are not that willing to disclose such information and they rarely remember how much they drink.

Second, and more important, it is a totally behavioral methodology; there is no nutritional element at all. But changing eating habits in an individual is one of the key signs of alcoholism.

Third—like the previous scale, this one is pegged to a later stage of the disorder.

What is needed is a simple set of questions that a spouse can answer about her possibly alcoholic husband without interrogating him severely, and that will essentially provide a valid diagnosis without clinical data, even though that eventually will be necessary to confirm.

I am going to present one now. It is based on almost thirty years of clinical experience. I will keep, for simplicity's sake, the model of a nonalcoholic wife dealing with a husband whom she has reason to believe may be suffering from alcoholism.

QUESTION NUMBER ONE: *Does he drink every day?*

(While there are alcoholics who drink episodically, the overwhelming number of alcoholics drink every day. So in fact do heavy nonalcoholic drinkers but future questions will weed them out.)

QUESTION NUMBER TWO: *Has he, in the recent past, increased his consumption of alcoholic beverages?*

QUESTION NUMBER THREE: *Is he able to drink more without appearing 'high' or 'intoxicated?'*

(This is the behavioral analogue of tolerance formation. Most laypeople think that individuals who can drink a great deal without appearing intoxicated are not necessarily alcoholics. The reverse is true. Tolerance formation of alcoholics enables them to delay intoxication.)

QUESTION NUMBER FOUR: *Has he stopped eating regular meals?*

QUESTION NUMBER FIVE: *Has he increased his consumption of sugar?*

(These last two questions reflect the two most prevalent behavioral aspects of alcoholic malnutrition. There is always appetitive derangement and there is always a desperate need for quick energy fixes.)

QUESTION NUMBER SIX: *Has he exhibited diminished sexual interest and/or activity?*

QUESTION NUMBER SEVEN: *Has he begun to exhibit unusual (for him) mood swings between depression and elation?*

QUESTION NUMBER EIGHT: *Has he begun to act inappropriately in the face of common events—with aggression or with passivity?*

QUESTION NUMBER NINE: *Has he been exhibiting some motor problems—dropping things, etc.?*

QUESTION NUMBER TEN: *Has he been depressed or mentioned suicide?*

QUESTION NUMBER ELEVEN: *Has he experienced sleep disturbances?*

QUESTION NUMBER TWELVE: *Recent unexplained weight gain?*

If your loved one drinks, and you can safely say that at least seven out of the twelve questions are answered by a yes, then the individual is either on the cusp of the disorder or already suffers from it until proven otherwise. It is time for you to act.

Appendix 2

What Do You Do If You Discover
A Loved One Is An Alcoholic?

In the previous Appendix I presented a simple 12-question scale that will identify the disease in most drinkers under most circumstances.

They were, to repeat (we are keeping the model of a nonalcoholic wife and an alcoholic husband for convenience):

1. DOES HE DRINK EVERY DAY?

2. HAS HE, IN THE RECENT PAST, INCREASED HIS CONSUMPTION OF ALCOHOLIC BEVERAGES?

3. IS HE ABLE TO DRINK MORE WITHOUT APPEAR-ING "HIGH" OR "INTOXICATED"?

4. HAS HE STOPPED EATING REGULAR MEALS?

5. HAS HE INCREASED HIS CONSUMPTION OF SUGAR AND HIGHLY REFINED CARBOHYDRATES?

6. HAS HE EXHIBITED DIMINISHED SEXUAL INTER-EST AND/OR ACTIVITY?

7. HAS HE BEGUN TO EXHIBIT UNUSUAL (FOR HIM) MOOD SWINGS BETWEEN DEPRESSION AND ELA-TION?

8. HAS HE BEGUN TO ACT INAPPROPRIATELY IN THE FACE OF COMMON EVENTS—WITH AGGRESSION OR WITH PASSIVITY?

9. HAS HE BEEN EXHIBITING SOME MOTOR PROBLEMS—DROPPING THINGS, ETC.?

10. HAS HE BEEN DEPRESSED OR MENTIONED SUICIDE?

11. HAS HE EXPERIENCED SLEEP DISTURBANCES?

12. HAS HE HAD A RECENT UNEXPLAINED WEIGHT GAIN?

If you recall a seven out of twelve 'yes' total identifies the drinker as alcoholic until proven otherwise.

Now what do you do?

1. Recognize that an acute emergency exists. Alcoholism is analogous to bleeding to death. In addition to the medical consequences, the mental derangements of the disorder and the ensuing possibilities of murder, suicide, and assault place both you and him in great danger.

2. Understand that your response and reaction must be commensurate with the severity of the problem.

3. Make sure that he ceases taking all psychotropic medication under medical supervision until the alcoholism problem is solved.

4. Tell him that all signs now point to the fact that he is suffering from alcoholism and that he is now dangerously at risk for suicide, homicide, liver failure, cardiovascular disorder, G.I. bleeding, etc.

5. Do not attack him morally. Do not slip into that delusion that alcoholism is a moral disease. It is a metabolic disorder. The alcoholic is not smart or stupid, not good or bad, not weak or strong. He is sick. Like the diabetic.

6. Support your diagnosis of his disorder with pictures, figures, statistics, facts. Show him case histories. Be relentless in your presentation.

7. Explain to him that he must seek treatment immediately; that it is dangerous for him to try to stop drinking alone; that there are many organizations that exist just to help people in his situation.

8. Obtain the telephone numbers of the local Alcoholics Anonymous, Alanon, and Adult Children of Alcoholics chapters from the phone book. Obtain the telephone numbers of local detox units and treatment centers from your physician or from state or city health agencies. *You* do the preliminary work of contacting them.

9. Enlist the support of friends, coworkers, physicians, clergymen—anyone and everyone he respects—in order to get him to listen to reason.

10. If he refuses to seek treatment for whatever reason—contact your local Alanon chapter (in the phone book) which exists to help families deal with alcoholics.

11. If, even with the help of the organizations above, you are not able to persuade him to seek treatment, it is time for you to practice "hard love." This means simply that you must disassociate yourself from the alcoholic as long as he continues to drink. Either he must leave the home or you must leave him and take your children along. By such action you will protect yourself, your children and your husband from the near certainty of alcoholic violence. You will also show him the consequences of his alcoholic behavior—the breakup of the family. If you are threatened or attacked, you must contact the police immediately and get a protective order. Above all, you must not be caught up in a current and very pervasive fantasy about the disease: that alcoholics can engage in safe "social" drinking or sustained "normal" drinking. The alcohol-drinking person must receive the strong, clear message that you are not going down with him.

No matter what your husband tells you when you confront him with the evidence of his disorder—DO NOT ACCEPT THE "I will cut down" ARGUMENT. Your husband, or any alcoholic, can no more cut down on his drinking than he can change the color of his eyes at will. Metabolism is stronger than free will.The current controversy over social drinking was heated up by a Rand Corporation study advocating social drinking as a sort of pseudo treatment policy. That report has now been discredited. The controversy, however, had its origin in a classic study by Dr. L. Davies in 1962 reporting that seven alcoholics returned to normal drinking over a follow-up period of 7-11 years.

A recent study of Davies' report by Griffith Edwards of the Addiction Research Unit at London's Institute of Psychiatry (1985:186) located the participants in that study and found that the long-term significance of the 'normal' drinking was often catastrophic and that the short-term evidence may have been mistaken.

"Case 2. A retired shopkeeper aged 74. The catastrophic outcome of this man's drinking can be in no doubt. He has been hospitalized continuously since 1975 with Wernicke-Korsakoff syndrome. Although the subject himself could not give a coherent account and no other informant could be traced, there was a great deal of hospital information with which to piece the story together. He was discharged from Maudsley (where Davies began his study) in 1950."

"In 1955 the subject was seen at a psychiatric unit and was said to be drinking '3 doubles/day and mild and bitter.' On one visit it was noted that he 'has had 2 gins and 3 beers before coming here.' In the same year he was admitted to the hospital with a peptic ulcer. In 1957 outpatient notes quoted him as saying: 'Starting early morning, I have a couple of doubles before I can do any work at all.' Notes made at that time and in 1958 refer to his recently drinking '4 double brandies and 2 Guinnesses.'"

"There are numerous outpatient and inpatient notes relating to subsequent years. In 1965 he was described by his GP as a compulsive drinker, and in 1966 and 1967 he was admitted to hospital with DT and convulsions. In 1967 he was said to be drinking 20-25 pt. of beer and one-half bottle of distilled spirits per day. In the late 1960s he was taking up to 100 mg of diazepam daily. He was readmitted to a psychiatric hospital in 1969 and then again in 1975 with eventual transfer to a long-stay hospital because of his Wernicke-Korsakoff syndrome."

"The story is a tragic one because of the subject's seeming inability to deal successfully with his drinking despite many efforts. He continued over many years to suffer from phobic anxiety symptoms.'"

So it is now obvious that there are two things you must avoid at the outset: you cannot do nothing; you cannot merely ask him to cut down on his drinking.

If you wish to 'head him off' before the inevitable catastrophe arrives you must work hard, gently and persuasively.

Above all you must know the disease you are dealing with and be able to impart that information to your loved one who is suffering from it. That is what this book is all about.

Appendix 3

Guidelines For The Minimal
Treatment of Alcoholism

The necessary first step for your loved one, once it has been determined that he is suffering from the disease of alcoholism, is to detoxify him in a hospital under the supervision of someone who is certified as a specialist in the treatment of alcoholism and drug dependency by the American Medical Society on Alcoholism and Drug Abuse or a physician who has special competence in the field.

The locale must be a hospital because the detoxification procedure is a very serious matter in that the patient, when the alcohol which has been reacting with the receptors in the brain is taken away, is at risk for:

- Grand Mal Seizures. The individual shakes and has convulsions, may bite his tongue, usually urinates and defecates, and can, if they have been eating, vomit and aspirate their vomitus into their lungs and die of respiratory failure. Convulsions are a major problem when withdrawing from alcohol.
- Delirium Tremens. Approximately 15% of patients go into this state and mortality can be as high as 20% even in the hospital. It is a state where the mind is so used to the metabolism of alcohol that, once the drug is removed, it actually begins to malfunction. Blood pressure, pulse rate, and temperature may go up very high. Unable to take fluids or nourishment of any kind, by mouth, the patient may hallucinate and act on their hallucinations. In other words, if they think a truck is running into the room, they may run out of the room. If they hallucinate that someone is trying to hurt them, they may try to hurt someone else as a reaction to their hallucinations. This is a severe medical condition which requires detailed and specific types of medical treatment.
- Cerebral Vascular Accident. Heart attacks and cerebral vascular incidents may occur as a result of rapidly rising blood pressure and pulse rate stemming from improper detoxification procedures.
- Alcohol Cardiomyopathy. A condition where the heart muscle fibers actually begin to either atrophy, swell up or malfunction. The heart is weak, the beat is weaker and the drug also affects the electrical

discharges of the heart so a patient at any time during alcoholism, but particularly during alcoholism withdrawl, can go into a form of cardiac arrhythmia where the electrical discharges of the heart are not coordinated and the heart stops beating in a synchronized fashion.

- Brain Damage. The patient is already suffering from toxicity and malnutrition of the brain from alcoholism so, during withdrawal, the alcohol must be replaced by all the B-complex nutrients, calcium, magnesium, etc. or the patient may suffer severe brain damage.

The hospital should at the onset begin to deal with all the complications of alcoholism that we delineated in the text—from cardiac to liver to brain to gastrointestinal damage and a treatment plan formulated to correct all these factors. And an immediate program of intensive nutrient supplementation should begin—by mouth, by intramuscular injections and intravenously, on occasions.

The patient needs to be confronted with the severity of the disease; it is a life threatening illness. He must be educated with great intensity about the nature of the disease and he must understand that getting and staying sober is a process that one has to learn.

Work should begin immediately with the family because they may be as sick as the primary patient and it is important for them to understand that they must provide an alcohol free environment until the patient regains enough brain functioning ability to sustain himself alcohol free over periods of time.

If your loved one is an alcoholic and you have helped him decide to seek treatment—what type of facility should you choose?

1. You should look for a hospital which treats alcoholism as a medical illness involving body, mind and soul and which understands the genetic components of the disease. This is vitally important, because all patients with alcoholism manifest all kinds of psychiatric symptoms which can easily justify psychiatric diagnoses—but these symptoms, until proven otherwise, must be understood and treated as if they are secondary to alcoholism. For example, a patient with depression should be watched carefully but no psychiatric diagnoses should be made during the acute phases of

alcoholism, during detox, or during the first few months or recovery. We have shown in the text the many dangers of treating depressed alcoholics with psychotropic drugs unless absolutely necessary (During the first five days of detoxification it is usually necessary and frequently imperative to use sedative-hypnotic drugs in order to facilitate a smooth, safe and as pain-free a withdrawal as possible).

2. The facility should be related to a medical institution which has support mechanisms such as oxygen, suction, a trained nursing and medical staff and which has arrangements with cardiac and intensive care units. This will be very important if the patient develops acute symptoms in these areas, either during the detox or in subsequent treatment.

3. The facility where treatment is taking place should be set up to maintain ongoing aftercare or continuing care after the patient leaves the hospital. The hospital staff should understand that their patient, while in the hospital, is analogous to the baseball player in Spring training. The real season starts when they get out and play the game for keeps. The real season for the alcoholic—the real game conditions—start the moment they leave the closed environs of the hospital. That's why there must be continuing support mechanism for at least a year.

4. The patient should be seen in an aftercare program on at least a weekly basis after he leaves the hospital for about six months, then on a monthly basis for the next six months. During this period, problems that arise can be worked out.

5. Ongoing medical care should be available after leaving the facility to handle residual medical problems and to prevent problems before they occur. If a patient develops a craving or other kinds of problems in the first year period, these can immediately be diagnosed and effective treatment can be administered. This follow-up should be carried out by a physician trained in Addictive Diseases.

6. The facility should be strongly associated with AA or AA-type spinoff organizations such as NA and Cocaine Anonymous. Preferably the patients should be introduced to AA while they are in the hospital with meetings and before they leave the hospital they should be introduced to AA units in their communities and have a temporary sponsor assigned to them.

7. The alcohol facility should treat every patient as an individual. Some patients require only short hospital stays and basic follow-up. Some patients require from three months to a year of inpatient treatment in order to have hope of getting well and then very carefully supervised outpatient programs. In general, most patients who are initially diagnosed as having alcoholism should, in addition to their being detoxified, go into an intensive three-week period of rehabilitation. There are several good reasons for this time period. First, the patient stays sober for at least one month. Second, the patient can, with his mind cleared,finally see and understand the nature of his disease. The patient can begin to deal with his many family, job and other problems. In addition, the patient can receive the intensive nutrient supplementation that he requires and his medical problems can be dealt with in a closely supervised manner. Time is essential to allow the body to stabilize the neurotransmitters in the brain, the metabolism and the biochemistry of the body—and to deal with the disease with a clear brain.

The current tendency to cut rehab by government, private corporations, unions and individuals is in my opinion strongly counterproductive in terms of the care of the patient and it lacks the basic premise of being cost effective because the less the alcoholic patient stays in rehab the more he will turn up in general hospitals for some alcohol-related disorder.

A final and very important point must be made about the selection of a facility. As I have shown in the text, problems of the immune system, including allergic type environmental reactions, toxic reactions—and, particularly in the alcoholic—adverse food reactions are now known to be often of crucial significance in the treatment and cure of patients with alcoholism. Therefore, the facility you choose should have the orientation and capacity to make those diagnoses and give adequate treatment accordingly.

In general, the staff of the facility should be positive, supportive and as skilled in the management of alcoholism as one would expect in a coronary care unit.

What Private Corporations,
The Federal Government And Unions
Should Do To Deal With The
National Tragedy Of Alcoholism

The Federal Government, labor unions, corporations, individuals and the entire insurance industry must place alcoholism on a very high priority in regards to coverage for adequate treatment.

The current policy of three-five days of total treatment for alcoholism now adhered to by most of the HMO's is absurd because it is killing a lot of patients, prevents them from getting adequate treatment and winds up costing them enormous amounts of money if they wish to survive.

The government's current position under Medicare of only allowing three days treatment for the average detox unless specifically justified otherwise after the patient has had one rehab—is equally absurd.

Its impact is to basically deny people treatment and cause their disease to progress further and faster. It is the most "penny-wise, pound-foolish" policy ever initiated because while it does save some shekels on one side of the alcohol and drug treatment problem—on the other hand about one-third of all admissions to general hospitals are caused by alcohol and drugs and therefore the real cost of this policy of neglect runs into the billions of dollars.

The real cost effective policy is for private corporations to understand that alcoholism is the most treatable of all the chronic diseases and to make sure that all insurance plans they enter into have adequate coverage for at least detoxification and rehabilitation of 30 days for the treatment of alcoholism on an annual basis.

The companies who fail to do this will suffer the consequences of vastly increased costs in terms of their other hospitalization, earlier disability, increased accidents, disruption on the job, theft, as well as a marked decrease in productivity. The cost of these for a company are immense as compared to the cost of adequate treatment for alcoholism.

Organizations should understand that at least 10% of their work force is in some stage of alcoholism at any point in time. Therefore, if a company employs 1,000 individuals, it should estimate that at least 100 of them are currently in some phase of alcoholism. Patients do not wake up with alcoholism appearing full-blown overnight, just as they do not wake up after developing diabetes overnight. They may present with acute complications of diabetes or acute complications of alcoholism overnight—but the disease process has been going on for months and in many instances for years before it gets to the acute crisis stage.

If one adds drug abuse to these figures, they would probably involve at least 15% of the work force but no real studies have been done to indicate how high these figures really are.

What should the company do?

First, every large and middle-size corporation should immediately set up an employee assistance program (EAP) and this EAP should be staffed by people trained as either counselors in alcoholism, MSW's, or psychologists who are fully aware of the diagnosis and treatment of alcoholism.

This EAP organization should be set up independently of the line operations of the rest of the company. A supervisor can, therefore, refer someone who he thinks is having problems of any kind to the EAP area and rest assured that the EAP counselor will maintain confidentiality.

The medical staff in the organization or its consultants should be people who have received special training and are particularly knowledgeable about alcoholism.

One must make quite sure that the medical staff —
• does not see alcoholism as a moral illness
• does not see alcoholism as a mental illness
• understands fully that alcoholism is a medical disease
with all of its ramifications

These individuals should be able to diagnose the illness properly and should maintain a high level of suspicion in their diagnosis. In fact, the annual medical screenings should be set up around having a high of suspicion for alcoholism or drug abuse. That way, even from the standard tests one would be able to notice toxicity from bone marrow, malnutrition, overweight, elevation in liver enzymes and many other signs which are clues to alcoholism. (In subsequent appendixes I describe several tests which are more or less specific for alcoholism but it is important always to remember that tests pertaining to alcoholism are only as accurate as the competence, knowledge and experience of the physician in the field).

In my opinion, all companies should carry out a sophisticated screen for alcohol/drugs including marijuana on all applicants who are making employment applications. In the event that any of these are positive I think that the applicant should be turned down unless thorough investigation reveals that there is not an underlying addictive problem. Recently, one major New York corporation instituted drug and alcohol screening of urine of all job applicants. Fifty percent of applicants tested positive and had to be turned down for employment. The area of random drug screens is currently a matter of legal controversy and there are important issues involving civil rights and the right to privacy, etc. However, in my opinion, a company has the right to ask employees to sign an agreement that will allow them to be tested on a random basis so that the workplace can be drug and alcohol free.

In the event that a company or union will not permit or does not choose to carry out alcohol and drug screening, if the company carries out an annual physical involving a complete blood count and a SMA 25 which is a simple inexpensive biochemical screen of the body, then using the techniques developed at the National Institute on Alcohol and Drug Abuse, a skilled medical doctor can identify the effects of heavy alcohol consumption over time from the way that they alter both these findings and the relationship of the findings to each other. A paper dealing with this for corporate medical directors interested in detailed information can be referred by us and we would also refer them to accounts of the diagnosis of alcoholism by quadrated analysis done at the National Institute of Alcoholism and Alcohol Abuse.

My staff and I are currently consulting on the development of many of these problems at major employers in the Metro New York area. We have found that they are highly effective and cost effective as long as the supervisors in charge understand the following factors and concepts.

Any time they notice actual impairment—word slurring, physically unstable, any manifestation of actual acute impairment—they should immediately report that worker to the medical division or EAP — *but at no time should that worker be identified as either an alcoholic or drug addict or being under the influence of any substance.* The supervisor is merely saying that something is wrong and checking out the employee for his own benefit.

Here are just a sampling of the behavioral changes that should be noted and reported to the EAP by supervisors.

1. Unexplained belligerence.

2. Sleeping or nodding off.

3. Major mood changes that occur for no explainable reason. For example: George was fine at lunch and then bit everyone's head off at 3 P.M. Is George withdrawing from something and therefore unable to maintain a stable mental state?

4. Obviously, the odor of alcohol.

5. The deterioration of the appearance of a person over time—both in terms of dress and personal hygiene.

6. Excessive absenteeism. If there is excessive absenteeism the first thing that should be suspected is alcoholism and/or drug abuse particularly if the absenteeism occurs on Monday mornings, after holidays, or around paydays. Several companies have now set up actual computer programs to discover employees who exhibit these patterns of absenteeism.

7. Employees showing manifestations of financial problems, and who bring these problems to other counseling areas in the firm.

8. Unexplained absence from job or home. If a person frequently leaves work for period of 15-30 minutes at a time and his absence is unexplained, one should immediately consider that said individual may be treating their addiction outside of the work area.

9. Deterioration in performance. Any individual who exhibits a sudden deterioration in performance or productivity should be carefully observed.

10. Accidents. Any accident of a reportable nature should be considered alcohol or drug related until proven otherwise. It is imperative that this extend down also to what seems minor accidents so that the severe life-threatening accident can be avoided.

Not only should all supervisors be aware of the above factors but they should also understand that alcohol and drugs are as prevalent in the board room as the mail room—all levels of employees are at risk.

For example, recently I was consulted by a corporation in order to set up the kind of program we've been sketching here. They called me in because they have been hurt badly by their own neglect of the problem. They had made a decision to put through an important sell order. They assigned one of their senior people to do this. The next morning they discovered that the executive had not followed through and the company lost $18,000,000 overnight. Further exploration revealed that this individual had chronic alcoholism complicated by cocaine abuse and was in a blackout at the time of the meeting and had no recall of any sell order. This company had paid a severe price by not being able to monitor their higher executives.

All organizations which initiate alcohol programs for staff and employees should make sure that the programs are characterized by sensitivity to the privacy and autonomy of individuals; a strong belief in alcoholism as a medical disease and not a moral failing; and, above all, by a commitment to the overall health of the individuals and their families. These programs are not espionage units—they are care centers within large corporations where troubled individuals can and must seek help.

Organizations should openly endorse, sponsor and cause to occur AA and NA type meetings on their actual premises and provide the physical space necessary.

Appendix 5

Guidelines For Staying Sober

I want to reiterate again that alcoholism is a disease at the present time for which we have no cure. The AA axiom goes: *once you become a pickle you will never be a cucumber again.*

Therefore, if a person has alcoholism they have alcoholism for life. Persons in this category must remain alcohol free and drug free unless specifically indicated and closely supervised because the possibility being cross addicted is always present and that is very dangerous.

The individual needs to organize his or her life around alcoholism as the first priority because if he or she can maintain sobriety and do the things we delineated, and had Cooper do, the individual will reach a new level of well-being; sobriety becomes wellness. This is something AA calls serene sobriety. The individual must constantly set himself up a mechanism of reminding himself that this disease is the difference between living and dying—and the disease will rapidly progress in the event he begins drinking again no matter how long he has been sober. It must be the first priority, because all other priorities are lost in the patient with alcoholism who continues to drink.

In my opinion, from my review and research of the medical literature, and from my own experience with this disease over the past 25 years—total sobriety is the only safe rule to follow. Anyone who tells you that a patient can go back to controlled drinking after the diagnosis of alcoholism is made, is in my opinion on very, very flimsy ground and this type of advice should be shunned.

To maintain sobriety, the patient with alcoholism needs to maintain an active program of good health so that their neurotransmitters in the brain remain stabilized. The advice given Cooper as to diet, exercise, etc. is the kind of advice that every alcoholic should follow.

We are learning new things every year which decreases the craving for alcohol and decreases the probability of patients needing to resume drinking again. These will be included in updates of this book.

It is very important that patients with alcoholism tell the people under whom they are receiving medical or psychiatric care that they are in the process of recovering from alcoholism. If a person does not feel free enough to reveal this data about themselves they should either seek therapy immediately or change physicians. It can be a life-threatening situation for a patient to be under the care of a physician when said physician is not aware that the patient has alcoholism.

Patients must be actively educated that they should stay off any type of addictive drug unless they are actually dealing with some type of life-threatening situation or for the control of pain over a short period of time. Any medication given to the patient should only be on the basis that the physician is aware of the patient's history. The danger of cross addiction, as we have shown in the text, is always there and when an alcoholic cross addicts, sobriety is almost impossible.

Patients should be trained so that if a physician tries to give them an addictive drug, they should get a second opinion from someone more knowledgeable about the disease before they accept the drug. The responsibility is with the patient, has to be with the patient, because, unfortunately, many physicians do not understand the importance of the above facts.

Ultimately, patients with the disease of alcoholism can turn it into the best thing that ever happened to them in their life. It will given them a chance to take stock of their lives through the steps in AA and other areas and to begin to really explore and develop their full potential as a human being. Patients can have more fun and more of everything in an alcohol and drug free state.

The patient who is in a solid recovering state is intellectually, emotionally, spiritually and sexually superior to any previous state he has ever experienced. Recovery is hard, yes, but it is also joyous, and should be shared by all: patient, family, coworkers, medical staff and society at large.

Appendix 6

Interrogating The Patient

In alcoholism, the 'taking of the medical history' is of enormous importance. First, it is an indispensable information source on those aspects of the patient which the physical examination and testing procedures simply cannot cover no matter how comprehensive they are.

Second, and equally important, it functions as a teaching tool...as a way to show the patient through his/her own answers, reflections, conversation, that alcoholism is a systemic disease with wide ramifications on all his/her body functions and organs. It forces the patient to think about his/her disease, to slowly understand that ethanol is uniquely toxic to all individuals but all individuals react differently to that toxicity.

What follows below is a comprehensive questionnaire which was originally developed at the University of Washington Medical School and has been altered somewhat by myself and my colleagues. It should be taken by the physician, with close family members present to help the patient's memory. It should be administered carefully, slowly, with the full realization on the part of the physician that this process is therapeutic as well as informational. In addition, a complete medical history should be taken.

INTRODUCTION

1. Why did you come to this agency/clinic/office?
2. What do you most want help with at the present time?

DRINKING HISTORY

3. How old were you when you started drinking alcohol regularly?
4. How long have you had problems with alcohol?
5. How often do you drink alcoholic beverages?
6. What kinds of alcoholic beverages do you drink?
7. How much of each alcoholic beverage do you drink?
8. When did you have your last drink?
9. When did you start your last drinking episode?

10. What have you been drinking during this last drinking episode?
11. How much alcohol did you consume each day during your last drinking episode?
12. Has your drinking created problems for you in any of the following areas? With spouse_____? With family_____? With friends_____? On the job_____? With children_____?
13. Have you ever been injured because of drinking? In fights_____? Accidental fall_____? Auto accident_____? Other_____?
14. Have you ever been arrested because of drinking? DWI_____? Fights_____? Drunk in public_____? Other_____?
15. Have you ever been in prison or jail because of drinking?
16. What previous treatment have you had for alcohol problems? Date_____ _____? Place_____?

QUESTIONS RELATED TO GASTROINTESTINAL SYSTEM

17. What have you been eating during this most recent drinking bout?
18. What is your usual eating pattern? When not drinking_____? When drinking_____?
19. Have you had recent changes in appetite?
20. Have you had any recent weight changes?
21. Are you on a special diet?
22. What fluids do you drink other than alcohol?
    Regular coffee_____? Tea_____? Water_____?
    Decaffeinated coffee_____? Juices_____? Milk_____?
23. Do you have frequent irritation of your mouth and throat?
24. Are you having pain in your stomach?
25. Are you bothered by heartburn or gas?
26. Are you nauseated?
27. Are you vomiting or having dry heaves?
28. Have you ever vomited blood? If yes, when?
29. Have you ever had stomach ulcers or other stomach problems?
30. How frequently and for what reason do you use aspirin?
31. What medications do you use to relieve stomach pain?
32. Are you having pain in your abdomen?
33. Are you having diarrhea or constipation?
34. Do you have hemorrhoids?
35. Have you had bleeding from your bowels?
36. Have you noticed a change in the color of your stool?
    Clay colored_____? Black_____? Bright red_____?

37. What problems have you had in the past with your bowels?
38. What medications do you use to relieve abdominal or bowel pains?
39. Have you ever had problems with your pancreas?
40. Has the skin or the white of your eyes ever turned yellow?
41. Have you ever had problems with your liver?
42. Do you have diabetes? If yes, what medicine do you take?

QUESTIONS RELATING TO NEUROLOGICAL SYSTEM

43. Have you noticed any change in the amount of alcohol it takes to get the effect you desire? If yes, describe the change.
44. What reactions occur when you stop drinking?
    Tremors_____? D.T.'s_____? Seizures_____?
    Hear or see things____? Other____?
45. Have you ever taken Dilantin or any other drug for seizures?
46. Have you ever experienced a period of time you don't remember when drinking?
47. Have you ever experienced tingling, pain or numbness in hands or feet?
48. Have you ever experienced muscle pain in your legs or arms?
49. Are you experiencing any difficulty in keeping your balance?
50. Are you experiencing any difficulty with your vision?
51. Do you have any problems with your sleep? If yes, describe.
52. How many hours do you usually sleep? When sober_____? When drinking____?
53. Do you feel rested after a night's sleep?
54. What do you do when you are unable to sleep?
55. Have you noticed any recent changes in your sex life? If yes, describe.

QUESTIONS PERTAINING TO CARDIOVASCULAR AND PULMONARY SYSTEMS

56. Do you have heart trouble? If yes, describe.
57. Do you have swelling of the hands and feet?
58. Do you have shortness of breath?
59. Do you have chest pain?
60. Are you taking any medication for heart disease?
61. Have you had pneumonia?
62. Have you ever had tuberculosis? If yes, are you taking any medication for it?

63. Do you have frequent infections (e.g. colds, flu, boils, sores) that don't heal quickly?
64. Do you have a chronic cough? If yes, describe.
65. Have you ever coughed up blood or phlegm?
66. Describe any other lung problems you have had.
67. Do you smoke? If yes, how many packs a day?

QUESTIONS PERTAINING TO PSYCHOSOCIAL STATUS

68. What is your marital status?
69. With whom do you live?
70. Does this person have alcoholism or use alcohol regularly? Yes___? No____?
71. To whom do you feel close?
72. Do your neighbors, relatives and/or friends use alcohol regularly? Yes_____? No_____?
73. How many children do you have?
74. How often do you see your children?
75. Describe the place you live: type of residence, cooking facilities, number of stairs, availability and type of transportation.
76. Have you had mental or emotional problems? Depression_____? Suicidal attempt_____? Nervousness (anxiety)_____? Loneliness_____? Other_____?
77. Are you currently involved in a counseling program?
78. Are you currently taking medication for emotional problems? If yes, describe_____.
79. Are you actively affiliated with a religious group?
80. What is your current employment status?
81. Do you have special job skills?
82. If employed, how does this period of treatment affect your employment?
83. If unemployed, what is your current source of income?
84. What hobbies or special interests do you have?
85. How do you spend a typical day at home?
86. What drugs do you take that you haven't mentioned? Prescribed drugs_____? Over-the-counter drugs_____? Drugs obtained on the street_____?
87. What is your usual manner of taking drugs? As directed_____? More than directed_____? Less than directed_____?
88. Are you allergic to any drugs?

FINAL QUESTIONS

89. What are your ideas for managing your drinking when you leave this agency?
90. Are there any further comments you would like to make?
91. Are there any questions you would like to ask?

Once this history is concluded, the physician then:

a) describes his or her impressions of the client—mood, attitude, intelligence, ability to relate, social skills, general physical and emotional health, level of orientation, reliability of information given
b) lists all the problems identified in order of priority
c) suggests a plan of action for each problem

Successful Therapy For
Alcoholics Depends on
Comprehensive And Exacting Testing!

As you have seen in the body of the text, Cooper was sober one year after commencing treatment for alcoholism because one of the key elements of that treatment was discovering through testing the exact picture of his metabolic, nutritional, neurological, cardiovascular etc. functioning.

Once identified, deficiencies were treated.

The following pages contain the blueprint of a testing program for persons with alcoholism, including treatment procedures.

I. PHYSICAL EXAMINATION

The following norms and standards are based on Hillman's approach to the clinical evaluation of metabolic status of patients with alcoholism during physical examinations. (1974: 513-581)

- *Physical Examination*
  - General impression: physical, intellectual, emotional
  - Anthroposcopic: body habitus, somatotype, gynandromorphy, etc.
  - Anthropometric: selected parameters—height, weight, girth, skin folds, etc., and derived indexes—and comparison with appropriate standards
  - Organ systems and tissues:
    - Signs suggestive of malnutrition (e.g., mouth, skin, nerves, lesions)
    - Signs suggesting conditioning factors (e.g., hepatic, cardiac)
  - Functional tests: physical, intellectual, emotional, strength, speed, stamina, reasoning, etc.
- *Detailed Evaluation*
  - Evident weight loss, notably reduced muscle mass and tone
  - Evident weight gain, principally of fat (increased skin folds)
  - Rhynophyma, acne rosacea

- Telangiectasis, spider angiomata
- Blepharitis, conjunctivitis, notably circumlimbal
- Premature arcus senilis and graying of hair
- Dyssebacca
- Angular stomatitis, reddened lips
- Poor oral hygiene, gingivitis, adentia
- Reddened tongue, fissures, altered papillae
- Hypervascularity, glossal undersurface
- Parotid enlargement
- Hepatomegaly
- Gynecomastia
- Testicular atrophy
- Hand tremor, poor grip, Dupuytren's contracture
- Palmar and plantar erythema
- Increased or decreased or absent ankle jerks
- Impaired vibratory (with intact position) sense, lower extremities
- Calf tenderness
- Plantar hyperalgesia
- Ecchymoses, purpura, petechiae
- Dermatitis of exposed and intertriginous areas
- Edema

II. ROUTINE LABORATORY SCREEN

Routine Laboratory Screen provides the nucleus of the Program's diagnostic testing for metabolic imbalance.

    A. Metabolic Laboratory Indications
    B. The Routine Laboratory Screen
    C. Optional Tests Available in the Screen

A. Metabolic Laboratory Indications

Hillman has delineated the minimal types of laboratory information required for the proper evaluation and management of the nutritional status of patients with alcoholism. The field continues to advance with the methodology moving more and more to biochemical and cellular assays of nutritional status as a guide to diagnosis and therapy. Indications consist of evidence, direct and indirect, about nutritional status and conditioning factors, including comparison with appropriate standards.

- Determinations in blood, urine, tissue, etc. of nutrients, derivatives, related substances and moieties reflecting conditioning factors; random postabsorptive or load tests, including:
  - Hematological parameters: blood and bone marrow
  - Proteins: fractions and ratios, including amino acids
  - Lipids: cholesterol, triglycerides, lipoprotein "typing"
  - Carbohydrates: sugars, lactic and pyruvic acids
  - Minerals
  - Vitamins
  - Metabolites: normal and abnormal
  - Enzymes: for vitamin adequacy, for tissue status
- Function tests: employing physical, chemical and other criteria of general, system or organ status (e.g., cardiopulmonary, hepatic, renal, visual, endocrine)
- Special adjunct procedures:
  - Estimation of body water and body density
  - Radiography: skeletal, soft tissue, visceral
  - Morphological studies: biopsy, histochemistry, electron microscopy
  - Electrocardiography, electroencephalography, electromyography
- Additional laboratory observations
  - Anemia, megaloblastosis, sideroblastosis, neutrophilic hypersegmentation
  - Megaloblastic bone marrow
  - Hypoproteinemia, decreased albumin/globulin ratio
  - Abnormal "liver profile"
  - Hyperlipidemia
  - Reduced pancreatic enzymes
  - Altered blood SGOT and SGPT
- Less frequently available information desirable if possible:
  - Reduced red cell transketolase
  - Increased LDH, Creatinine Phosphokinase (CPK)
  - Reduced blood vitamins A, C, B_6, B_{12}, folate, carotene
  - Altered blood amino acid pattern: decreased essential/nonessential ratio
  - Reduced urine content of thiamine, riboflavin, niacin derivatives and ascorbic acid
  - Abnormal formiminoglutamic acid (FIGLU)

B. *Routine Laboratory Screen*

The following tests should be carried out for all clients in the diagnosis of alcoholism:

- Glucose
- Blood Urea Nitrogen (BUN)
- Total Protein
- Albumin
- Total Bilirubin
- Cholesterol
- Alkaline Phosphatase
- Serum Glutamic Oxaloacetic Transaminase (SGOT/AST)
- Serum Glutamic Pyruvic Transaminase (SGPT/ALT)
- Magnesium
- Alb/Glob Ratio
- Amylase
- Carbon Dioxide (CO_2)
- Chloride
- Sodium
- Potassium
- Complete Blood Count
- Urinalysis

C. *Optional Tests Available*

Additional tests available in the routine medical screen which may be indicated for some patients.

- Creatinine
- BUN/Creatinine Ratio
- Uric Acid
- Globulin
- Direct Bilirubin
- Lactic Acid Dehydrogenase (LDH)
- Total Lipids
- Y-Glutamyl Transpeptidase
- Triglycerides
- Lactic Acid
- Phosphorus

As indicated by the history, physical and laboratory findings, the additional metabolic and nutritional diagnostic profiles depicted in the following sections may be carried out on patients referred for metabolic consultation and/or who manifest particular problems in the following areas. In general, when closely studied the pan-malnutrition and pan-toxicity manifested in alcoholism affects to some degree all of these systems in all patients with the disease. Due to biological individuality certain systems may be affected more than others in individual patients.

III. CARBOHYDRATE METABOLISM

A. *Tests Conducted:*

• Glucose - included in the Routine Laboratory Screen
• Glucose Tolerance

B. *Rationale*

Chronic alcohol ingestion decreases absorption and circulating levels of glucose. Reduced glucose tolerance is commonly found in chronic alcoholics.

Alcohol interferes with carbohydrate metabolism and can produce hypoglycemia by impairing gluconeogenesis; however, a significant degree of hypoglycemia will occur only if hepatic glycogen stores are depleted. Under certain conditions alcohol can also interfere with the peripheral utilization of glucose and produce hyperglycemia.

Maurice Victor, Raymond D. Adams, "Alcohol," in *Principles of Internal Medicine*, 9th ed., ed. T. R. Harrison (New York: McGraw Hill, 1980), 969.

A number of drugs have been implicated in hypoglycemia. By far the most common, apart from insulin and sulfonylureas, is alcohol. Alcohol only induces hypoglycemia after a period of fasting sufficient to deplete liver glycogen stores.

Daniel W. Foster, Arthur H. Rubenstein, "Hypoglycemia, Insulinoma, and Other Hormone-Secreting Tumors of the Pancreas," in *Principles*, Harrison, 1760.

Undoubtedly the commonest cause of hypoglycemia, after overdosage with insulin and the hypoglycemic agents, is overindulgence in alcohol.

Philip Felig, "Disorders of Carbohydrate Metabolism," in *Metabolic Control and Disease*, 8th ed., ed. Philip K. Bondy, Leon E. Rosenberg, (Philadelphia: W. B. Saunders Company, 1980), 364.

... chronic alcohol administration results in impaired transport of carbohydrates (7). Administration of alcohol has a priming effect on glucose mediated insulin release (8) and causes glucose intolerance (2). Chronic alcohol administration results in impaired glucose tolerance, elevated insulin levels and abnormal responses to glycogen (5). These effects were noted in alcoholics with fatty liver as well as in those with cirrhosis. Alcohol-induced pancreatitis may result in a transient or permanent glucose intolerance, because of damage to pancreatic islet cells or the secondary release of steroids and catecholamines. Alcohol has many effects on the intermediary metabolism of carbohydrates (9) which may contribute to impaired gluconeogenesis and in part explain the symptomatic hypoglycemia seen in human alcoholics with prolonged fasting following heavy drinking. Other mechanisms which may contribute to hypoglycemia include glycogen depletion and autonomic dysfunction (9).

Spencer Shaw, Charles S. Lieber, "Nutrition and Alcoholism," in *Modern Nutrition in Health and Disease* 6th ed., ed. Robert S. Goodhart, M.D., Maurice E. Shils, M.D. (Philadelphia: Lea & Febiger, 1980), 1228

C. *Signs and Symptoms*

Signs and symptoms of the hypoglycemias in the fed state can be readily understood when viewed as "over-utilization" during non-steady-state conditions. The relationships between insulin and glucose simulate those seen when hypoglycemia is induced acutely during an intravenous insulin tolerance test. Thus the symptoms are characterized by precipitous onset and by acute adrenergic features, e.g., tachycardia, tremulousness, sweating, piloerection, weakness, anxiety, nervousness and hunger. Although the hyperepinephrinemia is triggered by glucose deprivation in the central nervous system, the duration of hypoglycemia is usually too brief to elicit additional signs of central glucopenia other than faintness, inability to concentrate, and sometimes mental confusion or visual disturbance. Consciousness is almost always preserved.

... in subjects with compromised cardiovascular function, even evanescent hypoglycemia and hyperepinephrinemia may provoke angina, ectopic cardiac rhythms, pulmonary edema and episodes of transient cerebral ischemia.

Norbert Freinkel, "Hypoglycemic Disorders," *Cecil Textbook of Medicine*, 16th ed., ed. James B. Wyngaarden, M.D., Lloyd H. Smith, Jr., M.D. (Philadelphia: W. B. Saunders Company, 1982), 1073

D. *Treatment*

General objectives of treatment are to dampen the elevations in blood sugar which elicit the subsequent excessive hypoglycemic rebounds. Multiple small feedings have constituted one approach. However, regular meal-eating with diets high in protein (120 to 140 grams), low in carbohydrate (75 to 100 grams), and sufficient in fat to maintain caloric adequacy have been more efficacious. Diets high in complex carbohydrates and fiber may provide another promising means for diminishing postprandial spikes in blood sugar.

Freinkel, "Hypoglycemic Disorders," 1074

Therapy of other forms of recurrent hypoglycemia, apart from hormone replacement in pituitary or adrenal insufficiency, is dietary. In most cases avoidance of fasting is all that is required. A high-protein, low-carbohydrate diet is frequently prescribed for patients with postprandial hypoglycemia and often relieves symptoms. With true alimentary hypoglycemia it is probably important to keep the size of the individual meals small.

Foster, Rubenstein, "Hypoglycemia," 1762

IV. LIPID METABOLISM

A. *Tests Conducted:*

- Included in the Routine Laboratory Screen:
  - Total lipids
  - Cholesterol
  - Triglycerides
- Lipoproteins:
  - High-density (HDL)
  - Low-density (LDL)
  - Very low-density (VLDL)

B. *Rationale*

Alcohol has a number of effects on fat metabolism. For example, it can cause hypertriglyceridemia and lead to a fatty liver; levels of HDL are also frequently lower in chronic drinkers while the VLDL are increased.

In any individual the daily consumption of large amounts of ethanol can produce a mild, asymptomatic elevation in the plasma triglyceride level due to an elevation of VLDL. However, in a subgroup ethanol ingestion regularly produces massive and clinically significant hyperlipemia with elevations in both VLDL and chylomicrons (type 5 lipoprotein pattern). In most of this group, the VLDL level remains mildly elevated (type 4 lipoprotein pattern), even in the basal state after recovery from the severe alcohol hyperlipemia. This suggests that these individuals have a form of familial hypertriglyceridemia or multiple lipoprotein-type hyperlipidemia that is exacerbated and converted to a type 5 pattern by the ethanol ingestion.

Ethanol elevates the plasma triglyceride level primarily because it inhibits fatty acid oxidation and enhances fatty acid synthesis in the liver. The excess fatty acids are esterified to triglyceride. Some of this excess triglyceride accumulates in the liver, producing the characteristic enlarged fatty liver of alcoholics. The remainder of the newly formed triglyceride is secreted into plasma, resulting in an increased secretion of VLDL. In those who develop massive alcoholic hyperlipemia, there appears to be a partial defect in the catabolism of these VLDL particles. As the concentration of VLDL increases, the lipoprotein begins to compete with chylomicrons for hydrolysis by lipoprotein lipase, and the plasma concentration of chylomicrons also rises.

Michael S. Brown, Joseph L. Goldstein, "The Hyperlipo-proteinemias and Other Disorders of Lipid Metabolism," in *Principles of Internal Medicine*, 9th ed., ed. T. R. Harrison (New York: McGraw Hill, 1980), 517.

Alcoholic hyperlipemia, usually mixed, is seen in chronic alcoholics with fatty liver and good hepatic function. Diversion of fatty acids entering the liver to triglyceride synthesis accompanies oxidation of ethanol to acetate and appears to be the most important abnormality, but decreased activity of lipoprotein lipase has also been implicated. These patients almost always have underlying primary hypertriglyceridemias, and ingestion of ethanol is an important factor aggravating primary endogenous and mixed hyperlipemias.

Richard J. Havel, "Disorders of Lipid Metabolism," in *Cecil Text-book of Medicine* 16th ed., ed. James B. Wyngaarden, Lloyd H. Smith, Jr., (Philadelphia: W. B. Saunders Company,1982), 1090.

The metabolism of lipids in alcoholics is of special interest because of the frequency of fatty liver and hyperlipidemias seen in these patients. Ethanol metabolism in the liver by alcohol dehydrogenase results in excess hepatic production of NADH. Alcohol consumption also results in mitochondrial damage within the liver. These two effects may in large part account for the major alterations in lipid metabolism resulting from ethanol: decreased fatty acid oxidation, increased fatty acid synthesis and increased ketogenesis. (5,6) As a result of these alterations excess triglycerides may accumulate within the liver and produce steatosis or may be released into the blood as lipoproteins. Intestinal production of very-low-density lipoproteins has been observed (3), although the contribution of this mechanism appears to be only minor. (7) The serum cholesterol may also be increased in alcoholism, a fact which may be related to an ethanol-induced increase in hepatic cholester-ogenesis (8) and decreased bile salt secretion.

A characteristic feature of alcohol-induced hyperlipemia is that all lipoprotein fractions are increased, albeit to a variable degree.

Spencer Shaw, Charles S. Lieber,"Nutrition and Alcoholism," in *Modern Nutrition in Health and Disease*, 6th ed., ed. Robert S. Goodhart, Maurice E. Shils, (Philadelphia: Lea & Febiger, 1980), 1220.

C. Signs and Symptoms

In severe alcoholic hyperlipemia, eruptive xanthomas and lipemia retinalis are frequently present. The most serious complication is pancreatitis. Pancreatitis may be difficult to diagnose, since elevated triglyceride levels can interfere with the estimation of serum amylase. There is no solid evidence to indicate that pancreatitis itself can cause hyperlipemia; rather the hyper-lipemia is the cause of the pancreatitis.

Plasma from patients with alcoholic hyperlipemia is creamy in appear-ance. If a blood sample is drawn in EDTA and the plasma placed in the refrigerator at 4 degrees C overnight, the chylomicrons float to the top, and the infranatant layer is turbid, owing to the combined elevation of VLDL and chylomicrons (type 5 pattern).

Brown, Goldstein, "Hyperlipoproteinemias," *Principles,* Harrison, 517

Most commonly, individuals with endogenous hypertriglyceridemia are discovered when patients with ischemic vascular disease are screened for metabolic abnormalities. Although endogenous hypertriglyceridemia is commonly found in individuals who develop such disease prematurely, the incidence of vascular complications is uncertain. Obesity and glucose intolerance are common, but fasting hyperglycemia is rare except in the few individuals who have mixed hypertriglyceridemia. In those with mixed hypertriglyceridemia, eruptive xanthomas and pancreatitis may occur, as in familial lipoprotein lipase deficiency. The incidence of hyperuricemia and hypertension seems to be increased.

Havel, "Disorders," 1088.

D. *Treatment*

For obese patients, caloric restriction (including ethanol) usually reduces levels of both chylomicrons and VLDL effectively. Restriction of simple sugars may contribute to reduction of triglyceride levels in some patients. For patients of normal body weight, avoidance of intermittent excesses of sugar, fat or ethanol may be helpful . . . For those individuals with severe mixed hypertriglyceridemia that does not respond to diet or to p-chlorophenozyisobutyrate, nicotinic acid, begun at a dose of 100 mg three times daily and increasing gradually as tolerated to as much as 2.5 grams three times daily, is frequently useful.

Havel, "Disorders," 1088-1089

V. PROTEIN METABOLISM

A. *Tests Conducted:*

- Included in the Routine Laboratory Screen:
  - Total Protein
  - Albumin
  - Globulin
  - Alb/Glob Ratio
  - Blood Ammonia
  - Transferrin

B. *Rationale*

Patients with alcoholism manifest gross defects in protein metabolism.

. . . ethanol depresses the synthesis of whole liver proteins (1-8) and inhibits the synthesis of albumin (9-12) and other proteins, such as transferrin (11) and complement (13), causing a disaggregation of the endoplasmic membrane-bound polysomes (9-11). On the other hand, ethanol seems to stimulate the synthesis of lipoproteins in liver (14), although in some conditions it impairs their release (15).

Antonio Perin, Angela Sessa, Alfonsina Desiderio, "Ethanol and Liver Protein Synthesis," in *Developments in Nutrition and Metabolism - Volume 1, Metabolic Effects of Alcohol*, ed. Avogaro, Sirtori and Tremoli (Amsterdam: Elsevier, 1979), 281

Acute ethanol administration has been observed to result in decreased hepatic synthesis of lipoproteins (16) and albumin. (9-11) By contrast, chronic alcohol feeding is associated with increased protein synthesis. (17) Furthermore, chronic feeding results in increased accumulation in the liver of transport protein such as albumin and transferrin. (18) This effect may be mediated by the action of ethanol (or its metabolite acetaldehyde) on hepatic microtubules. (18) The accumulation of hepatic protein is comparable in magnitude, in terms of weight, to the accumulation of lipid.

Spencer Shaw, Charles S. Lieber,"Nutrition and Alcoholism," in *Modern Nutrition in Health and Disease*, 6th ed., ed. Robert S.Goodhart, Maurice E. Shils, (Philadelphia: Lea & Febiger, 1980), 1231.

Frequently, the intake of protein is more limited than that of calories. This occurs because dietary protein is more expensive than carbohydrate or fat; because protein of high biologic value (chiefly animal) is more expensive than protein of low biologic value (chiefly vegetable); because high-calorie, low-protein foods (many snack foods, ethanol, starchy root-based vegetables) are in frequent use in the United States and abroad . . . The deficiency state under these conditions is analogous to kwashiorkor in children.

Daniel Rudman, "Protein-Energy Undernutrition," *Principles of Internal Medicine*, 9th ed., ed. T. R.Harrison (New York: McGraw Hill, 1980), 408

Chronic alcoholism is the most common cause of fatty liver in this country and in other countries with a high alcohol intake. The severity of fatty involvement is roughly proportional to the duration and degree of alcoholic excess . . . The hepatic changes may be associated with other clinical and pathologic features of kwashiorkor.

Kurt J. Isselbacher, J. Thomas LaMont,"Infiltrative and Metabolic Diseases Affecting the Liver," *Principles*, Harrison, 1487.

The chronic alcoholic may have enough calories from ethanol to supply energy needs under usual circumstances, but they are "empty calories" without the many other ingredients of a balanced diet, such as essential amino acids or fatty acids, vitamins, minerals or electrolytes.

Marvin H. Sleisenger, "Gastrointestinal Diseases," in *Cecil Textbook of Medicine*, 16th ed., ed. James B. Wyngaarden, M.D., Lloyd H. Smith, Jr., M.D.(Philadelphia: W. B. Saunders Company,1982), 599

C. Signs and Symptoms

At all ages the body is wasted and may be edematous. Ascites is common. Subcutaneous fat may be totally absent (advanced calorie depletion) or variably preserved (protein starvation). Involution is most pronounced in adipose tissue, thymolymphatic system, spleen, exocrine glands, skeletal muscle, gastrointestinal tract, and pancreas. The gastrointestinal tract is thin and distended; rectal prolapse is common. The size and fat content of the liver are variable. Heart and kidney size are decreased in proportion to the loss of nonedematous body weight. Pituitary, thyroid, and adrenal glands are atrophic. Muscle atrophy is invariable. Skin is atrophic, dyspigmented, scaly, and frequently ulcerated. The cornea is dry, atrophic, and often ulcerated.

No microscopic lesions are specific in protein-energy starvation. Adipose tissue is atrophic. Mitotic figures in proliferating tissues are decreased compared with those of patients who die with normal nutriture. Enzyme granules and ribosomes are less prominent in exocrine glands. The liver is often fatty. Muscle and kidney show nonspecific hyalinization and cloudy swelling. Germinal centers are absent in lymph nodes. Columnar epithelium tends to become cuboidal, villi are flat, and the brush border atrophies in many cells.

The facies is drawn, temporal regions are concave and fleshless, intercostal spaces are excavated, and the skin hangs in folds on the wasted extremities. "Flaky paint" dermatitis and dyspigmentation of skin and hair are common. The patient is pale and may be edematous. Signs of deficiency of water-soluble or fat-soluble vitamins may be present.

Rudman, "Protein," *Principles*, Harrison, 409-410

Alcoholic cirrhosis, the most common variety encountered in North America and many parts of Western Europe and South America, is characterized by diffuse fine scarring, a fairly uniform loss of liver cells, and small (often less than lobule-sized) islands of preserved or regenerating parenchyma. The term Laennec's, micronodular, portal and fatty cirrhosis have also been used to describe this type of chronic liver disease.

J. Thomas LaMont, Raymond S. Koff, Kurt J. Isselbacher, "Cirrhosis,"*Principles*, Harrison, 1473

D. Treatment

The treatment plan to correct protein malnutrition includes abstinence from alcohol, plus a high protein diet, in the context of excellent overall nutritional program.

. . . treatment of cirrhotic patients with protein-rich diets often produces clinical and morphologic improvement.

LaMont, Koff, Isselbacher, "Cirrhosis," 1473

VI. VITAMINS AND ENZYMES

Hypovitaminosis is regularly noted when alcoholism interferes with an intake of established minimum requirements of protein and vitamins. (1) Alcoholics may also develop vitamin depletion syndromes because of defects in absorption or storage of ingested vitamins and a decreased ability to convert vitamins into metabolically active forms. These factors may also contribute to clinical abnormalities currently attributed to ethanol toxicity.

> C. M. Leevy and H. Baker, "Vitamins and Alcoholism," *American Journal of Clinical Nutrition*, 21 (1968), 1325

Literature since the 1930s has included numerous reports of recognized vitamin deficiencies in alcoholics. (2-4) Early case studies include elaborate descriptions of frank cases of beriberi, pellagra, and pernicious anemia in chronic alcoholics and since that time, deficiency states of varying severity repeatedly have been described for thiamine, niacin and riboflavin. (4) In addition, however, as nutritional knowledge and methodology have improved, deficiencies of other vitamins have been recognized, in particular, folic acid (6-9), vitamin B_6 (2,7,9,10) and vitamin C (4). Poor dietary intake and malabsorption are major factors promoting vitamin deficiencies in alcoholism, but progressive liver damage also plays a role in interfering with vitamin metabolism and storage, as previously defined.

The clinical problems associated with "vitamin deficiency" are numerous, non-specific, and dependent on the particular vitamin or vitamins that are lacking. Frequently, multiple vitamin deficiencies exist, and clear association between specific defined clinical symptoms and specific vitamin deficits is nearly impossible. Clinical patterns of avitaminosis vary not only in accordance with the vitamin involved and the response characteristics of the person in question but also with the intensity and duration of the nutritional stress imposed. Severe, acute lesions usually are more transient than more moderate, chronic lesions, but reversibility of symptomatology can generally be expected if appropriate vitamin support is provided during the rehabilitation period.

Thiamine deficiency is the most common vitamin deficiency seen in chronic alcoholics in the United States at the present time. Clinical manifestations of the deficiency vary and depend largely on the severity of deprivation of the vitamin. Muscle and nerve tissues are always affected, but other tissues may also demonstrate abnormal structure and function. The most serious form of thiamine deficiency in alcoholics is Wernicke's sixth nerve palsy, nystagmus, ptosis, ataxia, confusion and coma. Other symptoms of thiamine deficiency may also be evident, such as peripheral neuropathy and cardiac failure. Vigorous therapy with thiamine and additional supportive care are vital to the survival of affected patients. Even with effective treatment, however, some patients maintain a state of confusion with amnesic confabulation, a condition often referred to as Korsakoff's psychosis. (5,11)

Thiamine deficiency, as previously described, is considered the most significant problem in alcoholics, but folic acid and vitamin B_6 deficits are also of major importance. Folate deficiency seriously limits hematopoiesis, granulopoiesis, and thrombopoiesis. Vitamin B_6 deficiency adversely affects amino acid metabolism and protein synthesis, and by virtue of its role in the formation of serotonin and gamma-aminobutyric acid in the brain, deficiency may impair neurological regulation.

> Bonnie Worthington, "Alcoholism and Malnutrition," in *Alcoholism: Development, Consequences, and Interventions*, ed., N. J. Estes & M. E,.Heinemann, (St. Louis: C. V. Mosby Co.,1977), 93-96.

226

A. *Thiamine (Vitamin B₁)*

1. *Tests Conducted:*

Assays for Thiamine Status

2. *Rationale*

Chronic ethanol consumption is frequently associated with thiamine deficiency. Subclinical to gross deficiencies are found in alcoholics.

3. *Signs and Symptoms*

The two major syndromes of thiamine deficiency involve the cardiovascular (wet beriberi) and nervous systems (dry beriberi and the Wernicke-Korsakoff syndromes). The typical patient has mixed symptoms involving both the cardiovasuclar and nervous systems, but pure cardiovascular, pure polyneuritic, and pure cerebral forms also occur. The factors that determine the relative preponderance of these manifestations are poorly understood but are related at least in part to the duration and severity of the deficiency, the degree of physical exertion, and the caloric intake. Thus, severe physical exertion, high carbohydrate intake and a moderate degree of chronic deficiency favor wet beriberi with little or no peripheral neuritis, whereas an equal deficiency with caloric restriction and relative inactivity favors the development of dry (polyneuritic) beriberi.

Beriberi heart disease comprises three major physiologic derangements: (1) a state of peripheral vasodilation leading to a high-output state, (2) a state of biventricular myocardial failure and (3) retention of sodium and water leading to edema.

Three types of nervous system involvement occur: peripheral neuropathy, Wernicke's encephalopathy (cerebral beriberi) and the Korsakoff syndrome. The neuropathy is characterized by a symmetrical impairment or loss of sensory, motor and reflex function affecting the distal segments of limbs more severely than the proximal ones. It may or may not be painful. The essential lesion is a noninflammatory, degenerative change affecting the myelin sheaths primarily.

> Jean D. Wilson, Leonard L. Madison, "Deficiency of Thiamine (Beriberi), Pyridoxine, and Riboflavin," in *Principles of Internal Medicine*, 9th ed., ed. T. R. Harrison (New York: McGraw Hill, 1980), 426

The WKS is characterized clinically by visual disturbances, ataxia, psychic alterations and vegetative symptoms. The pathologic findings are characteristic lesions of the brain stem. The illness is predominantly found in chronic alcoholics.

> D. Hell, P. Six, "Zur Klinik des Wernicke-Korsakoff-Syndroms," in *Praxis 65*, (1976), 707

4. *Treatment*

Administration of therapeutic dosages in thiamine deficient patients restores blood levels to normal (p < .01) and relieves deficiency symptoms.

> Administration of thiamine rapidly restores peripheral vascular resistance, but improvement in the myocardial abnormality may be delayed so that a low-output failure may supervene during treatment . . .
>
> Prompt administration of thiamine is indicated when beriberi is diagnosed or suspected . . . All patients should also receive other water soluble vitamins in therapeutic quantities.

Wilson, Madison, "Deficiency," 426-427

> For patients with the Wernicke-Korsakoff Syndrome thiamine supplementation reverses ataxia and visual disturbances in most patients and may prevent further development of amnesic disturbance if the therapy is begun at an early stage.

Hell, Six, "Zur Klinik," 707

B. *Riboflavin (Vitamin B$_2$)*

1. *Tests Conducted:*

Assays for Riboflavin Status

2. *Rationale*

Riboflavin deficiency occurs frequently in chronic alcoholic patients (p < .05). Ethanol acutely diminishes vitamin B$_2$ bioavailability.

3. *Signs and Symptoms*

> The deficiency syndrome is characterized by sore throat, hyperemia and edema of the pharyngeal and oral mucous membranes, cheilosis, angular stomatitis, glossitis, seborrheic dermatitis and normochromic, normocytic anemia associated with pure red blood cell hypoplasia of the bone marrow. All these features can be rapidly and completely reversed after riboflavin administration.

> Jean D. Wilson, Leonard L. Madison,"Deficiency of Thiamine (Beriberi), Pyridoxine, and Riboflavin," in *Principles of Internal Medicine*, 9th ed., ed. T. R. Harrison (New York: McGraw Hill, 1980), 428

4. *Treatment*

For treatment, an adequate diet should be prescribed, and 5 mg of riboflavin given orally twice a day. Symptoms disappear in a few days and the lesions clear up in a few weeks. In general, it is better to give a multivitamin preparation in treating ariboflavinosis because of frequency of simultaneous deficiency of other B vitamins. When signs suggestive of such deficiencies are present, therapeutic doses of the appropriate vitamins should also be given.

> Nevin S. Scrimshaw,"Deficiencies of Individual Nutrients: Vitamin Diseases," in *Cecil Textbook of Medicine*, 16th ed., ed. James B. Wyngaarden, Lloyd H. Smith. Jr.,(Philadelphia: W. B. Saunders Company, 1982), 1368

C. *Niacin (Vitamin B₃)*

1. *Tests Conducted:*

Assays for Niacin Status

2. *Rationale*

Pellagra, which is caused by a deficiency of niacin or its precursor tryptophan, has been found in chronic alcoholism.

> Pellagra is traditionally associated with maize (corn) diets because this cereal grain has a low tryptophan as well as low niacin content . . .
> In the 1930's it was still common in the Southern United States among low-income groups whose diets consisted mainly of pork fat and hominy grits made from degerminated corn, but the disease has now disappeared from the United States except in alcoholics.

> Nevin S. Scrimshaw, "Deficiencies of Individual Nutrients: Vitamin Diseases," in *Textbook of Medicine*, 16th ed., ed. James B.Wyngaarden, Lloyd H. Smith, Jr.,(Philadelphia: W. B. Saunders Company, 1982), 1368

3. *Signs and Symptoms*

Clinically, alcoholic pellagra does not differ in any appreciable way from endemic pellagra seen prior to 1930 in the southern United States. It is characterized by a bilateral photosensitive dermatitis, stomatitis, gastritis, diarrhea, encephalopathy and peripheral neuropathy. Lesions may appear on extensor surfaces of both hands and feet despite the lack of overt evidence of exposure to sunlight. Interestingly, in alcoholics the "Casal's necklace" is often absent. The tongue in pellagra is bright red with flattened papillae. The mucous membranes of the mouth and the epithelium of the whole gastrointestinal tract may be involved with characteristic diarrhea in 50 per cent . . .

The encephalopathy of pellagra may simulate any mental disease although depression and suicidal tendency usually predominate. Disorientation, hallucinosis and delirium, sometimes difficult to distinguish from delirium tremens, may be observed . . .

The peripheral neuropathy features a chronic sensory disturbance with prominent burning paresthesias of the feet.

> Robert E. Olson, "Nutrition and Alcoholism," in *Modern Nutrition in Health and Disease*, 5th ed., eds. Robert S. Goodhart, Maurice E. Shils (Philadelphia: Lea & Febiger, 1973), 1045-1046

4. *Treatment*

Pellagrins respond promptly to niacin therapy.

The treatment of pellagra is a diet adequate in niacin and tryptophan and the administration of therapeutic doses of the vitamin.

> Scrimshaw, "Deficiencies," 1369

D. *Pyridoxine (Vitamin B₆)*

1. *Tests Conducted:*

Assays for Pyridoxine Status

2. *Rationale*

The incidence of low serum B_6 in alcoholic subjects ranges as high as 50 to 80%.

3. *Signs and Symptoms*

Symptoms were restlessness and irritability, and some developed convulsions. Pyridoxine deficiency may be responsible for anemia in adults.

> Nevin S. Scrimshaw, "Nutritional Diseases," in *Cecil Textbook of Medicine*, 16th ed., ed. James B. Wyngaarden, Lloyd H. Smith, Jr., (Philadelphia: W. B. Saunders Company, 1982), 1357

Sideroblastic anemia occurs in about 30% of alcoholics who become ill enough to require hospitalization. It is particularly common in malnourished, chronically ill alcoholics as contrasted with binge-drinkers.

> Maxwell M. Wintrobe, "Sideroblastic Anemias," in *Clinical Hematology*, 8th ed., ed. Maxwell M. Wintrobe, (Philadelphia: Lea & Febiger, 1981), 661

4. *Treatment*

Administration of pyridoxine to alcoholics significantly improves B_6 status and the symptomatology.

> In the first group of 20 consecutive admissions all were given Pyridoxine. None of them had seizures. This compares with the usually expected frequency of 25 percent with seizures.
> In the second group of 46 patients, only one of those who received Pyridoxine had seizures compared with seven in the control group . . . These results are significant at the .02 level, using the chisquare test of independence in a contingency table.
>
> > Finn Lunde, "Pyridoxine Deficiency in Chronic Alcoholism," *The Journal of Nervous and Mental Disease,* 313, (1960), 78

> It has been reported that parenteral administration of pyridoxal-5-phosphate, the coenzyme form of vitamin B_6, leads to remission . . .
>
> > Wintrobe, "Sideroblastic," 661

E. *Cyanocobalamin (Vitamin B_{12})*

1. *Tests Conducted:*

Assays for Cyanocobalamin Status

2. *Rationale*

Vitamin B_{12} absorption is impaired by chronic ethanol consumption, leading to megaloblastic anemia and a variety of neurologic disorders.

> Most megaloblastic anemias are due to a deficiency of vitamin B_{12} and/or folic acid . . .
>
> The etiology of megaloblastic anemia varies in different parts of the world. In temperate zones, alcoholism and pernicious anemia are the common causes of megaloblastic anemias.
>
> > Bernard M. Babior, H. Franklin Bunn, "Megaloblastic Anemias," in *Principles of Internal Medicine*, 9th ed., ed. T. R. Harrison (New York: McGraw Hill, 1980), 1519-1520

> Megaloblastic anemia has been observed in about 20% of patients with alcoholic cirrhosis.
>
> > Maxwell M. Wintrobe, "Conditions Associated with Folate Deficiency," in *Clinical Hematology*, 8th ed., ed. Maxwell Wintrobe, (Philadelphia: Lea & Febiger, 1981), 581

231

3. *Signs and Symptoms*

Deficiency of vitamin B_{12} results in the development of megaloblastic anemia and signs of degeneration of the long tracts of the spinal cord. Sore tongue, paresthesias and amenorrhea may also be present.

Nevin S. Scrimshaw, "Nutrient Requirements," in *Cecil Textbook of Medicine*, 16th ed., ed. James B.Wyngaarden, M.D., Lloyd H. Smith, Jr.M.D. (Philadelphia: W. B. Saunders Company, 1982), 1357

4. *Treatment*

Vitamin B_{12} therapy results in a significant improvement in the vitamin status in alcoholics ($p < .001$) and amelioration of symptoms.

In most cases of megaloblastic anemia, the most important goal of therapy is the repletion of body stores of the deficient vitamin. Care should be taken to define the nature of the deficiency with precision so that the proper vitamin can be given in adequate amounts and over a sufficiently long period.

Wintrobe, "Management," 591

Therapy consists in the parenteral administration of vitamin B_{12} (hydroxocobalamin or cyanocobalamin) in amounts that are ultimately sufficient to provide the 2 to 5 mcg needed for the daily requirement and to replete liver stores and other reservoirs, which normally contain 2 to 5 mg of vitamin B_{12}. Because of its low cost and lack of toxicity, doses in excess of need are generally given.

William S. Beck, "Megaloblastic Anemias," in *Cecil*, 858

F. *Folic Acid (Folate)*

1. *Tests Conducted:*

Assays for Folate Status

2. *Rationale*

Studies of chronic alcoholic patients have shown low levels of folate in 50-80% of such individuals with up to 60% having associated hematological abnormalities (megaloblastic anemias).

Megaloblastic anemia occurring in chronic liver disease is usually due to folate deficiency resulting from poor diet and impaired hepatic storage of folate.

William S. Beck, "Megaloblastic Anemias," in *Cecil Textbook of Medicine*, 6th ed. James B. Wyngaarden, Lloyd H. Smith, Jr. (Philadelphia: W. B. Saunders Company, 1982), 859

Nutritional folate deficiency has also been found in relatively affluent populations living in temperate areas. Major factors contributing to the consumption of poor diets in such people were mental disturbances, chronic illness, alcoholism.

> Maxwell Wintrobe, "Conditions Associated with Folate Deficiency," in *Clinical Hematology*, 8th ed., ed. Maxwell Wintrobe (Philadelphia: Lea & Febiger, 1981), 581

3. Signs and Symptoms

As a general rule, the manifestations of folate deficiency resemble those of vitamin B_{12} deficiency. The major exception to this generalization is the occurrence of neurologic disease, which is more characteristic of vitamin B_{12} deficiency.

> Wintrobe, "Conditions," 581

Signs and symptoms of folic acid deficiency: pallor, glossitis, stomatitis, diarrhea, anemia.

> Daniel Rudman, "Nutritional Requirements," in *Principles of Internal Medicine*, 9th ed., ed. T. R. Harrison (New York: McGraw Hill, 1980), 400

4. Treatment

Supplementation of folate effectively repletes the vitamin levels to normal (p <.005).

> Like vitamin B_{12} deficiency, folate deficiency is treated by replacement therapy . . . The hematologic response is similar to that seen after replacement therapy for vitamin B_{12} deficiency—that is, a brisk reticulocytosis after about 4 days, followed by correction of the anemia over the next 1 to 2 months. The duration of therapy depends on the basis of the deficiency state. Patients with a continuously increased requirement (such as patients with hemolytic anemia) or those with malabsorption or chronic malnutrition should continue to receive oral folic acid indefinitely. In addition, the patient should be encouraged to maintain an optimal diet containing adequate amounts of folate.

> Bernard M. Babior, H. Franklin Bunn, "Megaloblastic Anemias," *Principles,* 1524

G. Pantothenic Acid

1. Tests Conducted:

Assays for Pantothenic Status

2. Rationale

Alcohol ingestion has been shown to increase urinary excretion of pantothenic acid. From 11-24% of malnourished alcoholics have below normal levels of circulating pantothenic acid.

Neuropathy associated with low serum pantothenic acid has been observed in alcoholic patients habitually consuming extremely poor diets.

Nevin S. Scrimshaw, "Nutritional Diseases," in *Cecil Textbook of Medicine*, 16th ed., ed. James B. Wyngaarden, Lloyd H.Smith, Jr., (Philadelphia: W. B. Saunders Company, 1982), 1357

3. Signs and Symptoms

Signs and symptoms of pantothenic acid deficiency are headache, fatigue, sleep disturbances, impaired coordination, muscle cramps, nausea and diarrhea.

4. Treatment

Supplementation with pantothenic acid is highly effective in correcting the deficiency. Rehabilitation of acute alcoholic patients with a diet containing ample quantities of pantothenic acid effectively returned the urinary excretion of this vitamin to normal ($p < .01$).

This decrease in urinary excretion of pantothenic acid during the progress of the rehabilitation program could indicate the repair of a disturbed metabolic state caused by the prolonged alcohol consumption.

As these patients gradually returned to normal due to the abstinence from alcohol and the consumption of an adequate diet more pantothenic acid was retained and utilized by the body and consequently less was excreted in the urine.

J. P. Bonjour, "Vitamins and Alcoholism: V. Riboflavin, VI. Niacin, VII. Pantothenic Acid and VIII. Biotin," *International Journal of Vitamin & Nutrition Research* 50 (1980), 438

H. Biotin

1. Tests Conducted:

Assays for Biotin Status

2. Rationale

The role of biotin in human nutrition is not fully understood. However, marked reductions in circulating levels and liver stores of biotin are found in 11-13% of patients with chronic alcoholism.

3. Signs and Symptoms

> Experimental biotin deficiency in man . . . results in the development of serious clinical and pathologic changes. These include scaly dermatitis, pallor, extreme lassitude, anorexia, muscle pains, insomnia, precordial pain and slight anemia.

> Nevin S. Scrimshaw, "Nutrient Requirements," in *Cecil Textbook of Medicine*,16th ed., ed. James B. Wyngaarden,Lloyd H. Smith, Jr. (Philadelphia: W. B.Saunders Company, 1982), 1356

As no effect of ethanol per se has been noted in the rat on circulating and hepatic biotin levels, the low levels found in alcoholics are then probably of nutritional origin: but no biotin deficiency symptoms have been reported in alcoholics.

> J. P. Bonjour, "Vitamins and Alcoholism: V. Riboflavin, VI. Niacin, VII. Pantothenic Acid and VIII. Biotin,"*International Journal of Vitamin & Nutrition Research* 50 (1980), 440

4. Treatment

Since the role of biotin in human nutrition has not yet been completely elucidated, it is not surprising that we have still to identify a specific study on the therapeutic administration of biotin to deficient alcoholic patients. However:

> Treatment of hypovitaminemia in the sick and injured patient is desirable to restore normal vitamin balance for proper enzymatic function. This will facilitate the return of a normal metabolic state. The frequency of multiple deficiencies, in the absence of telltale signs and symptoms, indicates the need to provide all known vitamins in malnourished patients. Provision of an adequate diet may be sufficient to replenish vitamin stores; however, oral or parenteral administration of the appropiate vitamin supplements is desirable with marked depletion.

> Carrol M. Leevy, "Incidence and Significance of Hypovitaminemia in a Randomly Selected Municipal Hospital Population," *Americal Journal of Clinical Nutrition* 17 (1965), 269

I. Ascorbic Acid (Vitamin C)

1. Tests Conducted

Assays for Ascorbic Acid Status

2. Rationale

Chronic alcoholics have significantly lower levels of ascorbic acid ($p < .05$).

The vitamin C status of an individual can be estimated by chemical measurements of ascorbic acid levels in leucocytes, serum, plasma and urine. (1) All these methods have been used for the assessment of the vitamin C status in alcoholics in whom significantly lower levels than in controls have been found. Not only the mean circulating ascorbic acid levels are lower but also the percentage with low circulating levels is larger in alcoholics than in controls. Thus 25% or 140 patients with Laennec's cirrhosis had an abnormal serum ascorbic acid level being 20% lower than the range (23-85 μmol/l) established for healthy controls (2), whereas in a randomly selected municipal hospital population only 11% of 120 patients had serum ascorbic acid level of less than 28 μmol/l. (3) Of 37 patients with alcoholic liver disease, 21 had leucocyte ascorbic acid levels of less than 113 μmol/10^8 W.B.C. (4) This figure is 2 S.D. below the control mean and may, therefore, be regarded as the lower limit of normal. Using the percentage of a test dose of ascorbic acid excreted in urine as a measure, then also a higher percentage (85%) of alcoholics is deficient in vitamin C as compared to controls (39%).

J. P. Bonjour, "Vitamins and Alcoholism,I. Ascorbic Acid," *International Journal of Vitamin and Nutrition Research* 49(1979), 435-436

3. Signs and Symptoms

In adults the characteristic features include perifollicular hyperkeratotic papules in which hairs become fragmented and buried, perifollicular hemorrhages, purpura beginning on the backs of the lower extremities coalescing to become ecchymose, hemorrhage into the muscles of the arms and legs with secondary phlebothromboses, hemorrhages into joints, splinter hemorrhages in the nail beds, gum involvement (only in people with teeth) that includes swelling, friability, bleeding, secondary infection, loosening of the teeth, poor healing of wounds, petechial hemorrhages in the viscera and emotional changes. The development of symptoms resembling those of the sicca syndrome has been noted. Terminally, icterus, edema and fever are common, and convulsions, shock and death may occur suddenly.

Jean D. Wilson, "Deficiency of Vitamin C (Scurvy)," in *Principles of Internal Medicine*, 9th ed., ed. T. R. Harrison (New York: McGraw Hill, 1980), 430

4. Treatment

The vitamin C status of alcoholics can be normalized by treatment with the vitamin.

If scurvy is suspected, samples of blood should be obtained, and ascorbic acid should be administered promptly. Scurvy is potentially fatal, and treatment should never be delayed . . . Generally, spontaneous bleeding ceases within 24 h, muscle and bone pain subsides quickly, and within 2 to 3 days the gums begin to heal. Even large ecchymoses and hematomas are resolved in 10 to 12 days, although pigmentary changes in areas of extensive hemorrhage may persist for months. Serum bilirubin becomes normal within 3 to 5 days, and the anemia ordinarily is completely corrected in 2 to 4 weeks.

Symptoms do not improve until the pool size is repleted, and the larger the therapeutic dose, the more rapid the repletion.

Wilson, "Deficiency." 429, 430

J. Vitamin A

1. Tests Conducted:

Assays for Vitamin A Status*

2. Rationale

It has been shown that nearly 60% of alcoholics have low plasma vitamin A levels.

3. Signs and Symptoms

Night blindness is the earliest symptom of deficiency, followed by degenerative changes in the retina. The bulbar conjunctiva becomes dry (xerosis), and small, grey plaques with foamy surfaces develop (Bitot's spots). These lesions are reversible with vitamin A. The more serious effect of vitamin A deficiency is keratomalacia and involves the cornea with ulceration and necrosis, leading to perforation, proplapse and endophthalmitis. The end result is impairment of vision. Patients may have associated dryness and hyperkeratosis of the skin.

Jean D. Wilson, "Deficiency of Vitamins A and K and Hypervitaminosis A,"in Principles of Internal Medicine,9th ed., ed. T. R. Harrison, (NewYork: McGraw Hill, 1980), 431

4. Treatment

Vitamin A supplementation results in significant increases in plasma vitamin A concentrations.

Vitamin A supplementation was associated with significant ($p < 0.05 - 0.005$) improvement in dark adaption and increased plasma concentration of retinyl esters, retinol and retinol-binding protein.

Robert M. Russell, Stanley A. Morrison, Frank Rees Smith, Edwin V. Oaks and Elizabeth A. Carney, "Vitamin A Reversal of Abnormal Dark Adaptation in Cirrhosis," Annals of Internal Medicine 88, (1978), 622.

---

*Since absorption of the fat soluble vitamins A, D and E is impaired when fat is poorly absorbed, an assay of beta-carotene levels is often conducted to indicate whether the deficiency of these vitamins may involve an absorption problem.

K. *Vitamin D*

1. *Tests Conducted:*

Assays for Vitamin D Status*

2. *Rationale*

It has been shown that up to 44% of patients with alcoholic liver disease have reduced serum levels of 25-hydroxy-vitamin D (25-OH-D).

> Metabolic bone disease is commonly seen in alcoholism and cirrhosis. Chronic alcoholics have been shown to have reduced bone mineral content, though bone pathology has not been extensively studied in this patient group. Patients with alcoholic cirrhosis frequently have osteoporosis as the predominant bone lesion, whereas patients with primary biliary cirrhosis often have a combination of osteomalacia and osteoporosis. Both osteoporosis and osteomalacia can result in reduced bone density measurements.
>
> D. B. Posner et al., "Effective 25-Hydroxylation of Vitamin D_2 in Alcoholic Cirrhosis," *Gastroenterology* 74 (1978), 866

3. *Signs and Symptoms*

> Osteopenia (osteomalacia and/or osteoporosis) is relatively common after gastric surgery, in disorders of the small and large intestine, and in chronic hepatic diseases . . . Characteristically, patients present with variable degrees of muscle weakness and diffuse tenderness and aching of the bones. Bone tenderness is usually elicited by tibial pressure or by compression of the rib cage. The tenderness may be localized to pseudofracture areas . . .
> Subclinical osteomalacia can only be diagnosed with certainty by bone biopsy. Low circulating levels of vitamin D3 and 25-hydroxycholecalciferol, wide osteoid seams, and the absence of calcification fronts in biopsied bone strongly support a diagnosis of osteomalacia, and the response to appropriate vitamin D therapy offers further confirmation.
> Osteomalacia is not uncommon as a complication of intestinal malabsorption; it often accompanies idiopathic steatorrhea, nontropical sprue, regional enteritis, prolonged biliary obstruction, chronic pancreatic insufficiency. . . . Dietary vitamin D and 25-hydroxycholecalciferol, which is produced by the liver and normally secreted into the intestine, are absorbed in the form of chylomicron complexes. This process is impaired in diseases with steatorrhea, such as chronic biliary obstruction in which emulsification of fat is disturbed. . . .
> Chronic pancreatitis, intestinal malabsorption, and steatorrhea frequently complicate the course of anicteric patients with liver disease. Moreover, since adipose tissue serves as a large storage depot for vitamin D, prolonged malnutrition, decreased sunlight exposure, and decreased fat stores which frequently characterize the clinical course of patients with chronic hepatic dysfunction may also contribute to a decrease in the body

---

*Assays for vitamin D are sometimes not conducted unless beta-carotene levels indicate a fat absorption problem. See note at J. *Vitamin A*.

stores of vitamin D. Patients with chronic liver disease and osteomalacia may also demonstrate unequivocal histologic evidence of osteoporosis. This form of bone disease is probably a result of cachexia and prolonged inactivity.

Louis V. Avioli, "Calcium, Phosphorous, and Bone Metabolism," in *Cecil Textbook of Medicine,* 16th ed., ed. James B. Wyngaarden, Lloyd H. Smith, Jr. (Philadelphia: W. B. Saunders Company, 1982), 1339-40.

4. *Treatment*

Treatment with vitamin D raises the serum levels of 25-OH-D and calcium ($p < .05$). Other manifestations of osteopenia also respond to appropriate vitamin D therapy. (1, 4, 5)

L. *Vitamin E*

1. *Tests Conducted:*

Assays for Vitamin E Status*

2. *Rationale*

Low serum vitamin E levels were found in 39% of patients with alcholic liver disease.

3. *Signs and Symptoms*

Although plasma vitamin E levels are often depressed in malabsorption, no specific signs or symptoms may be attributed to it.

Robert M. Glickman, "Malabsorption Pathophysiology and Diagnosis," in *Cecil Textbook of Medicine*, 16th ed.,ed. James B. Wyngaarden, Lloyd H. Smith, Jr., (Philadelphia: W. B. Saunders Company, 1982), 684

It is not known whether abnormalities in plasma tocopherol have physiological significance in man. Indeed no clear-cut evidence of vitamin E deficiency has been demonstrated in man, with one possible exception. Pappenheimer and Victor (2) have found "ceroid" pigment, muscular dystrophy and testicular atrophy, suggestive of vitamin E deficiency, in tissues obtained from patients dying of cirrhosis and non-tropical sprue, conditions in which low plasma tocopherol levels have been reported.

Gerald Klatskin, Willard A. Krehl,"The Significance of the Plasma Tocopherol Concentration and of Tocopherol Tolerance Tests in Liver Disease," *Journal of Clinical Investigation 29* (1950), 1528

---

*Assays for vitamin E are sometimes not conducted unless beta-carotene levels indicate a fat absorption problem. See note at J. *Vitamin A.*

4. *Treatment*

Administration of d-alpha-tocopherol acetate raises plasma tocopherol levels. In the absence of clear-cut clinical deficiency symptoms, the therapeutic goal is to restore the vitamin E levels to normal.

VII. MINERAL AND TRACE ELEMENT METABOLISM

A. *Tests Conducted*

*   Included in the Routine Laboratory Screen
    *   Magnesium
    *   Chloride
    *   Sodium
    *   Potassium
*   Copper
*   Zinc

COPPER

B. *Rationale*

Although copper is an essential trace metal for man, it is toxic at high levels. It has been reported that sometimes unusually high concentrations of copper can be found in wine. Chronic alcoholics have been found to have high circulating levels of copper. Liver contents of copper and serum copper are increased in patients with liver disease.

> Elevated concentrations of copper in serum are observed in a large number of acute and chronic diseases and appear to be a manifestation of response to stress. Increased copper accumulation is observed in Wilson's disease, primary biliary cirrhosis and prolonged extrahepatic biliary tract obstruction.
>
> > David D. Ulmer, "Disturbances in Trace Element Metabolism," *Principles of Internal Medicine*, 9th ed., ed.T. R. Harrison (New York: McGraw Hill, 1980), 433

C. *Signs and Symptoms*

Elevated serum copper levels have been found in cases of alcoholic intoxication. This may cause the classic symptoms of "schizophrenia" in alcoholics, including paranoia and hallucinations.

[In a study with 30 patients hospitalized for treatment of seizures during a period of alcohol withdrawal,] those patients who developed delirium tremens or a prolonged hallucinatory state had significantly higher plasma copper concentration ($p = 0.026$), significantly lower zinc concentration ($p = 0.004$), and significantly higher copper/zinc ratios ($p = 0.001$) than the patients who recovered uneventfully.

J. D. Bogden, R. A. Troiano, "Plasma Calcium, Copper, Magnesium and Zinc Concentrations in Patients with the Alcohol Withdrawal Syndrome," *Clinical Chemistry 24* (1978), 1553-56

D. Treatment

The first step in the treatment program is to identify and eliminate the source of excessive copper, e.g. copper piping. Improvement of the schizophrenic symptoms is obtained with the use of penicillamine, a chelating agent, to increase the urinary excretion of copper, and the concomitant trace metal dietary supplement (without copper).

ZINC

B. Rationale

Alcohol dehydrogenase, which catalyzes the oxidation of alcohol in the liver, is a zinc metalloenzyme. Therefore, zinc is indispensible in alcohol metabolism. Serum zinc has been known to be decreased in cirrhosis of the liver. In a recent study involving 119 hospitalized alcoholics with liver disease, plasma zinc levels were low in 82% of patients. Urinary excretion of zinc is increased in 33% of alcoholics. In another study, plasma zinc levels in chronic alcoholics with cirrhosis were decreased to 60% of normal levels. Since liver alcohol dehydrogenase and retinol dehydrogenase are the same enzyme, zinc influences vitamin A metabolism. It is important to include zinc in the treatment with vitamin A for alcoholic cirrhotics with abnormal vitamin A metabolism.

Zinc has been recognized as an essential element in the nutrition of animals and humans, and there is some evidence for the occurrence of zinc deficiency in man under some circumstances. Patients exhibiting anemia, hepatosplenomegaly, short stature, hypogonadism, and geophagia have responded to zinc therapy when tissue levels of zinc and zinc intakes were low.

Nevin S. Scrimshaw, "Nutrient Requirements," in *Cecil Textbook of Medicine*, 16th ed., ed. James B. Wyngaarden, M.D., Lloyd H. Smith, Jr., M.D. (Philadelphia, W. B. Saunders Company, 1982), 1358

C. *Signs and Symptoms*

More recently, several clinical observations have suggested an association between zinc deficiency and poor healing of wounds, anorexia, hypogeusia and behavioral disorders. Furthermore, zinc-responsive vesiculobullous dermatitis has been well described.

Richard B. Williams, M.D., et al.,"Alcoholic Pancreatitis: Patients at High Risk of Acute Zinc Deficiency,"*The American Journal of Medicine 66,*(1979), 889

The testis and the eye are unique organs in that they both require a specific form of vitamin A—retinol. The metabolism of retinol is mediated by alcohol dehydrogenase. Thus, synergistic effect of combined zinc and vitamin A deficiency could lead to an impairment of both testicular function and night vision.

Craig J. McClain, M.D., et al.,"Alterations in Zinc, Vitamin A, and Retinol-Binding Protein in Chronic Alcoholics: A Possible Mechanism for Night Blindness and Hypogonadism,"*Clinical and Experimental Research 3,*(1979), 135

D. *Treatment*

Alcoholic hypogonadism and night blindness are ameliorated by abstinence and zinc and vitamin A therapy.

Growth retardation, testicular atrophy and skin changes were major manifestations of zinc deficiency, which were reversed on supplementation with zinc sulfate in physiological amounts.

Ananda S. Prasad, M.D., et. al., "Essential Micronutrient Elements Biochemistry and Changes in Liver Disorders," *American Journal of Clinical Nutrition 23* (1970), 582

VIII. TOXICOLOGY

A. *Tests Conducted:*

The toxicity screen is administered to patients with a history or physical findings of exposure to the following toxic metals:

- Aluminum (Al)
- Arsenic (As)
- Cadmium (Cd)
- Cobalt (Co)
- Lead (Pb)
- Mercury (Hg)
- Nickel (Ni)

B. *Rationale*

As some of the clinical symptoms of trace metal poisoning mimic some of the manifestations of alcoholism, a screening for trace metal toxicity is carried out on patients when indicated by history or physical findings of exposure to toxic metals.

C. *Signs and Symptoms*

Incidence and clinical symptoms of toxicity from these trace metals are detailed in *Cecil Textbook of Medicine*, 16th Edition, pages 2218-24.

D. *Treatment*

The clinical treatment of trace metal toxicity is well established in the principles and practice of internal medicine.

IX. IMMUNOLOGICAL STRESS

A. *Tests Conducted:*

T-Suppressor and Helper Cell Determinations

B. *Rationale*

Patients with alcoholism are generally more susceptible to infections (especially pneumococcal pneumonia). In patients with alcoholism, and certainly where severe infection is present, the capacity of the metabolism to carry out an immune response is measured.

> Nutritional interference with humoral antibodies specific for infectious agents has, until recently, received the most attention because severe deficiencies of protein, vitamin A, ascorbic acid, riboflavin, thiamine, pantothenic acid, biotin, and niacin-tryptophan in laboratory animals have long been known to interfere with antibody formation. Serious protein deficiency in man can interfere with formation of antibodies . . . The same effect has been observed in cases of severe pellagra and moderately severe deficiency of several of the B vitamins.
>
> > Nevin S. Scrimshaw, "Nutrition and Infection," in *Cecil Textbook of Medicine*, 16th ed., ed. James B. Wyngaarden, Lloyd H. Smith, Jr.,(Philadelphia: W. B. Saunders Company,1982), 1362

C. *Signs and Symptoms*

The symptoms of immunosuppression are manifold and well known, including poor wound healing and collagen formation, changes in intestinal flora, etc.

D. *Treatment*

The therapy for impaired immune response due to malnutrition or vitamin deficiency involves improving the nutritional status of the patient and correcting the specific underlying deficiency.

> The changes in mitogen-induced lymphocyte responses in malnutrition are completely reversed to normal on dietary supplementation.
>
> R. K. Chandra, "Interactions of Nutrition, Infection and Immune Response," *Paediatrica Scandinavia 68*, (1979), 140

X. PSYCHOLOGICAL STRESS

States of severe or prolonged psychological stress, which are generally found in alcoholics, can cause secondary biochemical stress with interference in endocrine and reticuloendothelial functions. Patients identified as being under severe emotional stress are referred to the Psychological and Psychiatric divisions for diagnosis and management. At the same time, the secondary biochemical effects are treated through the reduction of stress and building up of the body's capacity to handle psychological stress.

GLOSSARY

Acetaldehyde
A toxic breakdown product of alcohol which the alcoholic may be unable to eliminate because of a liver enzyme difference which is characteristic of the disorder.

Acidosis
A condition caused by the increase of acid or the depletion of alkali in body fluids and tissues. Disturbs tissue function, particularly in the central nervous system.

Adrenergic
Relating to nerve fibers of the sympathetic nervous system which release norepinephrine.

Alb/Glob ratio
The ratio of protein constituents in the blood. An indicator of malnutrition secondary to alcoholism and other disorders.

Alcoholic Cirrhosis
A degeneration of functioning liver cells, it is the most common form of liver disease in the Western world and a leading cause of death; occurs in I0-20% of alcoholics.

Amblyopia
A reduction in visual acuity without detectable organic lesions of the eye. Can be caused by the toxic effects of alcohol in the orbital portion of the optic nerve.

Anergy
An absence of immune sensitivity to substances which are antigenic in most subjects.

Anorexia
The refusal to maintain a minimal diet standard; severe weight loss with no obvious physical illness; intense fear of becoming obese which does not lessen as weight loss increases.

Anorgasmic
Unable to experience orgasm.

Anoxia
The depletion or absence of oxygen in the blood, leading to an inadequate supply of oxygen to the body's tissues.

Antigen
A substance to which the body reacts by producing antibodies.

Antihypertensive
An agent or mode of treatment that reduces high blood pressure.

Apomorphine
A derivative of morphine which, when administered intravenously, induces instantaneous vomiting. Also can be used as an expectorant and hypnotic.

Arrhythmia
An irregularity in the normal rhythms of the heart.

Arrhythmogenic
Capable of promoting or producing arrhythmias.

Arteriosclerosis
A group of diseases characterized by sclerosis - the thickening and loss of elasticity of arterial walls. It is the underlying problem in most heart attacks and strokes.

Ascites
The accumulation of fluid in the abdominal cavity. Can contain suspended fat and blood. Also known as abdominal dropsy.

Ascorbate
A compound or derivative of ascorbic acid (vitamin C).

Aspiration
The removal, by suction, of unusual accumulations of gas or fluids from a body cavity, such as the lungs.

Ataxia
The loss of muscular coordination. An inability to coordinate the muscles in voluntary movement.

Axon
The part of the neuron through which nerve impulses travel. It is "insulated" by a myelin sheath.

Axonal
Having to do with the axon of a nerve cell.

Babinski Reflex
A reflex extension of the great toe, normal in young children but indicative of a disorder in adults.

Beriberi
A disease caused by a deficiency of thiamin in the diet. Characterized by polyneuritis (symptoms usually beginning in the feet), edema, and cardiac pathology.

Blood Alcohol Level (BAL)
A technique to measure the alcohol concentration in a blood sample, expressed in milligrams of alcohol per deciliter (dl) of blood (mg/dl). Legal intoxication in many states is 100 mg/dl or .10 BAL.

Biliary
Relating to bile, the bile ducts, or the gallbladder.

Biotin
A component of the vitamin B complex required by (or occurring in) all forms of life. Manifestations of deficiency include paralysis and dermatitis.

Bipolar
Having two poles or ends. In depression, a condition characterized by radical mood swings from elation to despair.

Cal/g
Calories per gram.

Calcitonin
A hormone secreted by the parathyroid glands in response to elevated calcium levels. It lowers blood levels of calcium and phosphate and inhibits bone loss.

Cardiomegaly
Enlargement of the heart.

Cardiomyopathy
A general diagnostic term for diseases affecting the muscle tissue of the heart.

Cardiovascular
Relating to the heart, blood vessels, and circulation.

Catecholamine
Any of the neurotransmitters of the sympathetic nervous system, including dopamine, epinephrine, and norepinephrine.

Cerebellar
Relating to the cerebellum, the brain region responsible for muscle tone, posture and coordination of movement.

Challenge Testing
The individual avoids the suspected item for 4-5 days, then undergoes acute reexposure to a pure form of that single food or chemical.

Cholelithiasis
The formation or presence of gallstones.

Clinical Depression
Poor appetite; insomnia; loss of energy and pleasure in usual activities; recurrent thoughts of death; psychomotor agitation or retardation.

CNS
The central nervous system - consisting of the brain and spinal cord.

Crohn's Disease
A chronic inflammation of the intestinal tract, particularly of the ileum. The cause of this disease is unknown, and the rate of recurrence is high.

Coeliac Disease
A disease characterized by a sensitivity to gluten, resulting in diarrhea, malabsorption, and nutritional and vitamin deficiencies. Usually responds to a gluten-free diet.

Conjugate
Pair; join; work in unison.

Cytochrome
A type of blood protein whose principal function is electron transport. Divided into four basic types: a, b, c and d.

Delirium Tremens
The most dangerous and dramatic consequence of alcohol withdrawal, usually seen in patients who are severely malnourished and toxic. The final stage is characterized by disorientation, delusions and delirium, often preceded by seizures. In the late stages it is life threatening.

Dementia
Severe impairment of mental function; deterioration of personality; inability to function independently.

Demyelination
The destruction or removal of the myelin sheath from the axons of nerve cells.

Diazepam
A skeletal muscle relaxant, sedative and antianxiety agent marketed under several trade names, including Valium.

Digoxin
A cardioactive steroid glycoside, related to digitalis, used to treat heart failure. It increases the force of heart muscle contractions while suppressing arrhythymias and slowing the heart rate, causing an increase in cardiac work with a decrease in metabolic strain.

Distal
In physiology, located away from the center of the body.

Diuresis
An increase in the excretion of urine.

Dopamine
A central nervous system neurotransmitter that also acts as a precursor of norepinephrine and epinephrine. A deficiency of this neurotransmitter is associated with Parkinson's disease. It has been theorized that an excess of dopamine is a causal factor in schizophrenia.

Duodenum
The first section of the small intestine, below the stomach.

DSM III
The official diagnostic and statistical manual of the American Psychiatric Association.

Dysarthria
A disturbance of articulation of speech. Can be the result of impaired muscular control arising from damage to the central or peripheral nervous system.

Dysrhythmia
A disturbance in rhythm.

Electrocardiography
A method for studying the action of the heart muscle. Uses an electrocardiograph to detect and graphically record the electrical activity of the heart.

Electrolyte
A compound that conducts electricity when it is dissolved in solution and which is decomposed by the electric current.

Electrolyte Imbalance
Loss of essential minerals in the stomach juices including sodium, potassium, magnesium, calcium.

Encephalopathy
Any disease of the brain.

Endocrine System
The network of glands which secrete hormones that are distributed throughout the bloodstream.

Endorphins
A group of polypeptides, found in the brain and throughout the nervous system, which are released in response to physical or mental stress. These "natural opiates" increase pain threshold and are responsible for the "high" produced by strenuous exercise. External opiates such as morphine bind to endorphin receptor sites.

Enkephalin
One of the endorphins.

Enteropathy
Any disease of the intestine.

Enzyme
A substance manufactured by the body which regulates the rate of speed at which metabolism occurs.

Epidemiological
Pertaining to the incidence and course of a disease in an actual population.

Epithelium
The cellular, avascular covering of the internal and external surfaces of the body.

Esophagus
The portion of the digestive canal between the pharynx and the stomach, approx. 25 centimeters long.

Ethanol
Alcohol; a transparent, colorless, volatile liquid obtained by fermentation of carbohydrates with yeast.

Etiology
The origin or cause of a disease.

Exocrine
Pertaining to a gland that secretes outwardly through a duct.

Extensor
A general term for any muscle that, upon contraction, extends and straightens a joint.

Folate
A salt of folic acid. Acts as a coenzyme.

Folic Acid
A water-soluble vitamin, found in liver, green vegetables, and yeast. Used to treat megaloblastic anemia.

Gastroenteritis
Inflammation of the mucous membrane of both stomach and intestine.

Gluconeogenesis
The formation of glucose from non-carbohydrate substances, such as protein or fats.

Gluten
A protein found in wheat and other grains.

Glycopeptides
A class of peptides containing carbohydrates.

GTT
The Glucose Tolerance Test measures, through blood and urine, the ability of an individual to metabolize the principal blood sugar. Should be done with concomitant insulin epinephrine levels.

Hematological
Pertaining to the blood or blood-forming tissues.

Hemiparesis
A slight paralysis affecting one side only.

Hemoglobin
The oxygen-carrying, pigmented element of red blood cells.

Hemolysis
The alteration or destruction of red blood cells, with a resultant release of hemoglobin into blood plasma.

Hepatic
Of or pertaining to the liver.

Hepatocyte
A liver cell.

Homeostasis
The state of equilibrium in the healthy body and the processes through which such equilibrium is maintained.

Humoral
Pertaining to any of the fluid or semifluid substances in the body.

Hydrolysis
The splitting of a chemical compound into fragments by the addition of water.

Hyperadrenalism
An abnormal increase in the secretions of the adrenal gland.

Hyperinsulinism
An excessive secretion of insulin by the Islets of Langerhans in the pancreas. Results in hypoglycemia.

Hyperkinesia
An abnormal increase in motor function or activity.

Hypertension
High blood pressure.

Hypoalbuminemia
An abnormally low concentration of albumin in the blood.

Hypochromia
An anemic condition in which the hemoglobin content of red blood cells is abnormally low.

Hypoglycemia
A low glucose content in the circulating blood supply. Can cause symptoms ranging from cold sweats to convulsions and coma.

Hypokalemia
Low blood potassium level. Clinically manifested by neuromuscular disorders.

Hypomagnesemia
Subnormal concentrations of magnesium in blood plasma, may cause convulsions.

Hypophosphatemia
Low concentrations of phosphates in the circulating blood. Manifested by hemolysis, weakness and convulsions.

Hypoproteinemia
Unusually small amounts of total protein in circulating blood plasma. Can cause edema.

Hypothalamus
The region of the brain which controls food intake, endocrine levels, water balance, sexual rhythms, and the entire autonomic nervous system. Through connections with higher brain centers, the hypothalamus also commands complex motivational states such as anger, hunger, and fatigue.

Hypothermia
A body temperature significantly below 98.6 degrees F.

Hypotrophy
The premature and progressive loss of vitality of a tissue or organ, leading to disorders and loss of function.

Hypovitaminosis
A state characterized by a deficiency of one or more vitamins.

Idiopathic
Of unknown cause.

Immuno-
Pertaining to the immune system and its functions.

Immunopharmacological
Pertaining to drugs that interact with or otherwise affect the cells and receptors of the immune system.

Immunosuppressive
Any substance or procedure which hampers the functioning of the immune system.

In vitro
In an artificial environment - usually refers to experiments and research in artificial media.

In vivo
In the living body.

Intragastric
Located in or occurring within the stomach.

Intraluminal
Located in or occurring within a tube, such as a vein or artery.

Isocaloric
Providing or containing the same number of calories as another substance.

K
The chemical symbol for potassium.

Ketogenesis
The production of acetone or other ketones.

Lactate
Any salt of lactic acid.

Laennec's cirrhosis
A type of cirrhosis of the liver associated with excessive alcohol ingestion. Characterized by fatty infiltration of normal liver cells, inflammation and progressive fibrosis.

Lateral
On the side; located away from the midplane of the body.

Limbic
Pertaining to the limbic system - the structures of the "visceral brain" at or near the wall (limbus) of the cerebral hemisphere. Through connections with other brain regions (including the hypothalamus) the limbic system exerts an influence on the endocrine and autonomic nervous systems and affects mood and motivational states.

Lipid
An operational term describing a group of substances which are water-insoluble and can be extracted from animal or vegetable cells by solvents such as alcohol. Lipids are easily stored in the body as a fuel source, are a major constituent of cell structure, and serve numerous biological functions. The essential fatty acids and fat-soluble vitamins are included in this group.

Lipoprotein
A compound consisting of lipid and protein. Almost all the lipids in blood plasma are in the form of lipoproteins, and are classified according to their densities. High density lipoproteins (HDL) contain high levels of protein and relatively little cholesterol. Low density lipoproteins (LDL) have moderate levels of protein and very high levels of cholesterol. Very low density lipoproteins (VLDL) contain little protein and moderate levels of cholesterol.

Lymphocyte
A white blood cell formed in the lymphoid tissues of the body (lymph nodes, spleen, thymus, tonsils, etc.). Lymphocytes synthesize antibodies in response to antigens.

Macrocyte
An abnormally large erythrocyte (red blood cell), frequently observed in cases of pernicious anemia.

Macrocytosis
The presence of unusually large numbers of macrocytes in the circulating blood supply.

Mast Cell
A connective tissue cell that contains histamine and heparin. During allergic reactions, mast cells release histamine, stimulating the secretion of mucus.

MCH
Mean corpuscular hemoglobin - an expression of the average concentration of hemoglobin, expressed in per cent.

MCV
Mean corpuscular volume - an expression of the average volume of individual red blood cells in cubic microns.

Mentation
The process of mental activity. Thought. Reasoning.

Merck Manual
A medical reference book.

Metabolism
The process whereby organisms process and utilize the nutrients necessary for survival and growth.

Metabolite
Any substance produced as a result of metabolism or a metabolic process.

Mg
The abbreviation for milligram.

Microcephaly
Abnormal smallness of the head, usually associated with some level of mental retardation.

Microsomal
Pertaining to microsomes, the spherical sacs (vesicles) of the endoplasmic reticulum which form after the destruction and centrifugation of cells.

Mitochondria
Tiny structures within each cell which are responsible for releasing energy from food.

Mitogen
A substance that induces cell reproduction, especially of lymphocytes.

Ml
The abbreviation for milliliter.

Morphology
The form and structure of an organism.

Motility
The ability to move spontaneously.

Mucosal
Pertaining to the mucus membranes.

Myocardium
The middle and thickest layer of the walls of the heart, consisting of cardiac muscle.

NADH
Nicotinamide adenine dinucleotide (reduced form) - a coenzyme which is involved in numerous enzymatic reactions throughout the body, including the metabolism of alcohol.

Neocortical
Pertaining to the neocortex, the most highly evolved section of the brain.

Neoplasm
An abnormal growth or tumor that grows more rapidly than normal cell proliferation and continues to grow after the stimuli that initiated the process are gone.

Neuritis
The inflammation of a nerve, most frequently accompanied by pain and tenderness, although also characterized by anesthesia and paralysis.

Neuroglycopenia
Chronic hypoglycemia so severe that it impairs the functioning of the brain, causing personality changes and intellectual deterioration.

Neuron
Any of the conducting cells of the nervous system.

Neuropathy
Any disorder affecting the peripheral nervous system.

Neurotransmitter
A chemical that diffuses across the gap from the end of one nerve cell to a neighboring one.

Niacin
A water-soluble B complex vitamin found in liver, yeast, bran, peanuts, poultry, fish and lean meats. It is an essential vitamin. Severe deficiency leads to pellagra.

Obtundation
The blunting of sensation or deadening of pain.

Opiate
Any preparation or derivative of opium; substances that have a chemical affinity to endorphin receptor sites in the brain and nervous system.

Pancreatitis
Acute or chronic inflammation of the pancreas. Caused by the autodigestion of pancreatic tissue by pancreatic enzymes. May be asymptomatic.

Pantothenic Acid
A growth substance found in plant and animal tissues, essential for the growth of yeast and some bacteria.

Paranoid Psychoses
Persistent persecutory delusions or delusional jealousy with behavior appropriate to the delusional system.

Parenteral
Administration through a route other than the gastrointestinal tract, such as intravenously or intramuscularly.

Paresthesia
Abnormal sensation, such as burning or tingling.

Paroxysmal Atrial Fibrillation
Spasmodic, randomized contractions of the atrial myocardium.

Pellagra
The clinical deficiency of niacin, characterized by the "three Ds": diarrhea, dermatitis and dementia.

Peptides
The constituent parts of proteins. A class of compounds with two or more amino acids.

Periodicity
The tendency to recur at regular intervals over time.

Peristalsis
Waves of muscular contractions in the intestines, by which intestinal contents are propelled through the tract.

Phenylalanine Hydroxylase
An enzyme that catalyzes the oxidation of phenylalanine (an amino acid) to tyrosine. Phenylalanine is necessary for growth in infants, and for nitrogen equilibrium in adults.

Phospholipids
A lipid which also contains phosphorus. Phospholipids are the primary lipids in cell membranes.

Plasma
The fluid, non-cellular component of circulating blood.

P.R.N.
Abbreviation for the phrase "pro re nata" (Latin) meaning "as circumstances may require."

Progressive Disorder
Any disorder in which existing symptoms grow more pronounced over time and new symptoms emerge.

Prostaglandin
Any one of a group of fatty acids that serve as vasodepressors, stimulate contractility of smooth muscle, lower blood pressure, regulate body temperature, and control inflammation and vascular permeability. Particularly prevalent in genital fluids and accessory glands.

Prothrombin
A glycoprotein blood clotting factor which is formed and stored in the parenchymal cells of the liver.

Pseudocysts
A false cyst; an accumulation of fluid or a dilated space which is not lined by epithelial tissue as is a true cyst.

Psychomotor
Pertaining to the production of voluntary motor movements; the motor effects of brain activity.

Psychotropic
Exerting an effect on the mind, specifically drugs that are used in the treatment of mental disorders.

Pyorrhea
The discharge of pus.

Pyridoxal Phosphate
A major coenzyme involved in the metabolism of amino acids.

Pyridoxine
One of the forms of vitamin B6. Deficiency can cause increased irritability, peripheral neuritis and convulsions.

Pyruvate
A salt of pyruvic acid. The end product of glycolysis, it can be converted to lactate or, in the case of yeasts, ethanol.

Quinidine
A stereoisomer of quinine, used in the treatment of atrial fibrillation and flutter. Also used as an antimalarial for patients who cannot take quinine.

Renal
Pertaining to the kidneys.

Retinal
Pertaining to the retina.

Secretin
A hormone secreted by the duodenum in response to the acid content of the stomach. Secretin stimulates the secretion of pancreatic juice.

Serotonin
A neurotransmitter that can be derived from the amino acid tryptophan.

Sinus Rhythm
The normal rhythm of the heart.

Sociopathy
An abnormal or pathological mental attitude towards society and/or the environment.

Somatic
Relating to or involving the body.

STAT
Immediately.

Steatorrhea
The presence of large amounts of fat in the feces. Characteristic of pancreatic disease and malabsorption syndromes.

Stomatocytosis
A rare form of congenital anemia characterized by the presence of abnormally shaped red blood cells (stomatocytes.)

Striatal
Referring to the corpus striatum.

Subclinical
Without clinical symptoms. Can refer to the early stages of the disease.

Substrate
The substance which is acted upon and altered by an enzyme.

Synergistic
A combined action, as of several drugs, greater in total effect than the sum of their individual effects.

Tachycardia
An excessively rapid heart rate.

Tachyarrhythmia
A disturbance in the heart's rhythm which results in a heart rate of over 100 beats per minute.

Thiamin
Vitamin B1. An essential water-soluble vitamin found in beans, green vegetables, the germ and husk of grains, egg yolk and liver. Deficiency results in beriberi.

Thrombocytopenia
An abnormal decrease of platelets in the circulating blood supply.

Titer
The standard of strength for a test solution. The amount of a substance needed to produce a reaction when combined with a given volume of another substance.

Tolerance
The ability of an organism to endure contact with a substance.

Triglycerides
Fats, synthesized from carbohydrates, which are stored in animal adipose cells.

Trismus
A firm closing of the jaw due to muscle spasms.

Tryptophan
An amino acid component of proteins, essential for growth in infants and for the maintenance of nitrogen equilibrium in adults. It is the dietary precursor of the neurotransmitter serotonin.

Tyrosine
An amino acid, synthesized from phenylalanine. It is needed for the production of thyroid hormones, catecholamine and melanin.

Vascular
Pertaining to or containing blood vessels.

Venous
Of or pertaining to the veins.

Ventricular
Pertaining to a ventricle (small cavity), particularly of the heart.

Wernicke-Korsakoff Syndrome
An encephalopathy commonly found in chronic alcoholics. Symptoms include vomiting, disturbed eye movement, pupillary changes, insomnia, hallucinations and psychosis. Primarily caused by thiamin deficiency, resulting in brain lesions and degeneration of brain tissue. Thiamin therapy relieves immediate symptoms but cannot reverse existing brain damage.

Xylose
A sugar obtained from wood or beechwood. Used as a diagnostic aid in assessing intestinal function.

Sources

APA 1980
American Psychiatric Association
Diagnostic and Statistical Manual of Mental Disorders, 3rd Ed. 1980

Abel & Zeidenberg 1985
Ernest L. Abel & Philip Zeidenberg
"Age, Alcohol and Violent Death: A Postmortem Study,"
Journal of Studies on Alcohol (46/3) May 1985: 228-231

Ablon 1976
Joan Ablon
"Family Structure and Behavior in Alcoholism: A Review of the Literature" in Kissin & Begleiter 1976:205-242

Abramsky & Litvin 1978
Oded Abramsky and Yair Litvin
"Autoimmune Response to Dopamine-Receptor as a Possible Mechanism in the Pathogenesis of Parkinson's Disease and Schizophrenia"
Perspectives in Biology & Medicine Vol. 22 1978: pp. 104-114

Abrahamson & Pezet 1971
E. M. Abrahamson & A. W. Pezet
Body, Mind, and Sugar
Holt, Rinehart & Winston, New York 1971

Alford 1980
Geary S. Alford
"Alcoholics Anonymous: An Empirical Outcome Study,"
Addictive Behaviors (5) 1980: 359-370

Arky 1971
Ronald A. Arky
"The Effect of Alcohol on Carbohydrate Metabolism: Carbohydrate Metabolism in Alcoholics" in Kissin & Begleiter 1971: 197-227

Avioli 1980
Louis V. Avioli
"Calcium and Phosphorus" in Goodhart & Shils 1980: 294-309

Axelrod 1980
A. E. Axelrod
"Nutrition in Relation to Immunity" in Goodhart & Shils 1980:578-591

Baekeland & Lundwall 1975
F. Baekeland and L. Lundwall, "Dropping out of Treatment: A Critical Review,"
Psychological Bulletin (82) 1975: 738-783

Bardos et al. 1981
P. Bardos, D. Degenne, Y. Lebranchu, K. Biziere, G. Renoux
"Neocortical Lateralization of NK Activity in Mice"
Scandinavian Journal of Immunology, Vol. 13, No. 6, 1981: 609-611

Bean 1983
Margaret Bean
"Clinical Implications of Models for Recovery from Alcoholism," *Advances in Alcohol & Substance Abuse* (3/1-2) Fall/Winter 1983: 91-104

Begleiter & Platz 1972
Henri Begleiter & Arthur Platz
"The Effects of Alcohol on the Central Nervous System in Humans" in Kissin & Begleiter 1972:293-343

Benowitz 1984
S. I. Benowitz
"New Predictor of Alcoholism?" *Science News* (126/12) Sep. 22, 1984: 181

Bissell & Haberman 1984
LeClair Bissell & Paul W. Haberman
Alcoholism in the Professions
Oxford University Press, New York 1984

Bjarnason et al. 1984
Ingvar Bjarnason, Kevin Ward & Timothy J. Peters
"The Leaky Gut of Alcoholism: Possible Route of Entry for Toxic Compounds," *Lancet* (I/8370) Jan. 28, 1984: 179-182

Bondy & Rosenberg 1980
Philip K. Bondy & Leon E. Rosenberg
Metabolic Control & Disease, 8th Ed.
W. B. Saunders, Philadelphia, PA 1980

Breggin 1983
Peter Roger Breggin
Psychiatric Drugs: Hazards to the Brain
Springer Publishing, New York 1983

Brennan 1975
Richard O. Brennan
Nutrigenetics: New Concepts for Relieving Hypoglycemia
M. Evans & Co., New York 1975; Signet, New York 1977

Broitman & Zamcheck 1980
Selwyn A. Broitman & Norman Zamcheck
"Nutrition in Diseases of the Intestines" in Goodhart & Shils 1980: 912-952

Bruun 1963
Kettil Bruun
"Outcome of Different Types of Treatment of Alcoholism,"
Quarterly Journal of Studies on Alcohol (24) 1963: 280-288

Carpenter & Armenti 1972
John A. Carpenter & Nicholas P. Armenti
"Some Effects of Ethanol on Human Sexual & Aggressive Behavior" in Kissin & Begleiter 1972: 509-543

CATOR 1986
Chemical Abuse/Addiction Treatment Outcome Registry
CATOR 1986 Report: Findings Two Years After Treatment, compiled by Norman Hoffman and Patricia Harrison, St. Paul, MN 1986

Cecil 1982
James B. Wyngaarden & Lloyd H. Smith, eds.
Cecil Textbook of Medicine, 16th ed.
W. B. Saunders, Philadelphia, PA 1982

Clark 1976
Michael Clark
"The 'Cocktail' That Gets Them Off the Bottle," *Prevention* (28)1976:126-133

Cohen 1950
Sir Henry Cohen
"Hypoglycemia and Hyperinsulinism," *Annals of the Royal College of Surgeons* (6) Jan. 1950: 3-27

Conn & Seltzer 1955
Jerome W. Conn & Holbrooke S. Seltzer
"Spontaneous Hypoglycemia," *American Journal of Medicine* (19)Sep. 1955:460-478

Covington & Kohen 1984
Stephanie S. Covington & Janet Kohen
"Women, Alcohol, and Sexuality," *Advances in Alcohol & Substance Abuse* (4/l) Fall l984: 41-56

Day 1973
Douglas Day
Malcolm Lowry: A Biography
Oxford University Press, New York 1973

Dorland's 1985
Dorland's Illustrated Dictionary, 26th ed.
W. B. Saunders Company, Philadelphia, PA 1985

Dreyfus 1974
Pierre M. Dreyfus
"Diseases of the Nervous System in Chronic Alcoholics" in Kissin & Begleiter 1974:256-290

Edwards 1985
Griffith Edwards
"A Later Follow-up of a Classic Case Series: D. L. Davies's l962 Report and Its Significance for the Present," *Journal of Studies on Alcohol* (46/3) May 1985: 181-190

Emrick 1974
Chad D. Emrick
"A Review of Psychologically Oriented Treatment of Alcoholism: I. The Use and Inter-relationships of Outcome Criteria and Drinking Behavior Following Treatment," *Quarterly Journal of Studies on Alcohol* (35) 1974: 523-549

Emrick 1975
Chad D. Emrick
"A Review of Psychologically Oriented Treatment of Alcoholism: II. The Relative Effective-ness of Different Treatment Approaches and the Effectiveness of Treatment Versus no Treatment,"
Journal of Studies on Alcohol (36/1) 1975: 88-108

Forsander et al. 1958
Olof Forsander, Juhain Kohonen & Heikki Suomalainen
"Physiological Alcohol Consumption," *Quarterly Journal of Studies on Alcohol* (19)1958: 379-387

French 1971
Samuel W. French
"Acute and Chronic Toxicity of Alcohol" in Kissin & Begleiter 1971:437-511

Goodhart & Shils 1980
Robert S. Goodhart & Maurice E. Shils, eds.
Modern Nutrition in Health and Disease, 6th Ed.
Lea & Febiger, Philadelphia, PA 1980

Goodwin 1976
Donald Goodwin
Is Alcoholism Hereditary?
Oxford University Press, New York 1976

Gordis et al. 1981
Enoch Gordis, Douglas Dorph, Vincent Sepe, and Harry Smith
"Outcome of Alcoholism Treatment Among 5578 Patients in an Urban Comprehensive Hospital-Based Program: Application of a Computerized Data System,"
Alcoholism: Clinical and Experimental Research (5/4) 1981: 509-522

Greenberger et al. 1983
Norton J. Greenberger, Alexander Davis & Roger Dreiling, eds.
The Medical Book of Lists: A Primer of Differential Diagnosis in Internal Medicine
Year Book Medical Publishers, Chicago, 1983

Gross 1973a
Milton M. Gross, ed.
Alcohol Intoxication and Withdrawal I. Experimental Studies
Plenum Press, New York 1973

Gross 1973b
Milton M. Gross
"Sensory Superactivity, A Preliminary Report on an Hypothetical Model for an Hallucinogenic Mechanism in Alcohol Withdrawal" in Gross 1973a:321-330

Guenther 1983
Ruth M. Guenther
"The Role of Nutritional Therapy in Alcoholism Treatment,"
International Journal of Biosocial Research (4/1) 1983:5-18

Harrison's 1983
Robert G. Petersdorf, Raymond D. Adams, Eugene Braunwald, Kurt J. Isselbacher, Joseph B. Martin & Jean D. Wilson
Harrison's Principles of Internal Medicine, 10th Ed.
McGraw Hill, New York 1983

Helzer et al. 1985
John E. Helzer, Lee N. Robins, John R. Taylor, Kristin Carey, Richard H. Miller, Terri Combs-Orme and Anne Farmer
"The Extent of Long-Term Moderate Drinking Among Alcoholics Discharged From Medical and Psychiatric Treatment Facilities," *The New England Journal of Medicine* (312/26) June 27, 1985: 1678-1682.

Hillman 1974
Robert W. Hillman
"Alcoholism and Malnutrition," in Kissin & Begleiter 1974: 513-581

Himwich & Callison 1972
Harold E. Himwich & David A. Callison
"The Effects of Alcohol on Evoked Potentials of Various Parts of the Central Nervous System of the Cat," in Kissin & Begleiter 1972: 67-84

Hughes & Brewin 1980
Richard Hughes & Robert Brewin
The Tranquilizing of America: Pill Popping and the American Way of Life
Harcourt Brace Jovanovich, New York 1979, Warner Books, New York 1980

Jankovic et al. 1980
Branislav Jankovic, Slobodan Jakulic & Jozef Horvat
"Schizophrenia and Other Psychiatric Diseases: Evidence of Neurotissue Hypersensitivity".
Clinical and Experimental Immunology, Vol 40, No. 3, 1980: 515-522.

Jankovic et al. 1982
Branislav D. Jankovic, Slobodan Jakulic & Jozef Horvat
"Delayed Skin Hypersensitivity Reactions to Human Brain S-100 Protein in Psychiatric Patients"
Biological Psychiatry, Vol. 17, No. 6, 1982: 687-697

Jellinek 1960
Elvin Morton Jellinek
The Disease Concept of Alcoholism
College and University Press, New Haven, CT 1960

Kahan 1975
I. J. Kahan
Questions and Answers About Alcoholism
Canadian Schizophrenia Foundation, Regina, Sask 1975

Kauffman et al. 1984
Janice F. Kauffman, Howard Shaffer & Milton Earl Burglass
"A Strategy for the Biological Assessment of Addiction,"
Advances in Alcohol & Substance Abuse (3/1-2) Fall/Winter 1983/1984: 7-18

Ketcham & Mueller 1983
Katherine Ketcham & L. Ann Mueller
Eating Right to Live Sober
Madrona Publishers, Seattle 1983

Kissin & Begleiter 1971
Benjamin Kissin & Henri Begleiter, eds.
The Biology of Alcoholism, Vol. I: Biochemistry
Plenum Press, New York 1971

Kissin & Begleiter 1972
Benjamin Kissin & Henri Begleiter, eds.
The Biology of Alcoholism, Vol. 2: Physiology and Behavior
Plenum Press, New York 1972

Kissin & Begleiter 1974
Benjamin Kissin & Henri Begleiter, eds.
The Biology of Alcoholism, Vol. 3: Clinical Pathology
Plenum Press, New York 1974

Kissin & Begleiter 1976
Benjamin Kissin & Henri Begleiter, eds.
The Biology of Alcoholism, Vol. 4: Social Aspects of Alcoholism
Plenum Press, New York 1976

Kissin & Begleiter 1977
Benjamin Kissin & Henri Begleiter, eds.
The Biology of Alcoholism, Vol. 5: Treatment and Rehabilitation of the Chronic Alcoholic
Plenum Press, New York 1977

Kissin & Begleiter 1983
Benjamin Kissin & Henri Begleiter, eds.
The Biology of Alcoholism, Vol. 6: The Pathogenesis of Alcoholism - Psychosocial Factors
Plenum Press, New York 1983

Klatsky 1982
Arthur L. Klatsky
"The Relationship of Alcohol and the Cardiovascular System" in NIAAA 1982: 173-209

Knochel 1979
James P. Knochel
"Pathogenesis and Effect of Phosphate Depletion in the Alcoholic" in NIAAA 1979:173-188

Korsten & Lieber 1979
Mark A. Korsten & Charles S. Leiber
"Hepatic and Gastrointestinal Complications of Alcoholism", in Mendelson & Mello 1979: 19-58

Krupp & Chatton 1982
Marcus A. Krupp & Milton J. Chatton, eds.
Current Medical Diagnosis & Treatment 1982
Lange Medical Publications, Los Altos, CA 1982

Landmann & Sutherland 1950
Heinz Richard Landmann & Richard L. Sutherland
"Incidence and Significance of Hypoglycemia in Unselected Admissions to a Psychosomatic Service," *American Journal of Digestive Diseases* (17) 1950: 105-108

LeMere 1953
F. LeMere
"What Happens to Alcoholics?"
American Journal of Psychiatry (109) 1953: 674

Lesieur et al. 1986
Henry R. Lesieur, Sheila B. Blume & Richard M. Zoppa
"Alcoholism, Drug Abuse, and Gambling," *Alcoholism: Clinical & Experimental Research* (10/1) Jan./Feb. 1986: 33-38

Lester et al. 1973
Body K. Lester, Orvis H. Rundell, Lawrence C. Cowden & Harold L. Williams
"Chronic Alcoholism, Alcohol and Sleep" in Gross 1973a:261-279

Lieber 1977
Charles S. Lieber, ed.
Aspects of Alcoholism
MTP Press, Lancaster, England 1977

Lieber 1979
Charles S. Lieber
"Alcohol-Nutrition Interactions" in NIAAA 1979: 47-63

Lieber 1982
Charles S. Lieber
Medical Disorders of Alcoholism: Pathogenesis and Treatment
W. B. Saunders, Philadelphia, PA 1982

Lieber & DeCarli 1977
Charles S. Lieber & L. M. DeCarli
"Metabolic Effects of Alcohol on the Liver" in Lieber 1977: 31-79

Lovell & Tintera 1951
H. Lovell & J. W. Tintera
"Hypoadrenocorticism in Alcoholism and Drug Addiction," *Geriatrics* (6) 1951: 1-11

MacDonnell & Ehmer 1969
M. F. MacDonnell & M. Ehmer
"Some Effects of Ethanol on Aggressive Behavior in Cats," *Quarterly Journal of Studies on Alcohol* (30) 1969: 312-319

Manschreck 1981a
Theo C. Manschreck, ed.
Psychiatric Medicine Update
Elsevier, New York 1981

Manschreck 1981b
Theo C. Manschreck
"Paranoid Behavior: A Psychiatric Medicine Perspective" in Manschreck 1981a: 65-76

Mansky & Neu 1981
Peter A. Mansky & Carlos A. Neu
"The Biological Treatment of Depression" in Manschreck 1981a: 47-64

Mapes et al. 1984
Bruce E. Mapes, Raymond A. Johnson & Kenneth R. Sandler
"The Alcoholic Family: Diagnosis and Treatment," *Alcoholism Treatment Quarterly* (I/4) Winter 1984:67-83

Mendelson & Mello 1979
Jack H. Mendelson & Nancy K. Mello, eds.
The Diagnosis and Treatment of Alcoholism, McGraw-Hill, New York 1979

Mezey 1986
Esteban Mezey
"Alcohol Abuse and Digestive Diseases," *Alcohol Health and Research World* (10/2) Winter 1985/86:6-9

Milam & Ketcham 1983
James R. Milam & Katherine Ketcham
Under the Influence: A Guide to the Myths & Realities of Alcoholism
Madrona Publishers, Seattle 1981; Bantam Books, New York 1983

Muhoberac et al. 1984
Barry B. Muhoberac, Roderick K. Roberts, Anastacio M. Hoyumpa & Steven Schenker
"Mechanism(s) of Ethanol-Drug Interaction," *Alcoholism: Clinical and Experimental Research* (8/6) Nov./Dec. 1984: 583-593

Murphy et al. 1984
S. M. Murphy, R. T. Owen & P. J. Tyrer
"Withdrawal Symptoms After Six Weeks' Treatment With Diazepam," *Lancet* (II/8416) Dec. 15, 1984: 1389

NIAAA 1979
National Institute on Alcohol Abuse & Alcoholism
Alcohol and Nutrition, Research Monograph No. 2, DHEW Pub. No. (ADM) 79-780;Dept. of Health, Education & Welfare, Rockville, MD 1979

NIAAA 1982
National Institute on Alcohol Abuse & Alcoholism
Biomedical Processes and Consquences of Alcohol Use, Alcohol and Health, Monograph 2, DHHS Pub.No. (ADM) 82-1191,Dept. of Health & Human Services, Rockville, MD 1982

Ober 1975
William B. Ober
"Swinburne's Masochism: Neuropathology and Psychopathology,"
Bulletin of the Meninger Clinic (39/6) Nov. 1975: 501-555

O'Keane et al. 1972
Maureen O'Keane, R.I. Russell, A. Goldberg
"Ascorbic Acid Status of Alcoholics"
Journal of Alcoholism (7) 1972: 6-11

Palm 1975
J. Daniel Palm
"Benefits of Dietary Fructose in Alleviating the Human Stress Response"
Physiological Effects of Food Carbohydrates, Allene Jeanes and John Hodge, Eds.
American Chemical Society, Washington, D.C. 1975 54-72

Patrick 1964
Adam Patrick
"Some Aspects of Hypoglycemia," *Lancet* (7371) Dec. 5, 1964:1230-1231

Pernanen 1976
Kai Pernanen
"Alcohol and Crimes of Violence" in Kissin & Begleiter 1976:351-444

Peters & Stanten 1965
Harry E. Peters, Jr., & Arthur Stanten
"Pancreatic Resection for Hypoglycemia in Children," *American Journal of Surgery* (110) Aug.1965

Pettinati et al. 1982
Helen H. Pettinati, Arthur Sugerman, Nicholas DiDonato, and Helen S. Maurer
"The Natural History of Alcoholism over Four Years After Treatment,"
Journal of Studies on Alcohol (43/3) 1982: 201-215

Register et al. 1972
U.D. Register, S.R. Marsh, C.T. Thurston, B.J. Fields, M.C. Horning, M.G. Hardinge & A. Sanchez
"Influence of Nutrients on Intake of Alcohol," *Journal of the American Dietetic Association* (61) Aug. 1972: 159-162

Rich et al. 1985
Eugene C. Rich, Constance Siebold & Brian Campion
"Alcohol-Related Acute Atrial Fibrillation: A Case-Control Study and Review of 40 Patients," *Archives of Internal Medicine* (145/5) May 1985:830-833

Sackler 1984
Arthur M. Sackler
"One Man & Medicine: America & Alcohol"
Medical Tribune Oct. 24, 1984: 37

Sherlock 1984
Sheila Sherlock
"Nutrition and the Alcoholic," *Lancet* (I/8374) Feb. 25, 1984: 436-438

Shive 1984
William Shive
"Development of Lymphocyte Culture Methods for Assessment of the Nutrition and Metabolic Status of Individuals," *Journal of the International Academy of Preventive Medicine* (8/4) May 1984: 5-16

Sipila 1985
Risto Sipila
"Atrial Fibrillation Precipitated by Alcohol," Letter to the Editor, *Lancet* (I/8425) Feb.16,1985: 391-392

Smith 1979
J. Cecil Smith
"Marginal Nutritional States and Conditioned Deficiencies" in NIAAA 1979:23-46

Sokolow 1982
Maurice Sokolow
"Heart & Great Vessels" in Krupp & Chatton 1982: 159-255

Solomon 1983
Joel Solomon
"Psychiatric Characteristics of Alcoholics" in Kissin & Begleiter 1983: 67-112

Stein 1981
Marvin Stein
"A Biopsychosocial Approach to Immune Function and Medical Disorders," *Psychiatric Clinics of North America* (4/2), Aug. 1981: 203-221

Steinglass 1977
Peter Steinglass
"Family Therapy in Alcoholism" in Kissin & Begleiter 1977: 259-299

Sugerman et al. 1982
A. Arthur Sugerman, D. Loren Southern, and James F. Corran
"A Study of Antibody Levels in Alcoholic, Depressive, and Schizophrenic Patients," *Annals of Allergy,* (48) Mar. 1982: 166-171

Thomson 1978
A.D. Thomson
"Alcohol and Nutrition"
Clinics in Endocrinology and Metabolism (7) 1978

"Tranquilizer" 1985
"Tranquilizer Should Be for Short-Term Use Only," *The Addiction Letter* (I/4) Apr. 1985: 6

Vaillant 1983
George E. Vaillant
Natural History of Alcoholism
Harvard University Press, Cambridge, MA 1983

W 1968
Bill W
The Vitamin B-3 Therapy: A Second Communication to AA Physicians
Published privately, Feb. 1968

Welte et al. 1979
John Welte, Gerard Hynes, Lloyd Sokolow and Joseph Lyons
Outcome Study of Alcoholism Rehabilitation Units
Research Institute on Alcoholism: New York State Division of Alcoholism and Alcohol Abuse 1979

WHO 1978
World Health Organization
"The International Classification of Disease/ 9th Revision — Clinical Modification (ICD.9CH)
Commission on Professional and Hospital Activities, Ann Arbor, MI 1978

"Why" 1985
"Why Stressed Fish Are Prone to Disease," *New Scientist* (105/1450) Apr. 4, 1985: 20

Williams & Salamy 1972
Harold L. Williams & A. Salamy
"Alcohol and Sleep" in Kissin & Begleiter 1972: 435-483

Winick 1980
Myron Winick
Nutrition in Health & Disease
John Wiley & Sons, New York 1980

Zinberg & Fraser 1979
Norman E. Zinberg & Kathleen M. Fraser
"The Role of the Social Setting in the Prevention and Treatment of Alcoholism" in Mendelson & Mello 1979: 359-385

Zivin 1970
Israel Zivin
"The Neurological and Psychiatric Aspects of Hypoglycemia,"
Diseases of the Nervous System (31) 1970:604-607

INDEX

Manschreck, T. C., 106
Medicare, 143, 201
Milam, James R., 59
Mueller, L. Ann, 78

National Council on Alcoholism, Inc., 24
Natural History of Alcoholism, The (Vaillant), 44

Ober, William B., 83-84

Pellagra, 84
Phenylketonuria, 44-45
Phosphorus, 87-89
Pickering, A. D., 100
Polyneuropathy, 66-67

Rand Corporation, 192
Rush, Benjamin, 20
Ryle, Gilbert, 20

Sackler, Arthur M., 9-10
Shive, William, 89
Smith, Robert Holbrook, 137-38
Smoking by alcoholics, 52, 63, 68, 140, 148, 153, 177
Steell, Graham, 151
Swinburne, Algernon Charles, 83-84

Television, 34
Treatment of alcoholics
    aftercare, 171-75, 197-98
    and child care, 30
    and cost of health care, 10, 14, 25, 142-43, 178, 199, 201-02
    with drugs, 168-69, 176, 197
    effectiveness of, 178; statistics, 11-14, 48, 164
    elements of successful programs, 141, 161-62, 165, 167-78, 196-99
    and employers, 178, 201-05
    and insurance companies, 142-43
    use of nutrition in, 13-14, 53, 170, 172-73, 176, 196
    and women, 30

Vaillant, George E., 44, 59, 184-85
Vitamin B_6, 91-92
Vitamin C, 92

Wernicke-Korsakoff Syndrome, 84-85
Williams, Roger, 49, 54
Wilson, William Griffith, 137-38, 140-41, 144-45
Winick, Myron, 49-50